An Insatiable Desire for a Satisfying Love

FANTASY

BY BETTY BLAKE CHURCHILL

with Rick James

Contributions by Henry Cloud and Shellie R. Warren

WOMEN'S EDITION

CRU Press
100 Lake Hart Dr.
Orlando, FL 32832

An Insatiable Desire for a Satisfying Love

FANTASY

WOMEN'S EDITION

Written and Edited by Betty Blake Churchill

Book and Cover Design
Hydragraphik, LLC
info@hydragraphik.com
hydragraphik.com

Edited by
Eric Stanford

To Order
New Life Resources
1-800-827-2788
Crupress.com
campuscrusade.com

"Fantasy"

Cru Press is the publishing division of Campus Crusade for Christ's Campus Ministry.

International Standard Book Number: 1-56399-250-7

Thanks to…

There are several who have been involved in this project, directly or indirectly, that I want to thank…

Funny people: Rick James, Will Walker, Jana Holley, Brett Westervelt, Cheryl Fletcher, Randy Choy, Doug and Tiffany (apologies for not knowing your last names)

Filter people: Rick James, Shannon Compere, Stephanie Nannen, Will Walker

Affirming people: Rick James, Shannon Compere, Stephanie Nannen, Will Walker

Contributing people: their names are listed elsewhere, but I so appreciate their insight and wisdom, time and energy

Brilliant people: Rick James and Will Walker

Praying people: Shannon Compere, Stephanie Nannen, Shane Weber, Lori Hutto and pretty much everyone else I happen to run into in the final days and begged for your prayers (I'm sure Rick prays I've just never seen him).

Of course, God, Jesus, and the Spirit each in their unique roles in my life and in this project

CONTENTS

Introduction

Is he really looking at me? It's so hard to tell; there are at least five hundred people here. But I really think we just made eye contact. I think we just had a moment! I am so connecting with him.

After he finishes speaking, I "put my canoe in the water," as my friend Rhonda used to say, and manage to station myself in his peripheral view as I talk to some old friends I happen to run into. He talks to students lined up to tell him how much they like his books and ask him their profound and soul-troubling questions. As he works the crowd, he accidentally bumps into me and turns to apologize, and with a look of faux surprise, he says, "Have we met?"

I say something stupid and generic like "You don't know me, but I know you. I've read all your books." Which is actually a bald-faced lie. *I just lied! I've read one and hardly remember much other than I did actually laugh out loud a couple of times. Shoot! What if he asks me about something in one of his books? If this goes anywhere, I'm going to have to fess up, and then it's for sure going nowhere, because who wants to go out with*

a bald-faced liar? Anyway, all this is going on in my head while we exchange witty banter.

He ends up asking me out for coffee, and we go to a hip spot that I almost never go to in reality, but imply that I'm a regular in hopes of wooing him with my cool quotient. We have great conversation about substantive things, and he asks if he can e-mail me while he's traveling on his book tour. He's leaving town the next day, but maybe we could have lunch before he goes to the airport?

"Sure," I say as if he just asked to borrow a pen. "Meet you at 12:30?" I want to either throw up or call someone on the drive home, but it's 1:30 a.m., so the latter is not an option.

Lunch is even better than coffee. We discuss everything from C. S. Lewis to family stuff to favorite vacations. We laugh hard a couple of times and agree on just about everything, or at least everything that matters. We part with a tentative side hug.

He leaves for his next stop on the tour, but there's an e-mail waiting for me the next morning. "Just wanted you to know that I really enjoyed spending time with you. I appreciate your wit and challenging conversation—you're the highlight of my tour so far. Talk to you soon."

"So far"? That's not saying much—this was only his second stop. Is that even a compliment? How exciting are book tours, anyway? Does he meet a girl in every town? And "soon"? How soon is "soon"?

Well, apparently to him "soon" means within twenty-four hours. He calls the next morning. And then he calls the next day and the next. In a few weeks I fly to spend time with him and his friends in his hometown.

We're both nervous when he picks me up at the airport. I'm wearing my good jeans and the green sweater that make my eyes look like kiwi, so I've got that going for me.

We quickly lapse into comfortable conversation, after an incident in which he accidentally elbows me in the chest while putting my bag in the trunk and I respond with a quick-witted reply and we laugh off the nervousness. The weekend is fabulous—love the town and his friends and possibly him.

The last night, we're sitting on his bachelor sofa (highly flammable brown plaid—you've seen it) in his bachelor apartment after making a Martha-would-be proud meal out of remnants found in his bachelor pantry and fridge. I'm sensing it's coming. The "What are we?" talk (and about time—hello?!). Through some kind and endearing words that make a girl weepy, it's determined that I may just be the love of his life and he wants to "pursue me to the altar." So I let him.

A few months later, we're at a conference where he's the keynote speaker. As he's making a point about experiencing God's love and how the love one has for a spouse is just a taste, a dim reflection of God's love for us. He goes on to explain that, as he has recently begun to experience the love for and from a certain woman in his life, he has begun to experience God's love in a new and deeper way.

That's me! He's talking about me! Publicly! In front of all these people! I'm dumbfounded and my ears are hot, so I know my face is flaming red. My heart is thumping so loudly that I almost miss what happens next.

He continues talking about this love he has for me and comparing it to God's love for each of us. Then he talks about the marriage vow and compares it to the covenant we have with the Lord. And he begins to step down from the stage and walk toward me. Then he's standing in front of me, and right there in the middle of his talk—okay,

near the end, really—he proposes. He asks me to marry him as part of his talk! For crying out loud!

Of course, I'm weepy and embarrassed and there is a thunderous applause and I have to stand up and hug him and kiss him. And of course, I nod my head clearly in the affirmative—I can't speak for the shock of it all!

He puts a ring on my finger and then, amazingly, he has the wherewithal to finish up the talk with a couple of sentences driving his points home through his own weepy tears of joy. Then the emcee gets up and says what a powerful talk it was and congratulates us with more applause, and he comes down to sit next to me. After the closing prayer, our friends swarm us with hugs and congratulations, and then we are off to call the families.

We have a beautiful October wedding in Texas. I'm wearing an updated version of the dress I designed on a scrap of paper when I was twenty-three and stuck in the wedding file. The flowers are peonies and verbena, which is miraculous in itself, since peonies bloom in June. We have chocolate cheesecake for the groom's cake and a honeymoon in Europe. We live in the big house at Two Niles Road, as the iron lettering says on the front gate, and have two idyllic children, a girl

and a boy, Blakely (after my mom) and Abbott, respectively. And there you have it … we live happily ever after.

And it's all true. At least up until the part where he bumps into me and speaks. The rest of it I just dreamed up as I was driving home.

Okay, I wish I could say that I didn't dream up that whole scenario in my head. It's a little embarrassing. But I did. Later, as I was laughing at myself, I started thinking about how telling that is. What's funny about that whole fantasy is that it has so little to do with the actual guy. He's almost like a prop. In reality, the guy is an amazing thinker and communicator, and I wouldn't object to going for coffee with him, but he's not an extraordinarily handsome guy. Really, that whole thing was about me—about me being wanted, being wooed, being pursued (to the altar, no less).

That's what it's all about, ladies, isn't it?

Since Eve in the garden, women have been fantasizing about the man of their dreams sweeping them off their feet, whether he's a knight on a white horse, a shirtless Brad Pitt, a fumbling Ashton Kutcher, or [insert current male fantasy here]. Relationships are a God thing. Romance is a God thing. Intimacy is a God thing. And, believe it or not, sex is a God thing. He created it all. And He created us with a need and longing for it all. Our fantasies are only a smidgen of what God really wants for us. Ironically, it was in the moment Adam and Eve understood nakedness that all was lost.

Since the loss of Eden, we've been left with a huge, steaming heap of disappointment, insecurity, failure, miscommunication, rejection, heartache, addiction, and brokenness. But (and that's a big *but*), by God's grace, it is still possible to experience incredibly fulfilling, rich, and healthy relationships. However, it doesn't happen by chance. In this age of "friends with benefits" and "starter marriages," it is a challenge to navigate your way to marriage and sex as God intended.

WHAT TO DO WITH THIS

Hopefully, this book will be a tool to challenge and shape your thinking about what it looks like to have healthy, God-centered relationships and to experience hope and healing in broken places. I pray it makes you want to be a godly woman and to make wise choices. But most of all, I hope it helps you grow into an intimate relationship with our very real Bridegroom.

There are three major sections in this book. First, there is a small-group Bible study for you and some friends to work through together. Why? Because a key part of success in this area of life is finding a group of friends with the same values and perspectives and processing life together, both for encouragement and for accountability.

Second, there is a content section with articles by several contributors covering a wide variety of topics related to relationships, sex and sexuality, dating, beauty, being a woman, marriage, and falling in love with Jesus. Some of the topics may overlap slightly, but we want you to have the value of considering these ideas from several viewpoints and broadening your perspective. They are included because this is largely a mental game and wisdom, truth, and knowledge make powerful allies as you battle against the voices of culture.

Last, there is a month's worth of personal devotionals that focus on the heart of Christ. The hope is that as you begin to saturate your mind and heart with who Jesus is, you will grow closer and closer to Him and you will develop a habit of bringing Him into this and every area of your life.

Plus, if you buy now, we'll throw in a few bonuses mixed in here and there for your further benefit and reading pleasure.

Get started with the personal devotionals and then talk to your small group. See if they're willing to give this study a whirl. What women's small group doesn't want to talk about this stuff? If you're not in a small group, ask some friends to get together and start one.

Before you get into the reading and studying, stop right now and pray. Ask God to show you truth and wisdom. Ask Him to show you the broken places in your life and in your thinking. Make a commitment to pursue Him first, followed by personal purity, godly relationships, and a wise character. Ask Him to change your life. He certainly can and He probably will.

FACTS AND STATISTICS

2.3 MILLION WEDDINGS WILL TAKE PLACE THIS YEAR WITH 411 MILLION WEDDING GUESTS

ON AVERAGE MARRIED PEOPLE HAVE SEX 127 TIMES PER YEAR, SINGLE PEOPLE AVERAGE 49 TIMES PER YEAR

RECENT DATING STATISTICS SHOWS THAT ONLINE DATING SERVICES NOW HELP OVER 7 MILLION REGISTERED USERS A YEAR. 48% OF MEN AND 53% OF AMERICAN WOMEN HAVE USED SERVICES OF VARIOUS DATING AGENCIES.

53% OF WOMEN HAVE SEX BY AGE 18 AND 75% BEFORE THEY MARRY

43% OF WOMEN IN THE US WILL HAVE HAD AT LEAST ONE ABORTION BY THE AGE OF 45

ON ANY GIVEN DAY 45% OF WOMEN IN AMERICA ARE ON A DIET

$3,098,000,000 HAS BEEN SPENT ON PERFUME THIS YEAR

COUPLES WHO LIVE TOGETHER BEFORE THEY MARRY HAVE AN 80% HIGHER CHANCE OF DIVORCE THAN COUPLES WHO DON'T

THE AVERAGE AMERICAN WOMAN IS 5'4" TALL AND WEIGHS 140 POUNDS, THE AVERAGE AMERICAN MODEL IS 5'11" TALL AND WEIGHS 117 POUNDS, MOST FASHION MODELS ARE THINNER THAN 98% OF AMERICAN WOMEN

ONLY 48% OF FIRST DATES END WITH A KISS. OVER 90% OF SINGLES SAY FIRST KISSES MADE THEM A BIT NERVOUS.

1/3 OF AMERICAN WOMEN WILL BE PHYSICALLY OR SEXUALLY ABUSED BY A HUSBAND OR BOYFRIEND IN THEIR LIFETIME

AIDS IS THE LEADING KILLER OF AMERICANS BETWEEN THE AGES OF 25 AND 44.

AVERAGE AGE OF BRIDES IS 27 AND GROOMS IS 29

1 IN 3 VISITORS TO ADULT WEBSITES IS A WOMAN

THERE ARE 46 MILLION ABORTIONS AROUND THE WORLD EVERY YEAR, 126,000 EVERY DAY

40% OF WOMEN HAVE EXTRAMARITAL AFFAIRS, 60% OF MEN

EVERY MINUTE, 1,484 TUBES OF LIPSTICK AND 2,055 JARS OF SKIN CARE PRODUCTS ARE SOLD IN THE U.S.

80% OF WOMEN ARE DISSATISFIED WITH THEIR APPEARANCE

50% OF MARRIAGES END IN DIVORCE

Adam Bomb

By Rick James

In regard to the chapter title, I made the following comment to a female friend: "All kidding aside, men really *are* evil." To which she responded, "Please don't say that. I struggle as it is to think well of men." Referring to men as a ticking bomb is not meant to incite hostility or fear between the sexes but to surface the truth that, like a bomb (or a perhaps a chain saw), men must be understood and handled correctly or they may hurt you.

Men may, in fact, become an enemy, for only an enemy feigns care and commitment while scheming a way to rob you of your most prized possession (purity), keeping you distracted with conversation while hurriedly squeezing your sofa out the back door. You, my dear ladies, possess something your physiological counterpart needs—craves, really. And like a junkie, he will often do or say anything to get his sexual fix.

But perhaps Melissa (that's my friend's name) is right and I should be more careful with labels. Perhaps fire is a better metaphor, for not all men are ticking bombs, but all men are like fire, bringing warmth and light while at the same time remaining capable of blazing out of control. Leave those curtain pulls dangling too close to the candle, and the whole house may wind up in ashes.

While you'll hear from the perspective of women throughout *Fantasy*, I think it's wise to begin this journey with a look at the flame. I will be the self-appointed spokesperson for the entire inferno of manhood, divulging classified information and helping you to better understand how the flame burns. And it *does* burn.

For instructional purposes, we're going to do something one should never do: make broad, sweeping generalizations about humanity. This is allowable because we are stereotyping men and not women and because we have a good biblical basis for doing so.

In the third chapter of 1 Corinthians the apostle Paul describes three types of people: The unbeliever, the godly man, and the worldly Christian:

Unbeliever: "The man without the Spirit does not accept the things that come from the Spirit of God, for they are foolishness to him, and he cannot understand them, because they are spiritually discerned" (1 Corinthians 2:14).

Godly man: "The spiritual man makes judgments about all things, but he himself is not subject to any man's judgment" (1 Corinthians 2:15).

Worldly Christian: "Brothers, I could not address you as spiritual but as worldly—mere infants in Christ. … You are still worldly. For since there is jealousy and quarreling among you, are you not worldly? Are you not acting like mere men?" (1 Corinthians 3:1, 3).

Following Paul's logic, we want to collate all men into one of these three spiritual file folders: worldly non-Christians, godly Christians, and worldly Christians. And we want to take a look at how each generally thinks about and behaves in the sexual area of life. This in some way should inform how you should approach each of these types of men—or not approach them, as the case may be.

THE WORLDLY NON-CHRISTIAN

On one occasion the apostle Paul was asked, "How would you describe young American males of the twenty-first century?" He responded, "Having lost all sensitivity, they have given themselves over to sensuality so as to indulge in every kind of impurity, with a continual lust for more" (Ephesians 4:19).

That's not really true. I mean, it's accurate; it's just not true that this was the context for Ephesians 4:19. Nothing could be a better articulation of the mind of the unregenerate male (remember, this is a generalization, and, this is the *unregenerate* male) than this. Men lust and think incessantly about sex.

No, really?

Really. Whatever you are picturing, it is worse. And it's worse in several dimensions.

It's worse in frequency, with sexual thoughts continuously parading across our minds like news updates on CNN. It's walking past women on the way to class, women we've never seen before, and thinking about having sex with them. It's sitting in class and thinking about the women in the classroom and what they look like undressed. Heck, it's thinking about the teacher if she's under sixty. It's being in the weight room and imagining the girl on the rowing machine in bed with us, and

it's conversations with other males about the same. This is the thought life of a man—a dirty vagabond collecting refuse in a shopping cart whose broken wheels are fixed in the direction of an endless circle.

For most men, this sort of thought life will culminate in some sort of sexual activity that day or later in the week, as they troll the pornographic Internet at night or indulge their imagination while lying in bed. Only to awaken in the morning and start the trash cycle again.

Men's thoughts are also worse in deviancy, fed by the pornography, media, and messages of a sexually obsessed culture. When you go into Abercrombie & Fitch, it isn't just a man and woman on the posters anymore, is it? It's a group of teens in bed—Say "*cheese*," *kids*. That poster is there only because of an audience that is not scandalized by the concept but comfortable with it and attracted to it.

On a recent news show a sting operation for pedophiles was staged. The camera recorded an older woman going online and slipping into chat rooms posing as a fourteen-year-old girl, one who was a virgin but open to having a sexual experience. Mind you, she made it abundantly clear she was fourteen. After a few hours of

conversations with various individuals, she began giving out her address and making invitations, saying that her parents wouldn't be home over the weekend. After only a few hours online, do you know how many men responded to her invitation? One or two? Try *eighteen* men of assorted ages, sizes, and shapes driving to the home of this "fourteen-year-old girl" to have a sexual rendezvous.

This is *not* deviant behavior. Deviant behavior is just that: behavior that deviates from the norm. But behavior such as I have described is increasingly becoming the norm.

Lust itself is a flame, and men fan it all day long, The flame, in rapid time, ceases to be satisfied with burning twigs and quickly moves on to harder and larger objects to feed its insatiable hunger—like an alcoholic, it progresses quickly from beer to Jack Daniels. It is insatiable lust and minds bloated with sexual imagery that cause men's sexual appetites to deviate in an attempt to quench an out-of-control fire. So when men fantasize about sex, they could be thinking about things that, if they were spoken, would seem patently offensive. I realize that women, too, have sexual fantasies that involve more than hand holding and a picnic lunch of brie and berries, but the point remains: men's thoughts and fantasies on the whole are more debased.

Men's thoughts about sex also tend to be more compulsive or addictive. As men cultivate lust, their disarrayed needs and desires all seem to focus on one thing: sex. And when they satisfy themselves and actually climax, it provides an enormous release. But soon masturbation, sex, and pornography become the snake oil that cures a thousand ailments. Men become their own unscrupulous pharmacist dispensing sex, pornography, and masturbation to treat just about any negative emotion or experience. And when something becomes such an all-encompassing coping mechanism for dealing with life, you have ventured in the realm of addictive behavior. You don't simply want sex; you *need* it.

If all that didn't create a disturbing brew in the minds of worldly male unbelievers, you now need to sprinkle in a beaker full of technology: DVD players, the Internet, imaging cell phones, etc. Now man's uncontrollable fire is introduced to a forest—Fire, meet Mr. Forest; Mr. Forest, Mr. Fire. Anything they want to see is now a button or a keystroke away. With such a voracious hunger, few men can resist the temptation to fill their hollow eyes with candy, and so, as you walk along campus, the odds are good that the majority of men you see will have viewed pornography within the last forty-eight hours.

This thing—this mind of carnal man, this vile concoction—is now at toxic levels, chemically unstable, and set to blow. So let's just add one more ingredient and see what happens: a belief that women are wired just like men are. Through TV, pornography, reality dating shows, MTV, and women's rooms littered with posters of half-dressed males, men begin to think that you think like they think. This, in turn, fuels all kinds of unrealistic sexual expectations and assumptions.

Bring all these forces together in the mind of a man drifting independently from God, and what you have is the perfect storm.

Are there exceptions? You bet, many of them. This is simply the broad brush of the non-Christian mind. But the Scripture's distinction still remains: non-Christians approach all areas of life, particularly the sexual area, from a dramatically different perspective, and without Christ, most men will contour to the bentness of the culture.

BACHELOR NUMBER 2

But just when you thought it couldn't get any worse … it doesn't. It actually gets better. There has always been a marked difference between a worldly unbeliever and a godly man. (And, ladies, if you find a godly man, he is indeed your friend and is worthy of respect.) But with the torrent of sensuality in our culture, the gap has become larger and the differences more distinct between these two types of man.

Godly men do all within their powers not to meditate on sexual thoughts: they memorize Scripture, keep active, go to the gym, punch themselves in the groin—whatever keeps them out of harm's way. When drawn to sexual images on TV or the computer, their impulse is to turn it off, pray, get out of the room, or take any other available escape route. Godly men seek friendships with the opposite sex that are pure and God-honoring, trying to reorient their view of women in a way that is free of sexual distortions. They also seek accountability and encouragement from other men, sharing their struggles and employing various tactics to keep one another striving for moral purity. These men consistently take their desires, longings, and failures to God, seeking intimacy, empowerment, and forgiveness.

No doubt you have some Christian men in your church or fellowship who are immature and vulgar and who basically act like idiots. But take my word for it, if they really are following after Christ, they look at women and sex from a perspective that is radically different from that of the worldly unbeliever, no matter how nice the non-Christian may appear to be. (Remember, an elephant will dance on its hind legs like a ballerina if it thinks it's going to get a peanut.)

Now, having looked at Christian men through a stained-glass window, it's important to see a few stark realities.

Almost all godly men struggle with pornography. Men are lured through their eyes as you may be through touch or your emotions. Christian men, although they are declining to masturbate and are trying to abstain from sex until marriage, are bombarded by provocative images every day and have at their computer instant access to any image or video clip they could possibly conceive of (as well as many they could not). This, to put it mildly, is a challenge.

It should not come as a surprise, then, that most Christian men have to deal with some degree of failure, either in how far they went with their girlfriend, in what they clicked on while on their computer, or in what they thought about while lying in bed. What may surprise you is the degree of guilt they feel when they fall. A bad choice on the computer can spiritually sideline men for days, and their time with God can be consumed with trying to experience the forgiveness that is, at least technically, freely theirs. Lust becomes the defining battle, benchmark, and bottleneck of their walk with Christ.

Because the pull of gravity is so great in the sexual area, you need to remember that no matter how godly the guy, you should not put him or yourself in a situation where you could stumble sexually. Committed Christian men are heroes, but they aren't supermen, and even if they were, you are kryptonite.

BEHIND DOOR NUMBER 3

We move now to exhibit C, the worldly Christian: "Brothers, I could not address you as spiritual but as worldly—mere infants in Christ. … You are still worldly. For since there is jealousy and quarreling among you, are you not worldly? Are you not acting like mere men?" (1 Corinthians 3:1, 3).

In every fellowship, short-term missions team, or youth group there are Christian men who have not made it their goal to seek sexual purity. It could be because they are still young in Christ or because they have not fully submitted this area to the Spirit's control. But whatever the reason, you have a rogue comet within your orderly Christian universe.

There's nothing more pathetic in the circus than when they dress the poor chimpanzee like a man or woman and have it ape (mimic) human behavior. Unfortunately, it doesn't take long to catch on to the trade language of the Christian world so that everybody—praise the Lord!—sounds as spiritual as everyone else, and the result is that it's difficult to pick out the chimps.

Years ago, as a college student, I went to my first Christian conference. I wasn't strongly connected to my campus ministry, so, along with a close friend, I took a bus with another Christian group halfway across the country to attend the conference. We had met some interesting people on the bus and made a few new Christian friends. The first night of the conference, my friend and I got a knock at our hotel room door. It was two women we had met on the bus, nice Christian girls from such-and-such college who, after entering our room, proceeded to get into our beds.

There's a point to this story; I just can't remember what it was. … Oh, yes: you just never know.

Don't be naive. Just because someone has a fish on his car or is wearing a Jesus bracelet, that does not mean he is one of the tribe seeking moral purity. Men in this camp exist along a spectrum, ranging from those who have embraced some picture of sexual purity to those seeking to take advantage of naive Christian women. Their mind, commitment, and thought life exist somewhere in the gray netherworld between the godly man and the worldly unbeliever. Buyer, beware: do not spend significant time with a man until you have a solid basis for assuming he is not in this camp.

So, having stared into the flame, I want to show you a neat trick: how to pass your finger through the flame without sustaining any burns.

MODESTY

In my home is a wireless network where my airport base station sends out unseen signals to computers throughout the house. I have never seen the signals, but as I am concurrently on the Web, they must somehow be broadcasting. Likewise, how a woman dresses, talks, and acts sends out sexual messages whether she realizes it or not, and therefore it's critical to contemplate what exactly you're broadcasting, to avoid sending confusing signals.

I have two teenage daughters, so I thoroughly get the complexity of this issue: Where does stylish turn into sexy? Where does sexy turn into slutty? It's even more complex than you may realize. Depending on the total "look" of a woman, something as simple as a pierced navel or a tattoo can be cute or it can send out sexual signals like you wouldn't believe. Added to this cheesy mess is a thick crust of subjectivity: some things turn on some men but not others.

How do you navigate through this maze? Get in the habit of seeking a second opinion on what you're wearing, such as from your dad, your brother, or a female friend (not a guy). My daughter was heading out to school with a cute but short skirt, a jean jacket, and shoes that had high heels. She looked fine to my wife, but my wife asked, "What do you think?" I said, "Lose the heels." In the male mind there is a microscopic line between a cute schoolgirl look and seductive-Britney-Spears-sex-toy-schoolgirl look. When you are open to feedback, you avoid mistakes and grow in your own discernment. And, when in doubt, lean in the direction of dressing conservatively, or as Grandma would say, "If you're not serving it for dinner, don't put it on the menu."

Flirting isn't harmless either. There are more godly ways than flirting to let men know you have relational interest. Flirtatious messages can send mixed signals of both relational and sexual interest that, in the mind of a man, can be tightly braided—like Britney's hair when she's dressed like a schoolgirl.

I honestly care that you have a need for masculine attention, but believe me when I say there is good attention and there is bad attention. They can feel the same to you, but they come from different places inside me. One is the godly man in me giving you a thumbs-up; the other is the depraved-spring-break-gone-wild troll who also resides in me giving you a thumbs-up. One of these men is worthy of your efforts, while the other is worthy of a jail sentence (ignore him). You can make me fumble my words by a glance or an innuendo, but it doesn't mean I'm drawn to your mind or your soul. If, on the other hand, I'm drawn to your humility, zeal, modesty, faith, love, ideas, dreams, passion, or talents, then you really are a beautiful woman.

Words are the clothes worn by ideas and thoughts, and modesty applies to them, too. There is an old adage among unregenerate males: "If she smokes, she's probably willing to have sex." The same connection can be made by men in regard to profanity: certain strange synapses in men are connected when they hear women talking like dockworkers. Avoid innuendos, sexual joking, and crassness. There's a bent part of a man that equates verbal graphicness with sexual graphicness. Best not to connect those dots in his head.

CULTIVATE YOUR RELATIONSHIP WITH GOD

As much as it may wish to go mall hopping around the universe, the moon is stuck in the gravitational field of the earth. It cannot escape and is forever sentenced to being the lapdog of our planet. The only chance for liberation is if a planet the size of Jupiter moved into the neighborhood with a significantly larger gravitational field.

So, what can we learn from physics? The only way not to live for men is to live for God. The only way to resist the desires for male attention and intimacy is to find intimacy in God. As the saying goes, "Nature abhors a vacuum," and so does your heart; therefore, it will always seek to fill itself with something. If it's not God, it will usually be men.

In 2 Corinthians the apostle Paul addresses the issue of singleness. I've pulled out just a couple of the verses.

> Now to the unmarried and the widows I say: It is good for them to stay unmarried, as I am. (1 Corinthians 7:8)

> I would like you to be free from concern. An unmarried man is concerned about the Lord's affairs—how he can please the Lord. (1 Corinthians 7:32)

The gist of Paul's message on singleness is that it affords a wonderful opportunity to be singularly devoted to God.

One of the great tragedies of singleness is that it is wasted in a state of pining for couplehood. But the Scripture encourages you to see yourself as a couple right now: you and God. You have a unique opportunity to give your total attention, energy, and passion to God—something that is not possible when you are married with children.

Strangely enough, such commitment, strength, and independence are extremely attractive to men. While it is perhaps counter intuitive, the best way to attract godly men is to leave them for your marriage to God. Besides, He's a much better

partner and He doesn't leave His clothes all over the floor.

STAY WITH THE FLOCK

There's strength and safety in numbers. While my daughter is home in our house, our family forms a protective barrier of protection over her purity. The other line of protection is the believing community of Christians.

Pam was extremely involved with a fellowship I led some years ago. She met a guy. Let's call him Bob because, well, his name really was Bob. She spent more and more time with him, and her connections with other women became threadbare. Before long, she began making a series of wrong choices, drifting out to sea further and further from the light of shore. Getting involved sexually was a poor choice, but it was her second poor choice. The first was to allow herself to drift from community—from honest questions, sharing of struggles, confession, accountability, and other sources of relationship and intimacy.

There needs to be at least one other Christian woman in your life who knows what is going on with you in the dating and sexual areas. Women's small groups that relationally go deep have proved to be the most critical component in living a life of purity. This is the closest thing to an antidote against male infections.

But I don't want to traipse off the property laid out in this article: the mind of man. So what you need to realize is that men not only can sniff out those wandering outside the fold (I don't know how, but they can) but also, even innocently, can lead you away from these life-sustaining relationships. Oo-oo, baby, it's a wild world, and it's tough to get by just upon a smile, girl …

I'M A LOSER, BABY, SO WHY WON'T YOU DATE ME?

Not a "loser" in the way Beck means, but in this context, the term "loser" means any guy who is not fully devoted to walking with Christ. If he is without a passion for Christ and sexual purity, your odds of losing and getting burned in the relationship are off the charts.

I'd love to tell you that temptation in this area will come in the form of a 4'10" obnoxious pervert, but it may well be a 6'2" European songwriter/poet/model who has long hair and an unshaven face and who cries over animal cruelty. You must remember that the orientation of the non-Christian mind is still radically different from that of the Christian. Don't date this man. Buy his albums and collected works of poetry, but do not date him. Only date a married man—one who has said "I do" to Christ and lives for Him alone.

DON'T BANK ON MY SELF-CONTROL

There is a medical term called "learned helplessness," and it refers to just what it says. In certain situations learned helplessness can be a defense mechanism, a posture of passivity that allows you to do certain things or not do certain things while avoiding the guilt or responsibility of the failure.

This is an issue that relates to relationships with bachelor number two, the godly man. No matter how godly the man, he is not beyond making impaired sexual choices. His failure does not justify yours if you go too far in the physical area of your relationship.

But isn't he supposed to give spiritual leadership?

You both are responsible for spiritual leadership. The role of spiritual leader relates to marriage, not dating, and so that responsibility does not belong to the man in your life until there's a ring on your finger. Until then, entrusting spiritual leadership to him in the sexual area is like giving a wolf guard duty at the chicken coop—a praying, Spirit-led wolf perhaps, but a wolf nonetheless. You need to share ownership and enforcement of boundaries. You both are guarding the chicken coop, and it will take watchfulness on both your parts to ensure that it doesn't get broken into. (I'm a little confused myself by my chicken coop metaphor, but let's assume it stands for something like sexual purity.)

PORNOGRAPHY

Don't take a boyfriend or husband's struggle with pornography as a personal failure on your part. Pornography is many things, but personal isn't one of them. You could be gorgeous and meet every whim of his beating heart, and he would still find sexual imagery alluring.

Maybe this analogy will help. Right now I could be deeply in love with you, having a wonderful time of conversation, while at the same time begin to eat a delicious cheeseburger. The appeal of that cheeseburger is to a different part of my mind and body and it in no way negates how I feel about you or any lack on your part. Pornography is that cheeseburger.

Certainly, when pornography becomes an addiction, on many fronts it will hinder relationships and intimacy, and it can lead to unfaithfulness. But for most men, pornography functions on a visceral level like a juicy cheeseburger (I'm beginning to think I have a problem with cheeseburgers), and men instantly go into a trance like Homer Simpson—*Mmm*, donuts. While it is sin, and a damaging one, having looked at pornography does not mean your male friend is a sexual deviant or in any way mean you are inadequate.

My reasoning, in giving clarity to this issue, is not to downplay the harm of pornography. Rather, it is to free you from the sense of responsibility you may feel for a male friend's involvement. The old Puritan adage was "Idle hands are the devil's workshop"; for women, it's guilt, low self-esteem, and a sense of inadequacy that most easily lead to moral compromise. When it comes to pornography, have compassion on the men's struggle and pray for them, but assume no responsibility for their involvement.

END NOTE

There is so much more I could tell you, but I sense I have given away one too many party secrets. To talk anymore could upset the delicate balance of power between the sexes and have far-reaching and cataclysmic results—floods, tidal waves, etc. I hope these words, as well as the rest of the book, will inspire you to purity. And purity's great value is that it brings honor, glory, and praise to Jesus Christ, the One who has purchased us out of sin. Oh, to be that spotless bride.

RICK JAMES is the Director of Cru Press, the publishing arm of the campus ministry of Campus Crusade for Christ. He has been on staff for 17 years and currently lives in West Chester, Pennsylvania with his wife, Katie, and three kids: Avery, Whitney and Will.

My Own Worst Enemy

By Cheryl Fletcher

If men are as depraved and sexually self-serving as many claim to be, then what are we? Their pure, innocent, nonsexual prey? I don't think so.

I am a woman and I am a Christian. If you ask me, *I* am the enemy. It's not my point to paint women as worse than men or to paint men as worse than women. I just want to stop pointing the finger at the other gender and to take a deep look inside myself.

There are some things it is helpful for me to understand about guys, but a lot of the information they give (e.g., that they're visual, lustful, and sex-obsessed) doesn't always help me in my quest to stay pure. On a good day, I want to help them in their battle; on a bad day, I'm going to use these facts against them to get what *I* want.

And what I want cannot be captured on a bumper sticker. Someone somewhere came up with this phrase, and it's been way overused: *Men give love to get sex and women give sex to get love*. I wish it were that simple. What I hear in this is that men want sex and women want love. I can't speak to the male side of this platitude, but I can speak to the female side.

Yes, I want love, but I want so much more. I want love and sex and intimacy and the feeling of being desired. I want a relationship with a man—a boyfriend who might become a husband. I want to feel attractive and sexy. I want to be powerful and tender and independent and dependent. I want to be cared for and able to care. I want romance. I want to be respected and cherished. I want to be enjoyed and delighted in. I want a man to want me but not need me, but I want to be needed and to have my needs met. I want to be adored but not worshiped. I want to be sexually aroused. I want to be pure. I want to be physically intimate, because I want a man to love me. But sometimes I want to be physically intimate because I want to be physically intimate.

Women are complex. At least I am.

Men are too, really. I had a boyfriend who admitted that he wanted more than just a sexual encounter—he wanted to feel powerful (because he could arouse a woman) and he wanted to feel desired and admired and respected. On the outside, he appeared pretty simple—feed him, give him a U2 CD, and satisfy his sexual passion, and he's a happy camper. But peel back the layers and there is so much more: the complicated soul of a man.

But I digress. This is not about men; it's about women. It's about women and sex and all the things we long for. And when it comes to sex, it's about how we are our own worst enemy. But this is true only if our ultimate desire is for Jesus and for loving and honoring Him. One of the definitions of an enemy on dictionary.com is one who "intends injury to, or opposes the interests of another." If we are women who love Jesus with all our heart, mind, and soul, then we injure ourselves and oppose our greatest interest if we use our sexuality in a way that doesn't delight Christ. And then, as God-loving women, we become our own worst enemy.

SPELL IT OUT

Let me define my use of the word sex before we continue. When I say "sex" in this article, I do not just mean intercourse. I am including here all that is sexual and physical in our relationships with men. I mean kissing and all that follows. You may never have intercourse, but you might have an extremely sexual relationship with a man. I have heard sexual immorality defined as creating a desire that cannot righteously be fulfilled. And ultimately, the fire we play with before actual intercourse is foreplay—it's meant to lead us to the ultimate sex act. But all of it is sexual.

Sex is not bad or evil. I just think it has a safe place to be explored and enjoyed—marriage. I believe that Jesus delights in our sexuality and in sex. He created both. He made us women and men. He made sex for pleasure and procreation and intimacy.

We are women. We delight our Creator when we delight in being made as women. We delight Him when we act and dress like women. This does not mean we have to cook and sew and never wear jeans, but it does mean we enjoy our femininity. We enjoy looking like women. We aren't ashamed of our bodies. We don't need to dress like Britney Spears, but we're not wearing our grandmother's muumuu either.

We are sexual beings. As we mature, our bodies are wired to want sex. We will get aroused and our bodies will desire a physical intimacy that matches our desire for emotional intimacy. What is beautiful is that sex was God's idea and it is a powerful picture of His intimate relationship with His bride, the church. God initiates with us and enters us through the Holy Spirit, and, with trust, we receive Him. There is great joy and pleasure in this relationship.

Theologically, we know our relationship with God to be a covenant relationship. This means that His relationship with us is a committed relationship and our intimacy is enjoyed in and as a result of this commitment. He promises to never leave us or forsake us (i.e., there's no divorce). He is safe. God will never embarrass or shame us.

Sex was designed to be enjoyed and experienced in the context of a covenant like this called marriage. But most people today don't really like that idea. They don't like limits on their freedom.

FOR YOUR OWN GOOD

My dog, Grace, loves to dig and escape from our backyard. In this backyard there is grass to roll in, water to drink, a porch for shade, toys to enjoy, and a fence to keep her safe. But Grace doesn't see it this way. Through her dog eyes, the fence keeps her from all kinds of great adventures. Through my eyes, the fence keeps her from ending up a bloody mess of fur with a tire track over her sweet little nose. To me, the fence protects; to Grace, the fence prohibits.

To most of the world, God's mandate to restrict sexual activity to a marriage relationship is prohibiting. It's seems so limiting, so 1864. To God, it's protection. It protects the holiness of the sex act. It protects the intimacy and fidelity of a marriage. It protects the goodness and beauty of what He has created. It protects His glory.

But most of us are like my dog. We see limits as confining, legalistic, absurd. And the only way I can explain this mindset is by understanding my sin. At the heart of sin is rebellion toward the person and purposes of God. We don't trust God. We don't trust that His decrees are for our good. We're suspicious. We're convinced He's withholding something. As soon as He says no, we find ourselves saying, "But I must." Why is it I want to pull every fire alarm I see if it happens to have a Don't Touch sign across the plated glass?

For this discussion to have any significance, then, God must matter and His purposes and provisions must matter.

PREVIOUSLY ENGAGED

I started loving God when I was seventeen. It was then that I became a Christian. Some would say I "married Jesus," which seems like a cheesy way of saying that I joined myself to Him in a covenant relationship. I placed my trust in Him to be all that He says He is: God and Savior and the only One able to abolish the consequence of my sin.

Being married to Jesus does sound cheesy. It sounds like something Gretchen Slavinsky might have said.

Gretchen was a self-righteous girl at my high school who used to tell all the kids who smoked pot before first period that they needed to be saved or they were going to hell. I think they were too stoned to care, but she'd say stuff like that. I can still hear her saying in a pious tone, "I'd never listen to Zeppelin. I'm married to Jesus."

But if I can get Gretchen's voice out of my head, then the image of being married to Jesus is helpful. To be a Christian is to be the bride of Christ. I belong to Him in the way a wife belongs to a husband and a husband belongs to a wife. We are Christ's greatest priority and He is ours. He loves us; we love Him. This is the reason the Bible often compares our propensity to sin as adultery—we're messing around on our soul mate, our husband, our first love.

THE THINGS WE DO FOR LOVE

If it is our greatest desire to love and honor Christ, then when we oppose this desire, we are our own worst enemy. And this is definitely true when we dishonor His purposes for sex. Let me suggest three ways we do this:

1. We use sex as a shortcut to intimacy. In any dating relationship, we desire to feel close, connected, and known, and it is a temptation to speed this process up by being physical. But anyone who has tried this fast track knows that the connection is fleeting and the physical closeness doesn't satisfy the desire to be truly known. The reality is that it can create even greater insecurity. We wonder, *Does he really love me or does he just like making out? and Do I really like him or do I just like having someone to kiss?*

For a woman, true intimacy comes first from being known and enjoyed. Wisdom would say that physical intimacy should not get ahead of emotional intimacy, but unfortunately we often listen to movies and sitcoms more than wisdom. Our favorite shows tell us that we're not intimate until we've had sex. So we let sex, rather than long conversations and emotional connection, inform us that we're close.

2. We use sex to feel attractive and wanted and feminine. If you have any insecurity about your attractiveness or desirability—and it seems most of us do—then this will be a great temptation. And this is when that information about guys being depraved and sexually self-serving plays into our court. If we are dating a guy who desires to follow Jesus and keep the relationship pure, there is something wicked in us (at least in some of us) that wants to push him to the point where he's a bit out of control and has to pull back because we're just so sexy and desirable. Unfortunately, he doesn't always pull back. But for that fleeting moment, we get to feel just what we wanted to feel.

And then, in a twisted way, we lose all respect for him. Can I explain it? Not really, but I know it to be true. The self-serving guy thing allows me to put all the blame on him. Unconsciously, I decide that if he were worthy of respect, he would have stopped us. In a strange, sadistic, selfish, and most often unconscious way, I have set him up to fail the test.

3. We use sex to get a man and try to hold on to him. Welcome to the world of insecurities and fears. Desperately, we want a relationship, but comparison rears its ugly head. The girl next door is a supermodel, and for those of us who are not, depression and desperation set in. To stave off the sadness, we look into our little bag of tricks and pull out the dagger of sexuality: *If I can't give him the girl off the magazine cover, then maybe I can give him my body and that will hold him. If it takes dressing like I forgot to put clothes on over these undergarments, then that's what I'll do, dadgummit! Anything to not be alone one more Saturday night watching the complete third season of the* Gilmore Girls *on DVD.*

Unfortunately, this strategy can work and we find ourselves married to a man who is as far from being our soul mate as Jude Law is from being our husband. When only the physical holds a couple together while dating, it often implodes in marriage and we find ourselves in a hard place.

HELP

I have no formula for getting out of this cycle of self-destruction. I know it starts with Jesus. I know this picture of being married to Him is helpful to me. I'm a romantic—I believe in being true to the one I love, in staying together and honoring one another. I believe in not messing around. And I believe that sexual purity begins with loving Jesus.

My mother scared me into staying a virgin during my adolescence. I didn't want an STD and I didn't want to get pregnant and have to drop out of school and work at the Piggly Wiggly to support my baby. I didn't want to get naked with some random high school crush who would never really love me, then have to introduce him to my husband at the ten-year class reunion.

Then I went to college and mom's scary scenarios didn't seem to have the same effect. Call it love. Call it hormones. But the urge to merge seemed much more intense after I left home. In college and beyond, it was my love for Christ that kept me pure. Maybe I'm starting to sound like Gretchen Slavinsky, but it's the truth. I can remember driving alone down Airport Boulevard in the midst of one relationship and crying out, "Jesus, You'd better be real, because my love for You is the only reason I'm not having sex."

For me, loving Jesus is the starting point. Loving the Bible and believing it's true is also key.

Paul says in 1 Corinthians 7:1 that "it is good for a man not to touch a woman" (nasb). This could be translated "for a man not to touch a woman in a married way (a sexual way)." This is where it's suggested that sexual immorality might be defined more broadly than just intercourse—any touch that leads to sexual desire that cannot be righteously fulfilled might be considered sexual immorality.

Again, most of the kissing and touching we do is technically foreplay and it's playing with fire. The wise man in Proverbs 6:27, 29 asks,

> Can a man take a fire in his bosom
> And his clothes not be burned? …
> So is the one who goes in to his neighbor's wife;
> Whoever touches her will not go unpunished.

The author of Hebrews put it this way: "Marriage is to be held in honor among all, and the marriage bed is to be undefiled; for fornicators and adulterers God will judge" (13:4). Now, there's a warm, fuzzy verse to puff-paint on the side of your mug.

Ever wonder about God's will for your life? The answer shows up in 1 Thessalonians 4, and it is anything but veiled. Paul clearly states, "This is the will of God, your sanctification; that is, that you abstain from sexual immorality; that each of you know how to possess his own vessel in sanctification and honor, not in lustful passion, like [those] who don't know God" (verses 3-5).

Sanctification is the process of becoming more and more like Jesus Christ, and if we are to look more and more like Him, we are to abstain from sexual immorality. Basically, being sexually immoral—taking sex out of its proper context—doesn't look like Jesus. To look like Jesus is to be pure and holy and righteous, fully submitted to the Father.

If I want to look like Jesus (and I do) but I use sex outside its design, then I am my own worst enemy—I have opposed what I desire most, which is to imitate and love my Savior and bring glory and honor to Him.

So I want to fall more in love with Jesus. I want to seek to live out a life that is honoring to Him in this sex-is-everywhere-and-only-weird-people-are-still-virgins world. I need to confess my selfishness and idolatry (because wanting a relationship with a man is often the thing I bow down to most in this life). I need to pray. I need to ask some friends to pray for me. I need to go to church. I need to find a small group of people to encourage me on this path. And I need to avoid doing stupid stuff with guys. I also need to work on emotional intimacy—the process of knowing and being known. I need to memorize some Scripture. I need to date guys who love Jesus too. And—did I mention?—I need to stay away from doing stupid stuff with guys.

Nobody wants to be their own worst enemy.

CHERYL FLETCHER has worked with YoungLife and Campus Crusade for Christ. She is a conference speaker and currently the director of collegiate ministry at First Evangelical Free Church of Austin, TX.

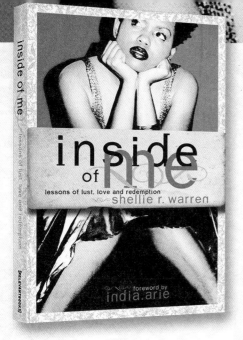

"Get Your Group On"…(Trying too hard)…
"Groupies"…(Too retro)…
"Groupers"…(That's a type of fish and it's too close to "gropers", which is interesting, but inappropriate) so…

Small Groups

(how very uninspired)

I'm going to guess that it would not be too difficult for you to gather a bunch of women to talk about men, sex, and dating on a regular basis. You may already have a group that does just that—your Bible study or roommates or sorority sisters—whatever. Why not be intentional about your discussions?

I truly believe that experiencing life as God intended it is impossible on your own. Apart from a collection of people who are committed to following Christ and living life together, we miss out on opportunities to grow and express our faith. We need each other to love, serve, encourage, speak truth, and spur one another on. These studies are intended for you to do just that with a group of friends. If you don't have a community, this is your chance to create one. Start taking applications now. I know it may seem overwhelming to start your own small group, but as I've often said, women's small-group success is when you laugh really hard and/or somebody cries. That won't take much, I promise. My hope is that these studies give you some structure and permission to get into each others' lives while each of you falls more in love with Jesus in the process.

Now, I also realize that there are quite a few questions for each study, and women being women, you may not get to all of them in the time allowed. So I'd suggest that whoever is facilitating the group go through ahead of time and pick out the questions she wants to be sure to cover, based on the needs of your group. There are answers in the back, but due to limited time, space, and caffeine drained from thousands of glasses of iced tea, they are brief. Many answers leave quite a bit of room for further discussion and additional passages and resources. So feel free to expound upon what we've started.

These studies are loosely tied to the articles, but not all the articles are connected to a study. So be sure you don't miss any juicy little nugget of wisdom or insight offered by our oh-so-wise contributors.

Lastly, I have this thought: the Bible would be whole lot different if it had been written by women. Men in general just record the basic, straight-up facts, and we have to assume much of the other elements. If women had written the Bible, there would be much less left to the imagination and much less confusion. We'd know what color their tunics were, what things smelled like, who was there and their relationship to one another, and most importantly, the tone and demeanor and full context in which things were communicated. Granted, the Bible would be twice as long, but it would be just that much more insightful (much like this book relative to its masculine counterpart, *Flesh*).

So, my point is this: …I don't really have one. Just that.

Study 1:
Quenched
Wants and Needs

Related Articles: Why Should You, What Bride Magazine Won't Tell you

When you think about life right now, and then five, ten, or fifteen years down the road, what do you hope for and dream about? What do you want in order to be fulfilled in your life? What are the things that each of your dreams has in common? Why do you think you share those things in common?

Read John 4:3-29.

1. Why does Jesus ask her for a drink?

2. Why was it surprising that Jesus would speak with the woman?

3. The sixth hour, by the Jewish clock, is noon. Why do you think she was there at noon?

4. What is Jesus really offering her by referring to "living water"?

5. Every woman is thirsty. In context, what was this woman thirsty for, and how had she tried to meet her thirst?

6. In what way have you sought to find life in relationships? Or what other things do you rely on for satisfaction?

7. Specifically, how have they left you thirsty?

8. With at least five previous relationships, and now in a sixth, she is obviously caught in cycle. How does this cycle work? What keeps women coming back?

9. When Jesus puts His finger on the issue, the woman changes the subject. Why would a woman be uncomfortable with being confronted on this particular issue?

10. In what ways have you seen Jesus meet your thirsts?

11. In what ways are you still thirsty? What do you do with those yearnings?

12. Describe how Jesus interacted with the woman—His tone and demeanor?

13. If Jesus came into the room where you are right now, how do you think He would approach and interact with you, and you with Him?

14. Jesus offers Himself to her as the substitute for her thirst and string of men. Does your spiritual life reflect that Jesus is your substitute or a means to get the relationship you seek?

Study 2:
Sex Offenders
Purity

Related Articles: I Gave My Word to Stop at Third, Adam Bomb, My Own Worst Enemy, The M Word

When it comes to the physical aspect of a dating relationship, how far is too far? What is the general consensus about this among your peers? What are some of the reasons or thinking you've heard others give for determining their standards in this area?

Read Matthew 5:27-28.

1. What is Jesus trying to communicate, exactly? Is thinking about it just as bad as doing it?

2. Reversing the gender roles and applying Jesus's teaching to women, what does lust usually look like for women? When, and/or in what situations, are you tempted to lust?

3. This passage is addressing adultery—having sex with another person's spouse. Do you think the same principle would apply to fornication—sex outside marriage?

4. What do you think is the intent behind Jesus's clarifying of the law, expanding His listeners' understanding of the definitions?

Read 1 Thessalonians 4:1-12.

5. Where are the two occurrences of the phrase "more and more" found? What does this tell you about Paul's primary purpose in writing these words?

6. Read again verses 3-5 and define the following words:
   • sanctified
   • sexual immorality
   • passionate lust
   • heathen

7. What are the specific challenges of our culture to remaining pure until marriage? Do you think we have it better, worse, or the same as others? What is the most difficult of all these factors?

8. Honoring God by controlling our bodies is a consistent theme in Paul's letters. Look up the following verses and record what they say on this issue:
   • Romans 6:19
   • Romans 12:1
   • 1 Corinthians 6:13-20
   • 1 Corinthians 9:24-27

9. What insights do these passages give you with regard to 1 Thessalonians 4:3-6?

10. Verse 6 says to not wrong your brother. How does sexual immorality wrong, or steal from, another brother (or sister)?

11. Imagine you are married and are having a discussion with your spouse concerning his sexual involvement before marriage. At what level of physical involvement will you begin to feel that someone has taken something from you?

12. How important do you feel it is to go back and apologize to people you have sexually wronged?

13. In verses 6-8, what further motivations to remain sexually pure do you see? In verse 8, why do you think Paul adds the parenthetical phrase "who gives you His Spirit"?

14. Why do you think God wants us to remain sexually pure until marriage?

15. In dating relationships, what levels of physical involvement do you think are clearly off-limits? What do you think is allowable? What are some of the gray areas?

16. How have you arrived at your standard?

17. Paul speaks about greeting other Christians with a "holy kiss" (Romans 16:16; 1 Corinthians 16:20). Some have suggested the principle of the holy kiss for dating relationships—showing physical affection with a commitment to not cause sexual arousal. It moves away from a standard of "What can I get away with?" or "How can I avoid all contact?" and asks, rather, "How can I physically express affection without sexually arousing either myself or my partner?" How do you feel about this as a guideline?

18. For you, personally, what are your reasons for pursuing sexual purity? Set aside a page in your journal and write out your guidelines, your reasons

for wanting to remain sexually pure, and a prayer of commitment.

Study 3:
Getting Back Together
Forgiveness and Restoration

Related Articles: The Beauty of Forgiveness, The Place of Faith, Spirit Filled

Of all of the sins we commit, nothing makes us feel more guilty than sexual sin. Why do you think that is?

Read John 8:1-11.

1. Obviously, there were two people involved. But only the woman is exposed. Why is there consistently a double standard for women?

2. Do you think God requires more of women than of men in exercising sexual restraint?

3. The woman obviously feels shame for what she had done. Write down on a piece of paper those things that have been the greatest source of shame for you.

4. Verses 4-6 mention that the religious leaders are hoping to trap Jesus. How does this form a trap for Jesus?

5. If convicted, the woman would have been stoned. In areas of shame, there is both a fear of judgment and a desire for it. Why?

6. In verse 7 Jesus says, "If any one of you is without sin, let him be the first to throw a stone at her." What might Jesus's motivations be for phrasing this statement the way He does?

7. Jesus writes on the ground with His finger twice. What significance might there be in Jesus writing with His finger as the law of Moses is discussed?

8. Jesus says, "Neither do I condemn you." I think we all know this is true for us, and yet somehow it is difficult to feel it on the emotional level as this woman must have. What have you found helpful in emotionally processing the truth of Christ's forgiveness?

9. Jesus tells the woman to go and leave her life of sin. Why would He tell her to do so?

10. So, what happens if she does sin again? Can we leave a life and then return, and is forgiveness still there?

Read John 21:15-24.

Often, because of our past sin, we feel that God can't use us to minister to others. But we see from Peter's case that restoration is possible, no matter how we've transgressed, sexually or otherwise. Peter, the cornerstone of the church, sinned hugely. He denied Jesus outright three times, even after being warned (John 18). It doesn't get much worse than that. But Jesus still had great plans for him.

11. The most obvious question is, why does Jesus ask Peter three times, "Do you love me?" Is this a rebuke or an opportunity for confession?

12. Why does Jesus ask Peter if he loves Him "more than these"?

13. What are the essential components of confessing our sin? If we are forgiven due to Christ's death, why do we need to confess our sins?

14. What role does faith play in feeling forgiven?

15. Rationalizing, vowing to never commit the same sin again, and berating ourselves all are human attempts to feel forgiven. How?

16. How is each a betrayal of faith?

17. It takes great courage for Peter to hear the painful truth from Jesus. It has been said that courage, or the lack of it, is what keeps us from repenting, growing in holiness, and feeling forgiven. Do you agree? If so, why? What was the most painful truth you've had to hear about yourself?

18. Earlier, you wrote a list of things you were ashamed of. How has that list affected your relationship with God? Take that list and, if you haven't already done so, go through the process of confession: Talk to God and own the sin; acknowledge that it was wrong. Thank God for His forgiveness. Turn from it and let it go. Ask the Spirit to be in control of this area of your life so that you might "leave your life of sin" (verse 11). After praying through those steps, write 1 John 1:9 across the paper, then tear it up and throw it away.

Study 4:
Bride by Design
Self Worth

Related Articles: M.A.C. and the Knife, Body Temple

If you could create the perfect soul mate for yourself, what would he be like and look like?

Read Colossians 1:16.

1. What do you think it means that you were created by Christ, through Him, and for Him?

2. What are the things that are uniquely you? What do you wish were different about your body or your personality and nature?

3. What difference does it make for you to know that Jesus created you exactly like you are for Himself, for His own purposes?

4. How could God use those things to glorify Himself?

5. Throughout Scripture, the metaphor of the bride is used for Israel and for the church. Isaiah speaks of God rejoicing over us in the same way that a bridegroom rejoices over his bride (Isaiah 62:5). How does a bridegroom rejoice over, or delight in, his bride?

6. How do you imagine that translates to Jesus rejoicing over you?

Read Psalm 139:13-16.

7. What does it mean that you are "fearfully and wonderfully made"?

8. How do you reconcile this verse with someone who has serious health issues or birth defects or even with things about your body that are not attractive?

9. Verse 14 says, "I know that full well" (another version says I know that "in my soul"), speaking of the fact that all God's works are wonderful. What do you think it means to know something full well, or in your soul, as opposed to just knowing it?

10. Does knowing in your soul that your body is a wonderful creation by Christ and for Him influence how you care for your body? Your eating habits? Rest? Exercise?

11. Is there any freedom or comfort or hope in the fact that all your days have been planned specifically for you before one of them came to be?

12. Take time to do exactly what verse 14 speaks of—praise God because you are fearfully and wonderfully made. In your journal, make a list of those things that are uniquely you—physically, personality, giftedness, even weaknesses and write a prayer of thanksgiving for those things. Take note of how God has used those things to build character, draw you to Himself, or help others.

Study 5:
Gripes, Complaints, and Compliments
Worry and Distraction

Related Articles: Waiting Room, All Worship

Describe your relationship with God.

Read Luke 10:38-42.

1. Why is Martha so upset and frustrated?

2. Read John 11:17-44. Combining that with the passage in Luke, describe the basic temperaments or personalities of the two women: Mary and Martha. (Notice in Luke who owns the home.)

3. Who do you identify with more: Mary or Martha? Why?

4. What are the strengths of being a "Martha" in life? What are the weaknesses?

5. Having lost her focus on the Lord, and having been consumed with worry, Martha lashes out and blames her sister when, according to Jesus, it was her own poor choice that is the problem. What are the common results you experience when you lose your focus on God? Who or what do you blame when your life becomes chaotic or doesn't go your way?

6. When have you found yourself recently in a state of Martha-like worry? What distracts you from devotion to Christ?

7. In verse 42, how does Jesus refocus Martha's perspective?

8. In verse 41, the passage more literally reads, "Mary has chosen the better portion." Look up the following verses and record what background they give concerning Jesus's use of the word "portion."
• Numbers 18:28-29
• Psalm 73:26
• Lamentations 3:24

9. One of the uses of "portion" is as daily food, which provides energy, focus, and motivation. What other things can become your "food source"?

10. In what way could you say that Jesus is your daily portion?

11. Briefly read through Luke 11:1-13. It is not accidental that Luke puts this story next. What things do you see in Jesus's teaching on prayer that could help Martha regain a proper focus?

12. List some practical ways for you to deal with distractions and maintain your connection with Jesus.

Study 6:
Lies that Bind
Believing Lies

Related Articles: Conflicts of Interest, God Fathers

Have you ever believed something that later on you found out was not true? Had you made decisions or acted on that false information? Describe the situation.

Read Luke 4:1-13.

1. Why does Satan choose this time to attack Jesus?

2. When are you most vulnerable to believing lies?

3. Jesus is tempted to meet His needs in a way that God had not sanctioned (verses 3-4). What area is the most difficult for you to wait on God and not provide for yourself?

4. The temptation to take a shortcut to the cross was a real one (verses 5-6). Satan never shoots blanks. Write out five lies you are most prone to believe about yourself and others.

5. Sometimes women's lies follow familiar patterns. Nancy Leigh DeMoss lists these lies as some of the most common women believe:
- God doesn't love me.
- God should fix my problems.
- I can't help the way I am.
- I should not have to live with unfulfilled longings.
- I can sin and get away with it.
- I can make it without consistent time in the Word and in prayer.
- I have to have a husband to be happy.
- If I feel something, it must be true.
- If my circumstances were different, I would be different.
- I shouldn't have to suffer.

Which of these are you most prone to believe?

6. What are some Scripture passages to combat the lies you believe?

7. Jesus audibly speaks the scriptural truth in response to Satan's lies (verse 8). Do you think there is any value in quoting Scripture and speaking the truth out loud or in a group? If so, what is it?

8. When you shared what lies you believe, why do you think it made you feel better?

9. The truth of Scripture is obviously the major way we combat lies. How else can we use truth as a defense?

10. Sometimes believing a lie is a journey that starts with small steps that move away from the truth. In what ways do you begin to migrate from the truth?

11. Jesus is tempted by Satan to ask God to prove His love and faithfulness, yet Jesus sees this as testing God (verse 9). Why?

12. One of the most common lies we believe is that God doesn't really love me as an individual. What are some legitimate ways to seek assurance of God's love for you, and what are not?

13. Spend some time journaling ways that you know that God loves you personally as well as addressing any of the other lies that you struggle with.

Study 7:
Group Date
Community and Accountability

Related Articles: Love Story, part 2

Share something vulnerable about yourself that you have never shared with anyone before. Afterward, discuss: How did that feel? What were the risks involved?

We know from Mark's account that when Jesus sent the disciples out to preach, heal, and cast out demons, He sent them out in pairs (Mark 6:7). Jesus knew the wisdom of community.

Read Ecclesiastes 4:9-12.

1. According to this passage, what are the benefits of living life with close friends alongside you? What are the negative consequences of living in isolation?

2. Can you think of a time in your life when you had to fend for yourself and when having a friend come alongside you really might have helped you? Can you think of a time when a friend did come

alongside you during a difficult time? What did she do? How did she help you?

3. What causes people to isolate themselves? What causes you to isolate yourself from others?

4. In your experience, do media outlets (movies, music, computers, and so on) relieve isolation or increase it?

5. The opposite of isolation is accountability and community. On a scale from 1 to 10, how would you rate your experience of community? Of isolation?

6. Verse 12 says that "a cord of three strands is not quickly broken." It is thought that the three strands in the cord represent two friends plus God. What is the benefit of having Christian community, specifically? How would you define Christian community?

7. Why are we drawn toward community?

8. What does healthy community look like?

9. The twelve-step Alcoholics Anonymous program was founded on Christian principles. Most people who make it through the program cite step five as the most critical one. It states: "Admit to God, to

ourselves and to another human being the exact nature of our wrongs." Step five is essentially James 5:16: "Confess your sins to each other and pray for each other so that you may be healed." With whom can you, or do you, share the exact nature of your wrongs?

10. The term used for Christian friendships that help one another in an area of life (such as sexual purity) is accountability. What does accountability mean?

11. What sorts of things might you do to hold one another accountable?

12. It has been said that a true accountability partner models both grace and truth. What do you think this means? Who models this for you?

13. Do you tend to be more grace oriented or more truth oriented?

14. Hebrews 10:24 says, "Let us consider how we may spur one another on toward love and good deeds."

Who could you spur on? List three things you could do that would spur a friend on to love and good deeds.

15. Are you part of a healthy community of Christ followers? What is your part in creating and maintaining that community?

Study 8:
Love Connection
Commitment

Related Articles: Love Story, part 1

How would you define love?

Read Luke 9:57-62.

1. Here are some common phrases spoken in wedding vows: "in sickness and in health," "forsaking all others," "till death do you part." What similarities do you see between these vows and this passage? What is Jesus really asking?

2. If love is measured by its duration, priority, and willingness to sacrifice, in what way do you feel that your love for Jesus is lacking and/or growing?

3. How has Jesus proven His love and commitment to us? In what ways have you personally experienced and internalized His love for you? Read John 14:21-24.

4. According to Jesus, what is evidence of your love for Him?

5. What is His promise for those who love Him?

6. It has been said that many Christians would rather date Jesus than marry Him. What do you think is meant by that?

7. The literal difference between dating and marriage is obvious. But emotionally, how do they feel different?

8. In dating, we are often trying to impress. In what ways are you still trying to perform for God?

9. When you think of a marriage that is successful, what would you say is the key ingredient?

10. Stagnancy is the death knell of a relationship. In what ways have you felt your marriage to Christ becoming stagnant? How have you tried to introduce life and passion into your relationship with Him?

11. Sometimes married couples renew their vows in the course of their relationship. Reread the passages and review the things you've learned about Jesus and His character and nature throughout this study. As you've learned more about who He is and what a marriage commitment involves, write your own vows to recommit to your relationship with Him. Sign and date it.

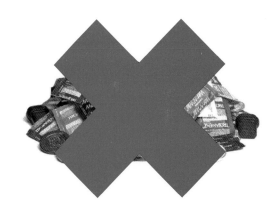

TOO BAD THEY DON'T MAKE ONE FOR YOUR HEART.

everystudent.com

Why Should You?

Because it's a natural part of being human.
Because it's part of who I am, and I need to explore and express my sexuality.
Because it's unhealthy to not do it.
Because how else will I know if I'm compatible with my partner before I marry him?
Because it's fun.
Because everyone else is doing it.
Because I need to connect more intimately with my boyfriend.
Because I need to show him I love him.
Because I really want to.
Because I can't help myself.
Because we're going to get married anyway.
Because I'm a freak if I don't.
Because I've already done it.
Did I say because it's fun?

At least that's what everyone says.

I just flipped through the channels and had the opportunity to watch the *Sunday Night Sex Show* (though it's not Sunday) with Sue Johanson, a grandma recommending sex toys—explaining some contraption that I chose to not let my imagination try to figure out. Somewhere between *Fear Factor* and *Law & Order* reruns, I saw actual sex in progress on *Nip/Tuck* and a bed full of topless women with the appropriately regulated blurs on the *Howard Stern* show. On WE there was a show about lesbian women who like to dress as men and do a little dirty dancing with other women. So I turned to the main network channels thinking they might be more tame. On *Inside Edition* they showed the controversial Carl's Jr. Paris Hilton ad several times over while discussing just how controversial it is. And then, of course, there was the obligatory and ubiquitous Victoria's Secret ad. Just another night of relaxing TV, and just what I need in my head before I go to bed—like I need a fungal disease. Frankly, it was tempting to watch most of it.

Between the ages of thirteen and twenty-three, the average person sees about a hundred thousand sex acts or implied sex acts on TV. Only 19 percent of those acts are within the context of marriage. We're saturated with images and ideas of sex, and little of it has anything to do with real sex—sex as God intended it. If it's true that our values and desires are shaped by what we're exposed to (and who needs to spend millions of dollars on a study to prove that, though it's been done), it's no wonder that statistics also say that 52 percent of women have sex by age eighteen and 75 percent before they get married.

For women, there is something in us that wants to be Paris Hilton (okay, maybe not her, exactly, but at least Jennifer Aniston, Lindsay Lohan, or the like), something that wants to be that sexy and desirable, to be that sought after, to be that ideal beauty. I think one of the best ways to explain the difference between men and women and our sexual desires is to say that when men look at a steamy sex scene in a movie they want the woman; when women see such a scene, it's not so much that we want the guy as much as we want to be that woman. We want to be wanted and known, physically and emotionally. Not to mention the time-honored truth that girls do just want to have fun. And if that means we have to look like that or act like that to get what we want, then all right. That seems to be the ticket, according to the wisdom of the world.

The World Health Organization estimates that there are 100 million sex acts performed worldwide every day. That seems like a whole lot of somethin' goin' on. I know you're thinking it, so let me do the math for you. There are 6.2 billion people in the world. Divide that by … that's actually only about 2 percent of people having sex every day. So, really, not so much is goin' on as one might think. (Though I'm sure a good part of that 2 percent is goin' on on your college campus.)

Regardless of participation, sex seems to consume a lot of people's brain energy—apparently guys think about sex every seven seconds or some preposterous statistic like that. (If that's actually true, how does anything ever get done in this world? I mean, really … seven seconds?!) People are driven by it, pay for it, sacrifice for it, are controlled by it, even kill for it. Wars have even been started over it. (Granted, not your major world wars, more like tribal disputes and such—but wars nonetheless.)

Is it really just those few seconds of pleasure that are so powerful? What is the power of sex? I'm going to wager that it's more about the emotions and meaning connected to the act—the intimacy, the passion, the sense of being as close to a person as you can possibly be for just a few moments. It's the feeling of trust and control because it involves exposing the most vulnerable part of one's soul. It's about the power it communicates and holds over a person's heart and mind.

Sex can make you feel more alive than ever before, and it can suck the life right out of you. It can literally create life and literally destroy it. It's beautiful and dangerous and powerful and risky. It's kind of like a wild animal that we treat like a big stuffed toy (very cute until you get mauled).

ARE WE ANY DIFFERENT?

I do not live in a vacuum, as has just been made evident by my cable TV viewing. Given the statistics listed earlier, I can only assume that there is a good chance you have already had sex and are currently doing so. (I mean, not right this minute. … You know what I mean.) You've thought and maybe even believe the reasons to have sex listed above. I know that everything you are about to read is contrary to what you hear, see, and read—on TV, in movies, on the radio, on the Web, in magazines, from your friends, from your professors, maybe even from your doctors, your therapist, and your parents. It could all easily be turned into a *Saturday Night Live* skit or be mocked on *The Daily Show*.

It is not my intent to rant about the downfall of our society. Really, why would we expect it to be any different? There is a place to speak out in an effort to turn the tide, but this is not it. My desire, rather, is to point you to the biblical challenge to live an alternative lifestyle, a life that goes against the mainstream, against your peers, against your sex ed teacher, and against your flesh—and it may even feel, at some level, like it's against your own heart. But I'm asking you to enter into the conversation. Consider the gravity of your choices before you allow yourself to be swept up in the current zeitgeist.

I'm also not naive enough to believe that, just because the Bible says we should or shouldn't do something, that is motivation enough for most people. Sadly, that's true even among many who claim to be Christ followers. Statistics show that those junior-high and high-school students who made a commitment to abstinence through the popular program True Love Waits waited on average only eighteen months longer than other students to have sex, according to Lauren Winner in her book *Real Sex*. Winner also referenced a study done in the 1990s showing that among Christian singles surveyed one-third were virgins. That means two-third weren't. Apparently we (the religious types) have not done a good job of motivating people to live differently than the rest of the world.

People who do make a commitment to abstain from sex before marriage are considered freakish and/or geekish. It did not take more than one episode for the Christian guy on *The Bachelorette* to get booted once he "came out" with his virginity and commitment to abstinence. (Interestingly, I work with hundreds of people who would have been booted off that show—shoot, maybe even thousands.) You know the producers were giddy with delight to discover a virgin in their midst. Now, that's some good TV, my friend.

WHY SHOULDN'T YOU?

So, why in the world would you want to read a book like this or, much less, make such a choice for chastity? What is going to motivate you to say no when he's looking at you with those big, beautiful "bedroom eyes," as my friend's mother used to call them? You had better come up with some good reasons now, in the light of day, that will hold up under the pressures of hormones, the desires of the flesh, and the heat of the moment.

Here's a truism: In order to deny yourself a desire, you have to replace that desire with a stronger desire, something you want more. For example, in order to deny myself a big spoonful of the chocolate frosting that's in my fridge right this moment—frosting that's calling my name—I have to desire to fit into those smaller-size jeans more than I desire that rich … fudgy … creamy … frosting …

I'm back. (*Oops*—a little bit of chocolate on the spacebar.) Back to the topic at hand.

So, really, why shouldn't you?

Because you could get pregnant?
Because you could get a disease?
Because you don't want to get hurt?
Because maybe sex isn't even *really* what you want?
Because you want to hold out for sex as God intended it to be?
Because you want to give your husband the gift of your virginity?
Because you don't want to lie in bed with your husband and have flashbacks of all the men you've been with and live with the guilt and comparison?

All good thoughts and valid motivations. Hopefully, the desires and consequences, both good and bad, will help you choose wisely. But in the passion of the moment you might be surprised by how your mind can weasel its way around just about any line of defense. In the long haul you've got to have some strong oars of truth to row upstream against the cultural current. You're going to have to have some serious resolve that comes from heart conviction. Motivations are good and helpful, but conviction—a certain and assured belief—is even better.

Sailing—now, there's an overused metaphor. But let's go with it, for lack of anything else coming to mind at the moment. If motivation is the wind in your sails, the power to make you move, then conviction is the rudder. Conviction determines the direction you're headed in. As long as you're headed in the right direction, motivations will keep you moving forward. In this case your convictions need to be about the character and nature of God and who you are in relation to Him.

Could you say no …

Because you love God?
Because you know God loves you and that's enough?
Because you value your relationship with Him above everything else?
Because you trust that He can meet your needs and desires in a deeper way?
Because you believe that He really does have your best interests at heart?
Because you believe He knows more than you do?
Because you want to pursue holiness and be more like Christ?
Because you value His glory above your own pleasure?

Those are some hard questions. For most of you, I'm guessing some days you may be close to answering yes to a few of those questions, or at least admitting that's where you want to be. I'm certainly not always there myself. It's a process. Hopefully, this book is going to start you down the road to getting there.

Peter writes that we have all we need to live a life of godliness.[1] I take that to mean that there is sufficient wisdom, encouragement, warning, and power in the Scriptures—if unearthed, if explained and applied—to accomplish the goal of motivation and conviction by the power of the Spirit that dwells within us. If that's true, and yet people who claim to be Christ-followers continue to make poor choices, that implies one of three things—either they honestly couldn't care less (which raises all sorts of other questions) or they do not have a clear understanding of God's love for them or they've just never had a clear explanation of how these principles apply to their life. I'm going to assume one of the latter and move ahead with great anticipation and expectation of the scripture's and the Spirit's work in your life.

[1] 2 Peter 1:3

The Same Page

Sometimes when you start talking about the Bible and morality in your average group of Jane Shmoes, certain phrases tend to pop up. Phrases that people think make them sound smart and make them feel better about themselves and their choices: "Well, the Bible doesn't really say that, exactly" or "It's all in how you interpret it" or "Culture is so different today; you can't really apply what the Bible says." It's funny because often, if you ask, "Have you read the Bible yourself, or do you know what it says?" the answer is a muffled no of some sort. These people are going with the word on the street, what they've heard others say, the cultural tide. God forbid that you would be in that ignorant camp. No, really: God forbids it.

Throughout this book, many of the articles will refer to passages of Scripture and develop thoughts and principles from those passages. But I want you to have a cheat sheet, your very own "quick reference user's guide to key biblical passages about most things sexual." (There should be a shortcut term for that—QRUGKBPAMTS doesn't roll off the tongue.)

You should know where to go to see what the Bible says for yourself. I've found this "quick reference guide" quite helpful, as I'm convinced I have early-onset Alzheimer's.

The Quick Reference User's Guide to Key Biblical Passages about Most Things Sexual

Genesis 2:24-25
A man will leave his father and mother and be united to his wife, and they will become one flesh. The man and his wife were both naked, and they felt no shame.

Leviticus 18
The whole chapter contains laws regarding incest, adultery, bestiality, and homosexuality.

You shall not lie with a male as one lies with a female; it is an abomination. (v. 22)

Proverbs 5
The whole chapter addresses the perils of adultery.

Let your fountain be blessed,
And rejoice in the wife of your youth.
As a loving hind and a graceful doe,
Let her breasts satisfy you at all times;
Be exhilarated always with her love." (verses 18-19)

Proverbs 6:27-28
In the context of adultery…

Can a man scoop fire into his lap
without his clothes being burned?
Can a man walk on hot coals
without his feet being scorched?

Song of Solomon
Pretty much the whole book is a picture of love, marriage, and sex.

Awake, O North wind,
and come, wind of the south;
make my garden breathe out fragrance,
Let its spices be wafted abroad.
May my beloved come into his garden
and eat of its choice fruits! (4:16)

Matthew 5:27-30

You have heard that it was said, "Do not commit adultery." But I tell you that anyone who looks at a woman lustfully has already committed adultery with her in his heart.

Romans 1:26-27

God gave them over to shameful lusts. Even their women exchanged natural relations for unnatural ones. In the same way the men also abandoned natural relations with women and were inflamed with lust for one another. Men committed indecent acts with other men, and received in themselves the due penalty for their perversion.

1 Corinthians 6:12-20

"Everything is permissible for me"—but not everything is beneficial. "Everything is permissible for me"—but I will not be mastered by anything. "Food is for the stomach and the stomach for food"—but God will destroy them both. The body is not meant for sexual immorality, but for the Lord, and the Lord for the body. By his power God raised the Lord from the dead, and he will raise us also. Do you not know that your bodies are members of Christ himself? Shall I then take the members of Christ and unite them with a prostitute? Never! Do you not know that he who unites himself with a prostitute is one with her in body? For it is said, "The two will become one flesh." But he who unites himself with the Lord is one with him in spirit. Flee from sexual immorality. All other sins a man commits are outside his body, but he who sins sexually sins against his own body. Do you not know that your body is a temple of the Holy Spirit, who is in you, whom you have received from God? You are not your own; you were bought at a price. Therefore honor God with your body.

2 Corinthians 10:5

We demolish arguments and every pretension that sets itself up against the knowledge of God, and we take captive every thought to make it obedient to Christ.

Galatians 5

The whole chapter is about how to live by the Spirit, not by the flesh.

Live by the Spirit, and you will not gratify the desires of the flesh. (verse 16)

Ephesians 4:17-19

I tell you this, and insist on it in the Lord, that you must no longer live as the Gentiles do, in the futility of their thinking. They are darkened in their understanding and separated from the life of God because of the ignorance that is in them due to the hardening of their hearts. Having lost all sensitivity, they have given themselves over to sensuality so as to indulge in every kind of impurity, with a continual lust for more.

Ephesians 5:3

Among you there must not be even a hint of sexual immorality, or of any kind of impurity, or of greed, because these are improper for God's holy people.

Philippians 4:8

Finally, brothers, whatever is true, whatever is noble, whatever is right, whatever is pure, whatever is lovely, whatever is admirable - if anything is excellent or praiseworthy - think about such things.

Colossians 3:4-6

When Christ, who is your life, appears, then you also will appear with him in glory.
Put to death, therefore, whatever belongs to your earthly nature: sexual immorality, impurity, lust, evil desires and greed, which is idolatry. Because of these, the wrath of God is coming.

1 Thessalonians 4:3-6

It is God's will that you should be sanctified: that you should avoid sexual immorality; that each of you should learn to control his own body in a way that is holy and honorable, not in passionate lust like the heathen, who do not know God; and that in this matter no one should wrong [defraud] his brother or take advantage of him.

Hebrews 13:4

Marriage should be honored by all, and the marriage bed kept pure, for God will judge the adulterer and all the sexually immoral.

1 Peter 4:1-6

Since Christ suffered in his body, arm yourselves also with the same attitude, because he who has suffered in his body is done with sin. As a result, he does not live the rest of his earthly life for evil human desires, but rather for the will of God. For you have spent enough time in the past doing what pagans choose to do—living in debauchery, lust, drunkenness, orgies, carousing and detestable idolatry. They think it strange that you do not plunge with them into the same flood of dissipation, and they heap abuse on you. But they will have to give account to him who is ready to judge the living and the dead. For this is the reason the gospel was preached even to those who are now dead, so that they might be judged according

to men in regard to the body, but live according to God in regard to the spirit.

HERME ... WHAT?

Okay, so now you've had all these random bits of Bible thrown at you. I realize these pieces may raise more questions than they answer in some cases. You may want to take some time out and study these passages on your own before you go any further and see what we have to say about it all, lest you claim you've been brainwashed in the end.

So, you may be wondering how does a person go about that—studying a passage of the Bible, figuring out what it all really means and what it has to do with you. There's a big, fancy term for that called *hermeneutics*, a.k.a inductive Bible study methods. People spend lots of time and money becoming proficient at such things. However, the beauty of it is that you can take a crash course for free. Go to **www.godsquad.com** and click on "Bible Study Resources." Everything you need to figure out what these passages mean and how they apply to your life is right there at your fingertips with some instructions on how to go about it. Also, **www.studylight.org** and **www.biblegateway.com** are excellent resources, but you might start with godsquad to learn the how-to's and then use the

resources available at the other sites. You can also use the book *How to Study the Bible for all Its Worth* by Gordon Fee and Douglas Stuart.

THE SHORTCUT

Some of you are not so motivated to do the work, but you want to know what the Bible says. Understandable—you're busy people. You usually have Cliff's Notes for things you don't have time to read. I get that. Here's the deal: go to www.biblegateway.com, look up a passage, and choose to read it in The Message version.

The Message is a paraphrase, as opposed to a translation, which is a word-for-word English translation from the original languages (Greek, Hebrew) in the manuscripts. In the case of The Message, Eugene Peterson has done the hard work for you—he's exegeted the whole thing, every last jot and tittle, and paraphrased the passages in contemporary language in a way that communicates the heart of what the biblical writers were trying to communicate to their audience. Really, it's worth buying a copy of The Message or one of the other paraphrased versions of the Bible for yourself. Such a Bible is a whole lot easier to understand as a quick and easy reference. However, you still need to know the context of the passages and to meditate on how they apply to you, so you're not totally off the hook, just slightly off the hook.

SEMANTICS

I want to help you out a little and give you a head start. Here are some definitions of some key words addressed in Scripture, some based on their original Greek and Hebrew counterparts. A few words are not from the Scripture passages but are words that may come up in our discussion.

The Sex Lexicon

Sex (Greek, *koite*)—Interestingly, this word is not used anywhere in Scripture. The biblical writers preferred to use euphemisms, such as "He went in to her" or "She lay with him." But for the sake of our discussions, sex is anything and everything that leads up to, but is not necessarily inclusive of, an orgasm. For all intents and purposes, it is anything that causes sexual arousal.

Intercourse (Hebrew, *shekobah* or *shekobeth*)—copulation, most often translated as "lie with carnally."

Lust (Greek, *epithumeo*)—to covet things forbidden, or as my friend Brett defines it, dwelling on What would hormones do? (WWHD?).

Fornication, Immorality (Greek, *porneo*)—illicit sex. You see where that's going. This can refer to adultery, but it also includes sex before marriage, homosexual sex, prostitution, incest, sex with animals, and so on.

Adultery (Greek, *moichos*)—unlawful sex with the spouse of another.

Homosexuality—sex with someone of the same sex. Again, the Bible uses terms like "men burning with desire toward other men" or "the exchange of natural functions for unnatural" rather than the direct label.

Sodomy—homosexual sex. It may also include anal sex between a man and a woman.

Orgy—sex with multiple partners at the same time (on my list of "words I don't like").

Incest—sex with family members. Again, in Scripture, terms like "uncovering the nakedness" of a blood relative are used.

Bestiality—sex with an animal.

Prostitution—receiving payment for sex.

Obscenity, coarse joking—inappropriate sexual comments or innuendos.

Impurity—living out thoughts, words, values, or actions that are secular or pagan in nature, not holy.

Pure—without contamination, undefiled, holy.

Defraud—take advantage of (steal).

Pornography—sexually explicit printed or visual materials intended to stimulate erotic rather than emotional feelings.

Love (Greek, *agape*)—unconditional love; (Greek, *phileo*)—brotherly love; (Greek, *eros*—romantic love). *Agape* is characterized in Scripture by things like laying down your life for one another, considering others more important than yourself—all that stuff in 1 Corinthians 13.

Celibacy—a lifelong vow of abstinence.

Chastity—a commitment to having sex in its proper place.

Abstinence—choosing to not have sex (in the secular realm, typically referred to as a form of birth control).

SO, IS THAT STILL GOING TO BE ON THE TEST?

It can be sometimes confusing to know whether a principle or guideline in Scripture is applicable today or whether it was just part of their culture at the time. There are a few basic principles of interpretation that you may want to keep your eye on.

The difficulty of application for many passages of Scripture lies in the relationship between the Old and New testaments. On one extreme are those who see complete "continuity" between the Old and New. The Old Testament provides a map as relevant for life today as does the New Testament, for we in the church are (more or less) Israel. And then there are those who hold to extreme "discontinuity." Apart from its historical value, much in the Old Testament is irrelevant to Christians and the church. Theologically, denominations fall somewhere along this spectrum.

The invaluable decoder ring is to see that when the Old Testament is squeezed through the keyhole of the Cross, it comes out the other side (the New Contract) transformed. Thus the New Testament becomes our interpretive key to understand what has changed and what has not. For example, the book of Hebrews says that Christ has fulfilled the animal sacrifices of the Old Testament. (That's a relief. We don't have to kill our pets to atone for sin.) Do we have a sacrifice like the Old Testament? Yes, but it is Christ, and His was a one-time sacrifice.

Here are a few more examples. Holiness (set-apartness) extended even to the food eaten by the Israelites. Yet we learn in the book of Acts, through a revelation given to Peter, that dietary laws are no longer in effect. (Another relief, because shellfish was on the list of unclean food, and shrimp scampi is a personal favorite.) Also, blessings in the Old Testament were often more material in nature, while in the New Testament "blessing" moves in a more spiritual direction.

While we're on a roll, perhaps the sexual restrictions against homosexuality and sexual immorality also expired. It's possible. Some of the Corinthians thought so. Here Paul quotes one of their slogans, "Food for the stomach and the stomach for food," the meaning of which was that neither food nor sex affected the spiritual life. Paul, obviously, does not buy the argument. " 'Food for the stomach and the stomach for food'—but God will destroy them both. The body is not meant for sexual immorality, but for the Lord, and the Lord for the body" (1 Corinthians 6:13).

As you read through the New Testament passages above, you will note that sexual purity is as foundational to the New Covenant as it is to the Old. While in biblical interpretation, there are nuances to be worked out in many areas in order to accurately understand how the period after Christ relates to the period before, the sexual area simply isn't one them. Annoying, perhaps. Tricky, no.

CULTURALLY BOUND

Because God's revelation was implemented within a culture, there are a few occasions where God's truth is bound to a cultural practice. In such cases, it is not the cultural practice that is timeless but the principle within. I do not affirm a covenant by killing an animal or exchanging my left shoe, as was the Israelites' custom, but I am certainly to be a person of my word.

We are also to be aware of what cultural practices communicate and be sensitive to our witness concerning them. A head covering, in certain locations during the first century, expressed respect for one's husband and his leadership; not wearing one expressed contempt. The apostle Paul says to the women at Corinth who had shelved their head coverings, "Wear the head covering and think about your witness and what you are communicating by your actions." In France, women sunbathe without their tops. If you chose to do so in America, it would injure your witness and cause men to stumble. Paul would have written, "Wear a top."

If you are looking for a cultural loophole on what the New Testament communicates on sex, I'm afraid the "head covering" is the only place you'll find an "out" clause. But enjoy it—go get yourself a perm and some highlights.

IT'S BEEN A COUPLE THOUSAND YEARS; THINGS CHANGE …

Not so much, really. As for the Bible in general being relevant to the culture today, have you read 1 and 2 Corinthians? Corinth was the Hollywood of its day, known for materialism and sex. It was at least as perverse as our culture is today. One Greek writer reports that the name Corinth was even slang for fornication. Instead of looking for a "hook-up," you might be looking for someone to "go to Corinth." Much of the culture of the day was similar to that in Corinth.

We often think that the Bible was written to a puritanical society. In reality, though, it was a wild and woolly era—pagans gone wild. In many ways, we're more civil and morally regulated than they were. We live in a culture that at least has a Judeo-Christian moral basis for law. In their era, the early Jews and the Christians were not so influential. (Slaves and prisoners usually aren't.)

The Bible always has been and always will be countercultural. Today we just have more high-tech manifestations of our debauchery. Most of the passages listed are New Testament teaching given directly to believers so that they would live a life honoring to Christ. These are timeless moral principles and most assuredly were as countercultural to their original audience as they are to us. No matter what you think about whether the Bible is totally true, nothing could be more applicable to people trying to live an "alternative" lifestyle today.

You should know that the reason God gives these and every guideline in Scripture is either to provide for you or to protect you. His intent in no way is to keep something good from you or to punish you. Like any good parent, He disciplines us for our own good. But He has drawn out these guidelines to protect your soul, your spirit, and your body—to give you the opportunity to experience sex in the way He intended it to be. When we follow the guidelines, there are great gifts to be experienced.

IN THE GRAY

Now you at least know where we're coming from, and I hope you're on the same page or at least in the same book. We've reviewed some passages and we've worked out the semantics, but when it comes down to it, some things still may not be clear in Scripture. Not everything is specifically addressed.

These fall into what some people like to call "gray areas." And we like to think that if it's not spelled out with a clear yes or no, we can make a judgment call based on what we feel is best for us. However (you knew that was coming) … however, if something is not specifically addressed, there is typically a broader principle that can be applied. The broader guideline may give some parameters, but it also may give some freedom within those parameters. Things tend to become less gray when we learn to think this way.

For example, clothes. The Bible says nothing about whether to wear clothes or not. So, for instance, wearing clothes in the shower is not wrong per se, but maybe it's not "wise" or "beneficial," as Paul advises. Not wearing clothes at the grocery store is not so much about you being embarrassed as much as it is about applying the broader principle of not causing your brother to stumble (or, in my case, the principle of considering others more important than yourself).

Another example from the realm of fashion. If your mother was any kind of mother at all, then you should know the fashion principle that white shoes are not allowed after Labor Day (with noted exceptions in the state of Florida and southern California, where fashion rules do not apply). So let's say you're shopping and come across a fabulous all-white ensemble on sale for a bargain price. It will be just the thing for your fall formal, which is, of course, post–Labor Day. There are no stated fashion principles against actually wearing a white outfit, given that it is not linen. (Apropos seasonal clothing is based more on style and fabric weight than color, unless, of course, you're in Europe, where black on black is always the most fashionable choice year-round.) The problem is that you know that if you wore this outfit it would require white shoes. Considering the broader principle regarding shoe color and season, you have to pass up the outfit and the bargain. (Note: if the example is "winter white," then all bets are off—make the purchase. Winter white boots are an added bonus to any wardrobe and are suitable for fall and winter.)

DON'T JUST TAKE MY WORD FOR IT (I MEAN, DO ... BUT DON'T)

Hopefully these passages, definitions, and principles give you a grid to develop some opinions on your own and discuss these matters with some measure of knowledge and, ideally, conviction. It is never my desire for someone to take my word for it (okay, actually that's always my desire, because I like to be right—or at least thought of as being right), but it's probably better for you if you do read the Word for yourself and figure these things out on your own with some consideration of what I and others say along the way.

"I Gave My Word to Stop at Third"

That's the slogan recently sighted on a T-shirt in the greater Austin area. I'm sure that kid made some commitment to abstinence at a church camp or a conference somewhere, and kudos to him. I hope he does stop at third. Similarly, I have a friend who made a vow to never kill anyone. Granted, he's beaten several people to a pulp, but to this day he's never killed anyone. I'm proud of him. He's a man of his word.

So, just because this kid gave his word to stop at third (and what exactly is third base these days?), does that mean all is well and right between him and his Maker? You're all good as long as you don't cross the line?

I like what my friend Will has to say along these lines: "It would be just like behavior modification to miss the point all together." My intent and the goal of this book is not to tell you what you can and cannot do. I am not a legalist. However, what you do and do not do is indicative of where your heart is. That's my real concern. My hope is that by talking about these things, and about God's desire and intent for you, you would want what He wants for you more than you want what your flesh wants. But I know it's hard to change your wants.

If faith is really about an intimate connection with God, then the idea is not to see how close to the line you can get but rather to see how close to God you can get. Closeness with God is not about following rules. It's about feeling comfortable with living life as He intended it. It's about being at ease with Him. It's about your heart toward Him.

There are two ends to this spectrum (as there are to any spectrum). On the one end, we are the bride of Christ and we have a loving submissiveness toward Him because He has loved us, because we trust Him, because we love Him. On the other end, we're God's children. And like most children, we're shortsighted, strong-willed, and don't know what's in our own best interest. As children, we need boundaries and guidelines for our own protection. The hope is that eventually we'll grow up and need fewer boundaries and guidelines because we've moved from a focus on rule-driven obedience to love-driven desire. But truthfully, few of us are at that point just yet.

NOT MUCH OF A DEBATE

So, in light of our childish nature, we probably should start with the boundaries. There's no getting around the fact that if you're using the Bible as your guidebook, sex before marriage is off-limits. More than thirty times in the New Testament we're admonished to avoid sexual immorality, which we have established includes sex outside marriage, among other things.

In more recent history, however, there has been much debate over what actually qualifies as "sex." Yeah, even our own United States Congress and former president had this debate. Apparently there's a lot that can happen between holding hands and actual intercourse.

Two informal surveys done by Lauren Winner in her research for *Real Sex* show that about 55 percent of the student participants did not consider oral or anal sex to qualify as sex. People, it's called oral *sex*. How can it *not* be sex?! I do know that, in this particular debate, that's too far. In fact, let's back up the love train quite a bit.

HEY, THAT'S MINE!

You've probably figured out by now that nowhere does the Bible say, "On the first date, thou shalt have a platonic side hug; the second date, hand holding; etc." (Do note that a side hug is a good place to start—see instructions.) So this is where the idea of applying the broader principles comes into play.

The Side Hug

1. To initiate, extend both arms as if making a face-to-face hug. As both parties converge, begin to turn your bodies so they are juxtaposed side by side.

2. Drop your outside arm to your side, and take your inside arm, wrap it around the other person's shoulder and clasp. WARNING: Do not at any time wrap your arm around their waist as you may send conflicting signals.

3. Lightly squeeze their shoulder and hold for a duration of 1-2 seconds. Your head should be facing straight ahead to ensure your lips do not come in contact with the other person's ear.

Let's take a look at 1 Thessalonians 4:3-6:

It is God's will that you should be sanctified; that you should avoid sexual immorality; that each of you should learn to control his own body in a way that is holy and honorable, not in passionate lust like the heathen, who do not know God; and that in this matter no one should wrong his brother or take advantage of him [defraud]. (NIV)

This passage is pretty self-explanatory.

1. It is God's will (everyone always wants to know God's will—here it is, spelled out) that you don't go anywhere near sex outside marriage.
2. Instead, learn to control your body in a way that honors God, not allowing it to be controlled by your sex drive, like those who don't know God.
3. And in this area, don't break the law (wrong) and don't take what is not yours (defraud).

Any healthy relationship is about considering the needs of others. It's about respecting and valuing the other person. In regard to avoiding sexual immorality, besides the obvious, one way you can think of it is as promising or suggesting something you're not going to deliver on. In other words, don't be a tease, don't get a guy excited for nothing—okay, just don't get him excited (though I realize we often have little or no control over such things). Not going anywhere near sex, and controlling your body in a way that honors God, means that you do not want to cause a guy or yourself to lust or be sexually aroused or, much less, actually go as far as to take what's not yours, his purity.

One way to keep your actions in check is to think of your boyfriend as another woman's future husband. How would you want another woman to treat your future husband? Imagine yourself at his wedding and being able to look both he and his wife in the eye with no shame or embarrassment, knowing that you have taken nothing from him that now belongs to her.

DRAW THE LINE

The first time I ever heard a "women's talk" at a conference, the woman giving the talk gave an illustration using an egg white to talk about how you know when you're sexually aroused. "Your body begins to produce something like this," she explained as she demonstrated the clear, sticky nature of the egg white. (Insert fingers in ears, close eyes tightly, "La-la-la-la-la.") Needless to say, I have hardly eaten an egg since. The image has stuck in my head, for better or for worse. Now it's in yours. Apologies.

Where you draw the line is the point at which you are starting something that cannot be fulfilled righteously. In other words, that is the place where you start something that starts you (or him) down the path to an orgasm. The line is where it turns from just being affectionate to being sexual arousal.

A helpful guideline is the "holy kiss principle" (as long as your Bible doesn't translate "holy" as "French"). For infants, children, and adults, physical contact is the primary way we show care, protection, affirmation, encouragement, and love for each other. Think about it. When your friend is miserable and discouraged, you may have nothing to say, but a hug goes a long way. I remember being cold in church and my dad putting his arm around me and then my snuggling in his nook—a genuine Hallmark moment, no doubt. A pat on the back or a slap on the butt says, "Good job" (in different realms, of course). When we think about physical standards for dating, it might be helpful to consider how we related to a brother or sister within our family, expressing affection without its ever being sexual in nature.

There's nothing wrong with physical contact; that's human nature and much of how we communicate. But the goal should be to express affection without causing sexual arousal. Hence the "principle of the holy kiss." There are affectionate kisses and there are passionate kisses. I trust you can figure out the difference.

As for how much affection, it should be stage appropriate. By that I mean that if your partner's arms are constantly surrounding you, that communicates protection and a degree of ownership of one other. Which is fine for a serious, exclusive relationship but inappropriate if it's not.

FOR YOUR OWN GOOD
Though I'd like to think I'm pretty spiritually mature, rather like the bride we discussed earlier, I also have to humbly admit that I am still childish in some ways—okay, probably in lots of ways. (For instance, I still find the word wienie in reference to a hot dog uncontrollably funny.) In light of that, I need to set up some parameters for my own protection, because, frankly, in the emotion of the moment, I can become like a bratty child and do what I want to do just because I want to do it, dadgummit. I need some boundaries and guidelines to keep me from getting to that place. Here are several questions and answer to consider:

1. At what point does affection turn to sex?
Wherever that point is, that's where I'm going to draw the line. But then I want to take two steps back. I don't even want to go near temptation. I may be able to handle it, but why would I want to tempt myself? It's like buying a chocolate cheesecake, putting it in the fridge, and telling myself I can't have any. Sooner or later, I'm going to have just a sliver (I hate that word). Then one day I'm going to find myself with my face in the fridge, a fork in my mouth, and a chocolate-glazed stupor written all over my face.

Now, the line is going to be a little different for everyone, based on their history and nature. But what I've observed in talking with women over the years is that the more sexual history a person has, the quicker she hits the line. I have one friend who has to be careful about holding hands with a guy.

2. Once you know where the line is for you, what are the situations that tempt you to cross that line? Once I knew a couple who decided they could not cook a meal together—too much heat in the kitchen, both literally and figuratively. For you, there may be some other situations that you know are high risk, causing you to walk right into the arms of temptation. For instance, let's take R-rated movies—it's probably not a good idea to watch other people having sex ever, but especially not with your boyfriend.

Here's a thought: avoid lying down in close proximity to each other. It may seem harmless when you're lying on the couch watching a movie—maybe, maybe not. (I confess that in college I spent many a night sharing a bed with my "best friend" when I would visit him for the weekend. It was no big deal, really. But then again, he turned out to be gay.)

Or here's another: set a curfew for yourselves. I know, I know—there's nothing more romantic than the staying-up-all-night-talking date. But as your grandmother used to say, "Nothing good happens after midnight." I hate to agree with your grandmother, but there's some truth in what she says. Late at night, you're tired. You say and do things you will regret in the light of day.

Here's a situation that seems to come up a lot. He's over late. He's tired. Why doesn't he just sleep on the couch? This is where the Ephesians 5 passage comes to mind: "There must not be even a hint of sexual immorality" (verse 3). His car in the driveway in the morning may raise an eyebrow or two. It's not about the rules; it's about protecting your heart, mind, and relationship with the Lord. I am certainly not saying you have to abide by these guidelines, but they're suggestions to jump-start your thinking.

3. What things are appropriate for you to talk about, and what should you not talk about?
We women want to be known, and we're prone to tell all. Often we say much more than what the guy asked—classic unsolicited TMI (too much information). All for the sake of intimate soul connection. Wait before you share those deep, intimate parts of your life.

I know you're thinking, *But ohmygosh, he so "gets" me.* Please trust me on this. Sometimes when you've had a great moment of verbal intimacy it makes you feel really close to a guy and you want to express that closeness physically. "Danger! Danger, Will Robinson!" (I know that no one under thirty-five got that classic TV allusion, but it was nostalgic for your mother and me.) Anyway, the point is—guard your words.

In a dating relationship there is no need to put all your laundry out there from the get-go. Wait until he pursues knowing you and asks questions (I know that's a rare guy, but give him a chance). Men like a little mystery; it's part of the pursuit. You and all your thoughts and life experience are a gift and a treasure. He needs to prove he's trustworthy for quite a while before you entrust yourself to him. Such conversations before their time can give a false sense of intimacy and make you think the relationship is further down the road than it really is. Don't give him your heart when he hasn't pursued it or asked for it or proven he's trustworthy to care for it.

There are some things that you do not need to talk about for a long, long time, not until you are in the "serious" dating zone, i.e. your sexual history. Really, there is no need to ever talk details about sex in any context with any man unless you are in premarital counseling or you are talking to your male gynecologist.

Now, here's a personal soapbox (and really, guys need to know this more than we do). *Do not talk about marriage until there is a ring in his pocket.* Now, granted, he may get to that place before you, and then you may need to talk about it. But here's what you need to know: guys really can think hypothetically. They're thinking, *What if we did get married—what would that look like?* He's just trying it on, seeing what it feels like, *hypothetically.* And he should. But he should not be discussing that with you. Ideally, he's discussing it with an older, wiser, godly married man.

Typically, we girls imagine the wedding within a few minutes of introductions, or we at least try on

FANTASY *"I Gave My Word To Stop At Third"*

APPROPRIATE OR INAPPROPRIATE!

1. DAISY DUKES
2. LOWRIDERS
3. DEEP V-NECK ANYTHING
4. SILK CAMI WORN AS A SHIRT
5. OVERSIZED RAINCOAT

6. MICROMINI
7. STILETTOS
8. UNIVERSITY OF TEXAS JERSEY
9. SHRINK WRAP T
10. DENIM JUMPER

11. TUBE TOP
12. SEE-THROUGH SHIRT WITH CAMI
13. STRING BIKINI
14. WIFE BEATER TANK WITH EXPOSED BRA STRAPS
15. PRAIRIE SKIRT

DAISY DUKES: Inappropriate at all times unless you're in Hazzard County. LOWRIDERS: Exposed thong – Inappropriate, no visual on the belly button -appropriate; DEEP V-NECK ANYTHING: Inappropriate – regardless of cleavage or not; SILK CAMI WORN AS A SHIRT: if it looks like lingerie , it should be worn as lingerie; OVERSIZED RAIN JACKET: appropriate – appropriate – a handy save to cover the outfit; MICRO MINI SKIRT: Inappropriate; STILETTO HEELS: depends on the outfit, can go either way – downtown – inappropriate uptown – appropriate; UNIVERSITY OF TEXAS JERSEY: always appropriate; SHRINK WRAP SHIRT: appropriate for the pre-pubescent; DENIM JUMPER: appropriate for the 50 and over crowd; TUBE TOP: no straps – no appropriate; SEE THROUGH SHIRT WITH CAMI: tank – sure, lingerie – nope; STRING BIKINI: on a deserted island - maybe; TANK WITH EXPOSED BRA STRAPS: appropriate – maybe , tacky - yes; PRAIRIE SKIRT: appropriate for this season only , next fall they will be so done his last name. Okay, not always; it depends on the time of the month and our current singlehood contentment level. But if there's remote interest, the thought of him in a tux runs across our subconscious at some point. We do not need his verbal wonderings to take our heart there any quicker than we do on our own. So please don't add your own verbal wonderings into the mix.

4. What are you going to wear? Always an important question. Last week I was watching *How Do I Look?* on the Style network, and there was a pitiful situation with a girl who by her ex-boyfriend's description "dressed like a tramp." She pleadingly explained to him that she dressed that way *for him*. She thought that if other guys thought she was hot, that would make her more attractive to him. He replied that it embarrassed him and it felt disrespectful.

Now, that's a good guy. That's the kind of guy you need to be looking for. In fact, as of the end of the show, he's available.

Along the lines of "not defrauding your brother" and determining some guidelines, this should be an area to consider. You really should think about how you dress all the time, but especially in light of your boyfriend. Certainly you should look your best for him; that communicates value and respect.

But you want to take his breath away, not force him to have to look away. Don't make him work to focus above the shoulders. I know that's hard to do with fashion these days. It's hard to find a pair of pants and a shirt that actually meet in the middle. But here's a general rule based on the previous principle of not causing sexual arousal: if he shouldn't touch you there, then don't show it to him, i.e. your upper thighs, lower back, belly button, cleavage (or where cleavage should be, in some cases). … You get the idea. Another principle is to not wear anything that will make him wonder if you're wearing a bra or not. He's got no business playing guessing games about your lingerie. Granted, for some guys, all of this might mean you have to wear Uggs, cargos, and a ski jacket year-round. But you can work out a compromise, I'm sure.

I'm sure there are other key questions to ask, but these four are a good starting point.

WHO'S GOT THE CHUTZPAH?

Ideally, you're dating a guy who has the maturity and chutzpah to bring up the topic of boundaries himself. But if that's not the case, then I say you need to throw it out there yourself in a gracious, sisterly love kind of way.

My friend dated just such a guy (one lacking in chutzpah). For several days, she was waiting for

the appropriate moment to raise the issue, and as it turned out, there was no such moment. So there they were, intertwined on the sofa at 2:00 a.m., watching *Titanic* in the dark. He's pretty sure the third-base coach is waving him home. That's when my friend—oblivious to the third-base coach—said what she'd been thinking about the whole time when Rose and Jack were freezing their bums off somewhere in the Atlantic: "You know, I really want this to be a relationship that honors God, and I want to respect you. Is that a high value for you? What do you think that looks like when it comes to our 'physical relationship'?" (BTW, I don't recommend the use of the finger-quote gesture here.)

"Huh?" (tripping over third base and falling flat on his face—*and heeeee iiiiisss outta here*). "Okay …"

(You should probably know that they had already crossed the line a few times, but since they hadn't drawn the lines to begin with, they were just now figuring these things out.)

"I've already put some thought into this for myself," my friend said, "and I've decided that this whole thing has really thrown a hitch in my relationship with God." (Note: she meant to say, "Thrown a wrench," but one of the funny things about my friend is that she often mixes metaphors.) "After we're together I feel like it's days before I can face Him, and I end up making all sorts of promises that I know I'm not going to keep. In a sort of weird and twisted way, it feels like I'm choosing you over Him."

"So … I could see that … now that you mention it …" (Translation: *Oh man, I'm such a loser. She's thinking about God, and I'm trying to figure out if this means there's no more lip gravy to be had tonight … or ever.*)

"So, I guess what I'm saying is that we need to step way back and sort all this out. Like, maybe we should keep the physical stuff to a minimum until we figure out what God wants this to look like."

"Yeah, sure. I mean I've sort of been thinking the same things." (Note: who knows if this is true or not? But it was a valiant effort to save face.).

So that's what they did. They took some time to pray and talk to friends about how far is too far. My friend started by thinking through the situations that start her engine, so to speak. Here's her short list (shared with permission):

1. Pretty much anything involving tongue(s).
2. Lying down together in the name of "snuggling"—includes all recliners as well as sofas and most certainly beds. However, the "sit and snuggle" is acceptable—in folding or ladder-back chairs.
3. Sharing a blanket is always risky.
4. When he wears those running shorts without a shirt …
5. His hands being anywhere south of shoulders and north of the knees, even if they're just resting there, with the exception of his putting his arm around the back. And especially if they're under the clothing.
6. Massages, except for feet. (My personal rule—no one touches my feet, and I don't touch theirs—blick!)
7. That thing he does.

She didn't exactly want to say all this to her boyfriend, at least not in those specific terms, lest he be tempted by such dangerous and powerful knowledge. So the question became "What boundaries would keep us from situations where these are likely to happen?" She wanted to keep it simple and make it not seem like she was writing a policy manual for their relationship. Here are some things she came up with:

1. Occasional affectionate kisses are allowed (not quite ready to give up kissing altogether, but try the affectionate/not sexual thing).
2. If no one else is in the house— no friends, roommates, etc.—then sit in separate chairs when watching a movie or hanging out.
3. Hands stay on the outside of clothes and only on the back, above the shoulders, and below the knees.
4. Honesty—speak up when you hit the line.

He did the same, I think, and they actually talked it over. Without getting unnecessarily graphic, they simply talked about how they could help each other stay connected to God in the area of physical purity. These conversations are awkward, but as I told her, "If you can't make it through some hard conversations, I'd say there is trouble down the road for your relationship."

So, hopefully, you can have a good discussion with your boyfriend and come up with some clear parameters for physical boundaries and perhaps broader guidelines as well. I'm not a stickler for rules (I see them as mere guidelines), but I do respect the spirit of the law. Don't put yourself in tempting situations or situations that would cause other people to wonder about your standards. Stay above reproach.

PROTECT AND PROVIDE

I realize you might not be motivated by Scripture alone to follow these guidelines, and you're thinking how unnatural it is to wait for marriage. Some would even argue that there are detrimental consequences if you don't find release for all those hormones. But I have to say that's a lie our culture has perpetuated—"It's unhealthy to not express your sexuality." As my pastor says, I don't think you've ever read a story about someone who died of internal hormonal combustion or from an explosion of organs due to lack of use. It's just not true. (Of course, sex within marriage does have its risks. I have a friend who busted his wife's nose during a little afternoon rendezvous.)

So, what are the consequences of crossing the line in this area? What is it that God is trying to protect us from and provide for us?

1. *Provide respect and trust for each other.* If the relationship does lead to marriage, there can be a freedom from fear and insecurity. If he can stop or say no to me while we're dating, then I know he can say no to others when we're married.

2. *Protect from flashbacks.* My friends who were sexually active before they were married tell me that one of the most painful things they have faced is telling their husband about the other men.

Basically, in their own words, "It's as though they're all right there in bed with us." Almost all say that flashbacks have been a struggle in their thought life, even in their dreams and when they're having sex with their husbands. They must deal with guilt, and both they and their husbands must carry the weight of comparison.

3. *Provide self-control.* This is what the passage in 1 Thessalonians talks about—learning to control your body and desires. If you can learn to say no when you're not married, it will help you when you are married to say yes when you don't necessarily want to. You're controlling your body rather than allowing your body to control you.

4. *Protect from future problems.* There is actually a medical consequence from repeatedly stopping yourself once you've started down that road toward an orgasm. It can lead to problems later on when you are married and you have the freedom to continue but have trained your body to stop. It has got to be frustrating to finally have the freedom and yet be unable to proceed, not to mention its being heartbreaking for your spouse.

5. *Protect from pregnancy outside marriage.* Sure, there's protection. It works most of the time. My friend with seven kids would tell you it doesn't work all the time.

6. *Protect from sexually transmitted diseases.* In the past thirty years STDs have reached epidemic proportions. Tons of statistics on this are available, and you can find detailed and unsettling information on several Web sites—some with pictures included as an added bonus. After surveying several myself, I discovered that they all seem to agree that every year between 12 and 15 million people contract a viral STD. If you are not in a relationship where both parties are monogamous, your chances are about one in five that you could contract a disease. The consequences range from the personal pain of the disease, to cancers, to birth defects for children. Condoms are not foolproof. In many situations they are totally ineffective.

7. *Protect from a loss of intimacy with God.* Like any sin you're not willing to let go of or turn from, premarital sex affects your connection with God. It becomes easier and easier to walk away from Him, and your sin begins to affect every area of your life.

TIRED BUT TRUE STORY

Claire was date-raped in high school and became pregnant as a result. On the counsel of her liberal pastor, she got an abortion. After that, she figured, what the heck—she's already had sex, so why not? She slept with anyone and everyone. In college she became a Christ follower and decided to give up sex. It was a struggle, and one night she gave in and slept with a guy she met at a party. It was just one night (actually, less than that—just a few hours), but she got herpes. There's no cure for herpes. Now she's married. She and her husband are facing infertility, as a result of either the abortion or the herpes. Even if she did get pregnant, she wouldn't deliver vaginally, for risk of blindness for the baby.

This is the part where I know it sounds like sex ed class. You've heard a hundred stories like Claire's, all intended to scare you into abstinence (or at least into using a condom). I confess that's my agenda too—the abstinence thing. I did not make up Claire's story, and I do hope it scares the somethin' out of you. The reason you've heard it so often is that it happens more often than anyone ever talks about or discusses publicly. It's not really information people share in casual party conversation. ("So, I just found out I've got a wretched case of genital warts. What's up with you?") You never see that story line on the WB. And the tired but real question still applies: Is it worth the long-term risk for a few moments of pleasure and a brief moment of feeling wanted? I'm sure you know Claire's answer to that.

GROWING UP

As I said in the beginning, I am not about rules. The rules are just a means to an end. Sexual purity is not about being good and staying within the lines. It's about being at home with God when it comes to your sexuality. There's nothing hidden or shameful about it. You're honest with Him about your struggles and trusting Him to give you wisdom and power to make choices that honor and please Him. A pure dating relationship is one in which a couple honors and respects each other, one that draws each of them to God rather than pushes them away.

I think a key principle of pursuing holiness in any area is to not spend energy and effort focusing on the limits and boundaries, trying desperately not to cross the line, but rather to focus on the positive— the freedoms you have within the parameters. Spend your time and energy on truth and on doing the right things. For example, some friends of mine who do premarital counseling encourage engaged couples, when expressing affection, to focus their minds on how much they love the other person, how much they respect the other, trust him or her. Think about how much you want to honor your boyfriend. If that's where your mind is, then it will be hard for you to put your hands where they shouldn't be or cross the line in other ways. Spend time praying together and talking about your

relationships with God. It's hard to follow that up with a mug session.

BECOMING HIS BRIDE

I know that some of the things I've said may seem extreme or ultra-conservative, but I can make a long list of women I've known over the years who were well on their way to falling in love with Jesus when "Mr. Right (now)" came into their lives, and they were quick to jilt the Savior in favor of a "savior" with skin on him. Some came to realize their misplaced expectations, but not all of them have figured that out, and these have settled for less than what could be. On the other hand, I've seen friends who are now married make wise choices and reap the benefits in their married lives and their spiritual lives. I want that for myself and for you.

Falling in love with Jesus as your first love, experiencing the fullness and delight of being His bride, is going to give you the convictions to live freely, to not worry about the boundaries as much as your relationship with Him. As you begin to build that relationship and learn His heart, developing some guidelines is going to keep you on the path of pursuing Him. He, more than anyone else, wants you to experience sexual purity so that you can reap the benefit in your own life as well as honor God and bring Him glory.

Biblical Proverb:
"Women should dress modestly, with decency and propriety."
Grandma's Proverb:
"If you're not serving it for dinner, don't put it on the menu."

The M Word

Masturbation …masturbation … masturbation. So, how many times in a month would you say that you masturbate?

When you go through training to be qualified to interview applicants to join Campus Crusade for Christ staff, they make you say the word out loud several times and then turn to the person next to you and use the word conversationally. You can imagine the blushing and nervous laughter as trainees say sex words like that out loud. It's comically, randomly ridiculous. Obviously, the point of the practice is to become comfortable with talking about topics that are taboo in polite dinner conversation but that are relevant to a person's character and walk with God.

Why is it that for guys there are all sorts of euphemisms and slang about sex—crass ways to get around using straight-up medical terms—but not so much for women? Scratch that, dumb question. I do, however, know of one girl who refers to masterbation as her "love button." I have

to say that term is a little easier to use. Maybe we should all practice asking, "So, have you played with your love button lately?" I will agree that masturbation is more of a struggle for guys than for girls—but it's not just a guy thing. The truth is, it's much more of an issue for women than has been historically assumed or publicly acknowledged. It is a real struggle for many women.

I realize that some of you are saying, " 'Struggle'? 'Issue'? What's the big deal? It's just a normal part of life. Everyone does it." And the famous Seinfeldian contest did turn it into dinner conversation (though perhaps it's still not a topic that's appropriate to discuss with your mother at the table). Elaine was right there in the running with Jerry, George, and Kramer.

Let me stop right here and acknowledge that there are a couple of you out there who have never realized that masturbation had anything to do with women and their sexuality. Just seeing the word in print has made you feel faint, and you can feel your face flush even if you're in a room by yourself. My former roommate was one of you until she got married she has been blessed with a fabulous sex life. So, for you, I'd say that you should forget you ever started reading this chapter. Close the book and go watch a Jane Austen film. Continue in your virtue, and kudos to you for guarding your eyes

and ears and, thereby, your mind and heart. But for most of us, especially for those who have been sexually active, masturbating is a real temptation, even if it's just out of curiosity.

THE SUPPOSED BOTTOM LINE

From my experience in working with college students and single women and discussing this issue, the bottom line is that everyone wants one thing—justification. "Just tell me it's not a sin!" For Pete's sake, I have to confess that as a thirty-something single woman, I'd like to find some justification for it myself. As my friend who married in her late thirties used to say, "My hormones are all dressed up with nowhere to go."

In the past year at my church we did a series on the Song of Solomon, a dating series, and in the main service, a series on sex—yes, in the main service. Each and every time, during the Q & A time, the topic of masturbation came up, and it was usually raised by a woman.

Likewise, my friend was one of the speakers at a women's retreat recently. Little did she know what she was getting into when she agreed to do Q & A with the singles. I'm so glad it was she and not me left to recover the room when one woman quipped, "Who needs men when you've got batteries?" The woman was only half joking.

Maybe even just a quarter or an eighth. (If you don't get it, that is probably a good thing.) To the relief of some and the chagrin of others, the Bible says nothing about the act of self-gratification. It falls into the abyss of "gray areas"—those topics not specifically addressed by chapter and verse. We like to think that fact gives us the freedom to do whatever we feel is right for us. But as with most gray areas, there are some greater guiding principles here that *are* clearly given and that tend to make things a little more black and white.

AND WHY NOT?

The broadest principle is this. God created sex for the purpose of allowing two people to experience intimacy and connection with one another. When you experience sex as God intended, the greatest pleasure is in pleasing your partner. Masturbation is self-serving (in every sense) and is not what God intended sex to be.

That's the short answer. There are, however, some other principles to consider as well.

My seventh-grade P.E. teacher taught us the mechanics of masturbation in a one-day sex education overview as required by the Board of Education of the fine state of Arkansas. (I know—there are so many things wrong with this story. But I wonder if she practiced saying the word out loud several times before she had to say it to a room full of seventh-grade girls.) Anyway, I confess I discovered that the pure mechanics of masturbation didn't do much, though I did not poll the class the next day to see if others had found the same. Later in life I learned that for women it's a mental game—it's about the things we think about, even dwell on, the fantasies we create in our mind that make us feel wanted, pursued, attractive, and sexy, *plus* the mechanics, that lead us down the path to pleasure.

Jesus said that if you even look at a woman (or a man, in our case) with lustful thoughts, it's the same as committing adultery (Matthew 5:27-28). Granted, the natural consequences of lusting are not necessarily the same as those for actually committing adultery. A spouse might be a little more upset by one more than by the other. Adultery is all the wrong of lust and then some. But the point is that just because you draw the line at actual adultery (or actual sex, in the case of single women with single men), that doesn't mean you're home free with God in the area of sexual purity.

That's the thing about Jesus. He's always much more concerned with our heart and mind than with just the outward actions. Having lustful thoughts is not in the game plan. Sexual fantasies that accompany masturbation certainly qualify as lusting, or coveting something forbidden. According to Jesus, thinking about it is not as far from doing it as one might think. As an alternative, Paul recommends this as a good overarching principle: "Whatever is true, whatever is honorable, whatever is right, whatever is pure, whatever is lovely, whatever is of good repute, and if there is any excellence, and if anything worthy of praise, dwell on these things" (Philippians 4:8).

I will acknowledge here that for people who have been sexually active in the past and who have made a commitment to chastity (now, there's a word from your grandmother's handbook), masturbation is a much greater struggle. Furthermore, for those who became aware of their sexuality at younger age through whatever circumstances—whether abuse, pornography, a lesson by their seventh-grade gym teacher, or just becoming sexually active—this is much greater temptation. In a sense, love has been awakened before its time, as it says in the Song of Solomon.

Some of the women I've discussed this topic with would say that they can masturbate without having lustful thoughts, that it is a purely mechanical release. This may especially be true for women in their thirties, when hormones are changing. And several well-respected Christian leaders—Dr. James Dobson of Focus on the Family fame among them—would say that if you can masturbate without lusting and without its becoming addictive, then go for it; it can be welcome relief for sexual pressure. So, there may be some freedom within parameters, according to some.

Another way to look at it, however, is to ask, "Is it out of bounds to have an orgasm if you're not married?" One sex therapist I know says it this simply: "There are two kinds of sex—married sex and unmarried sex." One is clearly in the green zone, the other in the red. Some want to believe that sex is only actual intercourse between two people, but I think that common wisdom would say sex is broader than that—it is anything that leads up to, but is not necessarily inclusive of, an orgasm. Really, it's anything that involves sexual arousal. The point, the motivation, the goal, the result, the climax of masturbation is the orgasm. So I think it's safe to say that masturbation is a sex act, though it may be a solo one, and thereby qualifies as "unmarried sex."

Contrary to popular belief, God is not the consummate parent wagging His Michelangeloesque finger and saying something is wrong "Just because I said so" (although, if you ask me, He certainly has every right to do so). If God draws a line and says not to cross it, that's because it's not a true reflection of His nature and character and/or because it's detrimental to us in some way—physically, emotionally, or spiritually. We know that orgasms per se are not bad. After all, God created them, and so that experience of intense physical pleasure is somehow reflective of how good God is. Yeah, it shows just a taste of His goodness and pleasure. (I know that's possibly a little freakish to think about, but it's true.) So then, the question becomes, are there detrimental consequences to masturbation?

WHAT WILL IT COST ME?

What is it that God is trying to protect us from? I'm not a sex therapist by any stretch, but I recently had a conversation with Marnie Feree who does counsel women with sexual issues. She gave me some insight into the risks involved.

One of the biggest risks in this area is addiction. Masturbating can become your drug of choice. When you feel lonely or frustrated or disappointed, masturbation becomes your outlet to feel better. Soon it can control you, as can any addiction. Certainly we all find ways to adjust our emotional thermostat. For example, when I'm depressed, I go for a long drive, often at high rates of speed, while listening to loud music, preferably U2. Not all emotional self-maintenance is bad or addictive, but some ways we cope are worse than others. So what I would say is that creating a link between negative emotions and sexual gratification is not wise.

It is clear in Scripture that we should be mastered by nothing, that we should learn to control our bodies.[1] Paul says we should "buffet" our bodies.[2] (That's not *buffet* as in all you can eat; that's *buffet* as in Jimmy and Warren—it means to discipline.) It is not our nature to deny ourselves what we want, but fortunately one of the fruits of a life with God is self-control.

Another consequence of indulging in masturbation is that you can train your heart, mind, and body to respond only to self-stimulation. Imagine the heartache and disappointment that might bring to your spouse when you are married and he is unable to satisfy you. "Thanks, honey—I'll take it from here." That would certainly inhibit your experience of sex as God intended it.

There is also the temptation of wanting more. This is the law of diminishing returns: what once seemed satisfying is now boring and doesn't do so much for you. It can get to the point where the fantasies are no longer exciting and you're tempted to act on them, to make them a reality, even if it is only a virtual reality via the Internet or romance novels or other forms of pornography. The risk is being drawn deeper and deeper into more destructive habits.

It only makes sense that self-gratification can lead to self-consumption: it's all about me. Sex was never intended to be all about one person. As God created it, it is the most intimate connection between two people. It's not about seeking to have one's own needs met but about giving and about satisfying another. Masturbation trains you to be self-serving in sex. That trait can spill over into other areas of life as well. And like any area of habitual sin, it can lead to a hard heart toward God.

THE REAL BOTTOM LINE

Not everyone who plays with her "love button" is going to end up a sex addict and never be able to have satisfying sex in marriage. But one of the overarching principles in this and every area of life has to do with our relationship with God, which is the source of all fulfillment in life. That relationship is not dictated by how much we can get away with and still be just to the right of the line, but rather it is about the condition of our heart toward Him.

I know that God's desire for me is to be able to experience this good gift of sex as He intended it in all its fullness within the context of marriage. I want what He wants for me. Granted, I may never marry (that's another chapter), but I still choose to honor sex for what He made it to be, which is not what I see on TV or movies or even the fantasies I could make up in my head. All of those are a poor reflection. I am hardheaded but am slowly learning that life is not so much about me and my pleasure and satisfaction as it is about knowing God and reflecting His glory. So, for me, the principle is to draw the line and take two steps back—not only for my own safety and protection but also to turn the other way and pursue being more like Christ, to pursue greater intimacy in my relationship with Him.

So, what does that look like—to turn the other way and pursue holiness? As with any sin habit, it means to bring it into the light (sin cannot survive in the light) and to own it, to tell someone. In fact, go ahead. Call Mom right now. Pick up your cell phone—speed dial 2. Okay, I'm kidding. I know that's an awkward conversation to have with anyone, especially Mom. But hopefully you have, or are developing, some heart-level friendships within which you can be real about the struggles in your life.

Then, quite literally, as the word repentance implies, "turn from it." Turn your eyes from things that make your mind go down the path of masturbation and lust—certain movies, TV shows, books, magazines, and Web sites. Maybe you need to get rid of cable TV. (Maybe I do.) Turn your thoughts from fantasizing about men and situations that make you feel sexy and wanted and valued. As Scripture says, "Take every thought captive."[3] Replace sexual thoughts with thoughts about God's love for you and the things He says are true of you. I know that sounds like a Sunday school answer, but if I had spent the same amount of mental energy on contemplating spiritual truth and memorizing Scripture that I've spent on daydreaming about men and relationships over the years, I'm pretty sure I'd be a different person by now, at least a little more Mother Teresa and a little less Cosmo. (Okay, not that I'm so Cosmo. But you know what I mean.)

Steer clear of situations and activities that stir wrong emotions and desires. For you, it may be flirting with men that makes you feel sexy and wanted. Crossing boundaries with your boyfriend can certainly start something you feel the need to finish on your own. Or it may be wearing a sexy outfit and slinky lingerie or sleeping in the nude or taking bubble baths by candlelight—whatever the romantic thing is that makes you a bit randy (apologies to those actually named Randy). Also, you might take note of your cycle. How very maternal that sounded. But it's true that most women tend to be in the mood more when they're ovulating and right before their period starts. It only makes sense that God would create us that way.

I know all this sounds a bit extreme, and I'm not saying that you shouldn't do things that make you feel attractive. Please do express your femininity and beauty and experience the fullness of being a woman. But if there are things that get your "love button" going, then you should flee. As you would with any sin, figure out what your triggers are and set up some boundaries for yourself, then get some accountability and encouragement.

Most importantly, ask the Holy Spirit to give you strength to resist temptation. Jesus modeled that we should pray that we would not be led into temptation, but rather delivered from sin and evil.[4] It is only through the power of the Spirit who lives within us that we can overcome any sin habit. Practice living the Spirit-filled life. Make a conscious decision to give Him control of this area of your life. I realize at this point you may not want to, because like most sin, masturbation is satisfying in the moment and seems harmless. However, the more you cultivate intimacy with the Lord, the more your desire for sin wanes. Pray that He would make you willing to be willing.

AND ONE LAST THING …

While not taking seriously our holiness in the area of sex is certainly a problem, there can be an extreme in the other direction as well. That is that we can feel a disproportionate amount of guilt when we fail in this area. A failure with masturbation is no different from a failure with gossip, overeating, or any other sin. If you have masturbated, there is no reason to allow a veil of guilt to remain for days, separating you from intimacy with Christ as you punish yourself rather than confess and accept God's forgiveness. In other words, don't let sin separate you from intimacy with Him, but don't let guilt feelings separate you either.

[1] 1 Thessalonians 4:4
[2] 1 Corinthians 9:27
[3] 2 Corinthians 10:5
[4] Matthew 6:13

From Fantasy to Reality

By Henry Cloud, Ph.D.

I was doing a radio show one day when a young woman called in and said she didn't know what to do with her boyfriend. When I asked what she meant, she said that she was struggling with whether to break up or to keep going, get more serious, and move toward marriage.

"Well, most times when people love each other and are thinking about marriage," I said, "it is pretty clear to them; otherwise, why would they even be thinking of such a commitment? But for some reason, with you and him, it is not. What are those reasons?"

"Well …" she started and hesitated. "There are some things that I just wish were different."

"That's pretty normal. No one person has everything we want," I reasoned, wondering if she might be a little picky. "What are the things?"

"Well, he just doesn't always pay attention to the relationship. It's like I am the one who always is pushing for time together or to talk about things that we need to talk about. It seems that his hobbies and buddies are a bigger priority than I am. Like sometimes when we have a date, he might just keep playing basketball, and not even call, and then come over later and think that is going to be okay.

"Also, he says he shares my values about physical limits, but he pushes me for sex and I don't want to, but I keep having to say no over and over. And I am the one that has to push for having a spiritual life. … I wish he was interested in spiritual things and just growing as a person."

"Wow," I said. "That's a lot to be concerned about. So, what's your question?"

"Well," she said, "I want to know if I should break up with him or go forward toward getting engaged."

"What have you tried to do about these things?" I asked.

"I have talked to him a lot," she answered. "I have told him that I want to feel more important to him and that I want us to have a spiritual life together and that I want him to respect my physical limits."

"That's pretty good," I told her. "And what happened?"

"He understands, he says. He agrees with me, saying that he wants the same things that I do. He is a really good guy," she said with a little drop in her voice. "But then nothing really changes. I still feel like I am always the one who is trying to get things to be better."

"Okay, question. If you have tried and tried and nothing has changed, and you are not happy, and the relationship isn't working like you want a relationship to work, then *why don't you end it and move on?* Why in God's green earth are you thinking about even being serious with him, much less marriage? He is not interested in changing and being what you are looking for, so why don't you get on down the road?"

And here it came, the moment that revealed what keeps a lot of young women stuck. "Because I love him," she said.

In one way, I could not believe my ears. And yet I have heard it so many times from women that I could easily believe it. It was the answer I was expecting. Nevertheless, I asked, "What does that mean?"

"Well," she went on, "I just love so many things about him. He is so good in so many ways. …"

"Yeah," I said, "but his character, and the way that he is in a relationship, makes all of those good things pretty unusable to you as well. You are really dissatisfied, but you have a big problem, and here it is: *you are leading with your attachment to him.*"

"What does that mean?" she asked.

"It means that what is driving your dilemma is that you have an attachment to him, instead of what is important to you: your *values*. Whenever we let our attachments drive us or guide us, we can get into all sorts of things that don't work well. And that is what is happening here. You feel so attached to him that that is what is driving your thinking, instead of what you really want and value in a relationship."

"But I really do love him," she said.

"I know, but let me ask you something. If you were not dating anyone and I said to you, 'Hey, Jill, I have somebody for you to go out with. I think you guys would be great for each other,' what would you say?"

"Well," she said, "I would want to know what he is like. I would ask you more."

"Fine," I said. "He is a fun guy, but he will use you for sex and he really won't pay attention to what you want. He will ignore you when it is convenient for him to do so, like going to play basketball with his friends instead of keeping his commitment with you, but he will call you later to see if you want his leftover time. And when you want to have a spiritual life, forget doing that with him. He is not interested, and you are on your own there. But don't worry, I am sure you will love him a lot and maybe even want to marry him."

The phone was silent for a moment. "Well, I don't think I would be that interested," she said. "Who would want that?"

"Exactly," I said. "That is because if you have not met him, you are leading with your values and not with your attachment. Since you are not attached to this hypothetical guy, you have no problem seeing it. But with Jason you do, because your attachment gets in the way. You are leading from the wrong place, like an addict who knows that getting high is destroying her, but she is so attached to the drug that she can't give it up."

"I think I know what I have to do," she said. "This is not what I want in my life. But how do I do it?"

"Let your values drive you," I said. "Say to him exactly what you just said to me: 'Jason, let me tell you what is important to me and what I am looking for. I want someone who makes a relationship with me a priority and where I feel wanted. I want someone who not only says he shares my values but actually lives them out and respects my wishes when I do. I want someone who is into spiritual growth and improving as a person and who is responsible in life. I want someone who keeps his promises. That is what I am looking for in a guy.

" 'Right now you are not that person. I want you to be that person—I really do. But you are not. If you become that person someday, you can call me, though I don't know if I will be there or not. Perhaps by then I will have already found him. But that is what I am looking for and I am not going to settle for less. So we have to break up.'

"If you say that," I said, "then you are truly leading with your values and not letting your attachment to him get in the way. Then you let go and move on, period. No looking back."

She told me she got it, we hung up, and I hoped she did get it. I will probably never know. But I do know, from working with a lot of women, that if she doesn't get it, she is in for a world of hurt. Why is this, and how can you avoid this kind of pain in your own dating relationships? Let's look at some of the biggest causes of "date diseases" that take women places where they don't want to go.

MISTAKE NUMBER ONE: NOT KNOWING WHAT YOU WANT BEFORE YOU KNOW WHO YOU WANT

This was Jill's problem. As I told her, she had not gotten clear about her values and what mattered to her before she got attached to someone. So she found herself deeply attached to Jason and yet continually disappointed. But she was letting how she felt for him keep her stuck. Or at least sort of.

In reality, she was letting *half of what she felt* keep her stuck. She was letting the half of her that loved him and wanted him keep her in the relationship. But she was *ignoring* the other half of her, the part that was hurt, disappointed, and left wanting more. This huge part of reality was a sign to her that things that matter were not present in the relationship—things that she really wanted in someone she was going to be serious with and potentially end up with for the rest of her life. Those are the things that come from our values.

To value something means to "assign great weight" to it. The things we value are weighty issues. They should command our attention more than anything else. And they should dictate whether or not someone gets through the gate to our heart. It is easy to have feelings for someone you are attracted to, but if the things you truly value are not present in him, then you will find that those things render all the things you find attractive about him spoiled in the end. You will not be able to enjoy them, or even have them sometimes, because the things that make a relationship truly work are not present.

So, before you even meet him, ask yourself what your nonnegotiable things are. I like the way David expressed some of his in Psalm 101. He said that things like honesty, faithfulness, and purity were important and that he would have nothing to do with people who did not possess those qualities. I wish all single women everywhere would date that way! Even if David liked someone, or that person possessed things that would be attractive to him, he would not trust such a person or give his heart away without the essential values being present. Have you thought about what those are for you? Here are some things to think about, and you can add your own as well:

- The ability to connect emotionally, to empathize, and to be present with you
- The ability to give freedom and not control you
- The ability to be real, and allow you to be real, instead of requiring perfection or having impossible standards
- The ability to be equals and show mutual respect

- Having a spiritual life of his own that you respect
- Honesty, faithfulness, dependability, sexual purity, integrity, responsibility, financial responsibility, compassion, forgiveness

These are the kinds of things that make relationships work in the long run. You will find many people you can be attracted to for a variety of reasons, some good and some not so good. But when you find yourself attracted, make sure that before you let your heart get involved, or let it stay involved, you make sure they possess the things you value most. Know what you want before you know who you want.

MISTAKE NUMBER TWO: DATING FROM A VACUUM

When I have talked to women like Jill who are not finding what they want, or who are settling for what they don't want, there is a common theme: they are trying to fill something inside them with that relationship. There is some sort of loneliness or a need to find validation of themselves—or even meaning—in a relationship with a guy. Many women give men way too much power to prove to themselves that they are lovable and desirable and even to make life worth living. They feel as if life is somehow not complete if they are not in a relationship with a guy.

When this happens, it makes letting go of someone, or not getting involved with someone, more difficult. The mantra seems to be that a not-so-good relationship is better than no relationship at all. But are those the only options?

The answer is that women who attract the best men, and who pick the best men, are women whose lives are complete *without being in a serious relationship*. "Aw, come on," you might be saying. "What a killjoy!" No, I don't mean to be, as I want a good significant relationship for you as well. That is a wonderful thing to be in. But the truth is that if you need it to be happy or to be complete, then you are not ready for one. Only a person who does not need the other person to be whole is whole enough to make a relationship work and to attract a truly whole person also. So make sure of a few things:

- Make sure that you are in a good, close-knit group of friends, male and female, so that all your relational needs are being met. If this is true, you have intimacy, connectedness, and support and you are not lonely at all. You will not be so needy that you "can't live without him," if he is not the right one. You will be perfectly happy in your community.

- Make sure that you are growing spiritually. Many times people try to fill a spiritual vacuum with a romantic attachment. Since romance itself is something of a transcendent experience, it can masquerade as having the ability to fill parts of your heart and soul that only God can fill. If you are growing close to Him and being fulfilled in your spirit, you will not ask a relationship to do something for you that it cannot. And you will be able to trust God to bring the right person along.

- Make sure that you are growing as a person and doing fulfilling things. Often someone dates poorly because life feels empty. She tries to fill an empty life with a person, trying to gain meaning from a relationship, when the real problem is a real lack of purpose and fulfillment. Find out what your talents and gifts are and develop them. Step out and grow in new areas and activities, and find your real passion and pursue it. When your life is full with purpose and with pursuing the gifts that God has given you, you won't ask romance to fill an empty life. You will be so busy and fulfilled that it is going to take a really special guy to get you to make room for him in your wonderful life!

MISTAKE NUMBER THREE: NOT DATING ENOUGH PEOPLE

I hear it all the time. Women start dating someone, quickly get interested in him, and then stop dating everyone else. Then, when the relationship does not pan out, they repeat the cycle. They start dating again and find one guy and get serious. When that relationship does not work, same thing again. As a result, they have a string of exclusive relationships but not much experience in dating a lot of people casually.

If you read my book *How to Find a Date Worth Keeping* (Zondervan, 2005), you will see what a big proponent I am of dating a lot of people. Dating is not about "finding the one"; it is about having fun and getting to know different kinds of people. If you have not dated a lot, then chances are that you really don't even know what you want or need. You may be stuck in looking for some "type" and not getting to know real people and through that process getting to know what kind of "type" you really need.

You should get more involved with someone only when he stands out in the crowd. It is easy to stand out in a crowd of one! Anyone can look good. You need to know what a lot of different kinds of people and experiences are like to chose well. How do you know you want the athletic type if you have never dated a brain? Get out there and discover the world.

MISTAKE NUMBER FOUR: NOT BEING ACTIVE ENOUGH TO MEET A LOT OF PEOPLE

It may be that the suggestion above seems out of reach, because you are not getting the chance to have a lot of dates. Is that true? If it is, then ask yourself and your close friends why. Why is it that you are not dating much or meeting many good guys? Is it your schedule? Is it your traffic pattern that keeps you around the same few people over and over? Maybe it is time to get out and try some new things or new circles. If you keep doing the same thing over and over, expecting different results, chances are that you will be dissatisfied.

Or are there more *internal* issues that are keeping you from dating? Are you not giving off signals that you are open? Are you not talking to guys at social gatherings or other places? Are you afraid of rejection or self-conscious in some way? Have you been hurt, and is that still affecting you? Whatever it is, be open to the fact that you may be doing some things that are reducing your chances of having dates, and do something about those issues. Talk to your friends or to a counselor about whatever that is. I can tell you that I see women all the time overcoming those kinds of things and turning a stagnant dating life around. God can heal those things in your life, but you have to ask Him to help you and get with someone else who can provide that kind of help.

MISTAKE NUMBER FIVE: LEAVING THE FOLD

It is the lone sheep who gets grabbed by the wolf. But if you stay in the pack, you will find safety. How does this turn into a dating mistake? Often when women begin dating someone they like, they drop out of life, in terms of their community and friends who ground them. So they gradually lose their greatest source of protection, feedback, and strength. As a result, they can find themselves deeper in a not-so-great situation than they would want to be and can find themselves unable to get out.

Stay connected to your friends throughout your dating experience. Talk to them about your dates and let them evaluate your dates for you. Get their feedback on how a guy treats you or what his issues are. Listen to them, for they might see things your smitten eyes have missed. Use their support to be able to deal with those things. I wish I had a nickel for every woman I have heard say, "I wish I had listened to my friends." Your friends are your best protection. You might hear them say, "What are you thinking?!" If they do, then listen.

Also, date in the context of your friends. Do things with them on your dates so that they can meet the guy and see him directly. That is where your life is, and he must integrate into your life. If he will not, or if he is not interested in getting to know the people you love, then something is wrong. Let that be a red flag. Remember, your community is your family. If he is interested in doing things only in his own circles, that is not a good sign. He must come your way, too.

MISTAKE NUMBER SIX: NOT RECOGNIZING WHERE YOU CAME FROM

Often, unfulfilling relationships are in some way a repeat or a symptom of family-of-origin issues. The classic example is the woman who is attracted to emotionally unavailable men and never realizes that she learned how to do that from an emotionally unavailable father. She is still longing for the detached dad to finally love her, and she keeps on finding him in the guys she dates, always striving to get someone who is incapable of love to somehow wake up and "get it."

It could be other patterns as well. Sometimes when someone grows up in a family where one or both parents were perfectionists or were critical, for example, she finds herself drawn to people who can't ever be pleased. Or she falls into other attractions, such as being drawn to addicts or self-centered people who are living out the ways that Mom or Dad did. What is happening is that she is repeating relational patterns she learned growing up, and she is failing to connect the dots. God designed us to learn our relational patterns in our families, and we do. If it goes well, we learn healthy patterns, and if there is dysfunction, we learn that as well.

Make sure that you have done what the Bible teaches and have grown past the generational patterns that have been handed down. If necessary, get counseling. Talk to your good friends about your patterns and see how you may be repeating some old hurts. Get involved in a new family, your community of friends, or your spiritual community, where you can learn new ways to relate and rise above the ones that are not working. Learn what you did not learn in your family of origin, and then you can find it in your dating life.

MISTAKE NUMBER SEVEN: BEING RESPONSIBLE FOR SOMEONE ELSE'S SPIRITUAL DEVELOPMENT

I talk to women all the time who are disappointed with the spirituality of the guys they are dating. But they did not think about that in the beginning. They just got serious about someone and then found they were driving the spiritual train, having to nag him into keeping up. Remember, if your spiritual life is important to you, then you are the one motivating that, not someone else, right? No one is making you care about your growth. In the same way, you have to find a guy who is self-motivated as well. If he is not, you are just going to get frustrated trying to get him to be different. That does not mean you can't expose him to your spiritual community, and things like that, and see if he wants to grow—that's great. But to have to push someone is going to get old in the end.

Get to know guys who are at the same level of motivation and growth that you are, and then you will have spiritual compatibility. You will love growing together and you won't be unequally yoked in your dating experience. Of course, you will probably go out with all guys at many different spiritual levels, but if you are going to get attached or serious, then you have to be more discerning and look for spiritual compatibility after some amount of time.

REALITY IS BEST

We know that women fantasize about relationships. That's not all bad, for you fantasy comes from your deepest desires. And we know that it is God's desire that your deepest desires are met. He even says that when they are not, it can make your heart sick: "A desire accomplished is sweet to the soul, but hope deferred makes the heart sick." (Proverbs 13:12) So, when you dream about having a good relationship, that can be a good thing.

But for a good relationship to materialize, the fantasy or the dream has to be rooted in reality. You have to be dreaming for the things that turn those dreams into real, tangible relationships. You can't, like Jill, be dreaming for someone without character and values to provide a good relationship for you. If you are, then you are just dreaming.

For dreams to become reality—and they can—they have to be rooted in real things that make them real. Get your dating life rooted in a deep relationship with God, deep relationships with friends who love you and give you feedback, deep and important values, and a fulfilling life of expressing your talents. As you are doing those things, you will be a grounded person who can find the kind of person who is like you and with whom your best fantasies can find themselves in the real world.

DR. HENRY CLOUD is a clinical psychologist and best-selling author or co-author of over eighteen books, including How to Get a Date Worth Keeping and Boundaries in Dating. He also conducts seminars across the country and co-hosts a radio program called New Life Live. He's the president of Cloud-Townsend Resources.

What *Bride* Magazine Doesn't Tell You

By Paula Keels

Does anyone *really* know what they're getting into when they get married? Is it really all about that ever-evasive kind of being "in love" that causes Tom Cruise to jump up and down on Oprah's couch for the love of Katie? Is it possible to find that one soul mate, the one you've felt like you've known your whole life? Can we end up like that old couple that's still holding hands at seventy-five as they walk through the park?

I don't think there is any other topic that occupies our thoughts as a whole more than relationships. Who is with whom? Who broke up with whom? Who is interested in me? How do I get rid of who I'm with? How do I make this work? Our society has turned such age-old questions into a multimillion dollar business in the form of advice books, therapists, gossip magazines, Jerry Springer–type shows, Dr. Phil, and so on. We are, as a nation, obsessed with relationships. If we took a poll, most of us would probably say that we just want to be married and live happily ever after. Judging from our divorce rate, we aren't good at that.

When I married fifteen years ago, I thought I had an advantage. My husband and I are both committed believers in Christ. We both have a personal relationship with the architect of marriage itself. We thought we knew what it was all about. Looking back, I don't think we had a clue. The divorce rate for believers is no lower than that of unbelievers. In fact, in some cases it's higher, according to a recent George Barna poll. I don't know one married person, even the most happily married, who has not at some point in her relationship been surprised, shocked, or even disappointed in all that the institution encompasses. It would seem society is obsessed with something it doesn't understand, and both believers and nonbelievers in Christ are equally confused.

IT'S NOT ABOUT THE ICING

Like most women, I long to have the closest, most intimate marriage possible. That's much harder than you might think. The only thing my husband and I had right when we said our vows was that we loved each other very much and that divorce was never an option. Interestingly, it is not the conferences or books on marriage or conversations with wise people that have helped me understand and improve my marriage. The most helpful thing to me has been a year-long, in-depth Bible study on the book of Revelation (warning—do not read this book without a "road map"; it can be freaky). I think that to truly understand the purpose of marriage, you have to understand the bigger picture—the purpose of life.

There is not enough space in this article, or even in this book, to examine Revelation or the meaning of life. But let me sum it up by saying that life is not about me—or you, for that matter. It's all about Him—God, I mean—His glory, His honor, His purpose. My marriage (any marriage) is not about being in love, sharing my life, experiencing fulfillment, ending loneliness, having children, or having all my needs met, etc., contrary to popular belief. It's about bringing honor and glory to God. That doesn't sound very romantic, does it? Not exactly the chick flick plot line. And yet romance and joy and love and passion and children and security and on and on are all elements of my marriage. But they are not the purpose of it.

It's somewhat ironic that the very things that most people pursue, the things they believe will satisfy them—happiness, romance, security—are actually not the end in and of themselves. When one pursues intimacy with God as the goal, those things are the byproducts, the bonus, the icing on the cake. One of the many paradoxes of the Christian life is this: by not pursuing selfish gain, you have your needs and desires met.

METAPHORICALLY SPEAKING…

God loves symbolism. The Bible is full of it. In his book *Sacred Marriage*, Gary Thomas writes,

> In fact, both the Old and New Testaments use marriage as a central analogy—the union between God and Israel (OT) and the union between Christ and his Church (NT). Understanding the depths of these analogies is crucial, as they will help us determine the very foundation on which a truly Christian marriage is based. If I believe the primary purpose of marriage is to model God's love for his church, I will enter this relationship and maintain it with an entirely new motivation, one hinted at by Paul in his second letter to the Corinthians: "So we make it our goal

to please Him." (2nd Cor. 5:9). More than seeing marriage as a mutual comfort, we must see it as a word picture of the most important news humans have ever received—that there is a divine relationship between God and his people.

We all long to love and be loved. We all experience desire and passion. We all want security and companionship. These desires are good and real and from the Lord. Where we go wrong is in expecting our mate to be the fulfillment of all of these things and more, instead of finding fulfillment in a relationship with a very real God. I speak from experience. I have spent several frustrated years expecting Jeff to meet all my needs (expecting him to meet some, I think, is fair). It is an incredible and unfair onus to place upon another imperfect person to meet all of my needs. I am the most in love, passionate, and content in my marriage when my relationship with God is rich.

With all of that in mind, in order to experience marriage as intended, we have to shift our paradigm on marriage from what our culture has taught us to what God has designed. We can start by examining our longings and emotions, and even the practical wants and needs for relationships, in light of God's design and intent for them. Hear carefully what I am saying so as not to get disillusioned. The romance and love and companionship that you have been dreaming of since you were a little girl (or the sex, for that matter) is completely available within God's design for marriage. It is just that most of us are looking to the wrong source. We think we have to have a husband to provide the emotional energy, right priorities, compassion, sacrifice, and wisdom required for those things to happen. Yes, you can have it all, as long as you find your all in Him. Anything else is counterfeit and ultimately unfulfilling. In other words, when both my husband and I are well connected in a healthy relationship with God—meaning we read the Bible with a teachable heart and spend time in humble prayer—God changes us and gives us His understanding, joy, and peace (Eph. 4). If we are both aligned with Him, then we are aligned with each other. It's really a three-way relationship in the purest sense.

WHAT IF GOD DESIGNED MARRIAGE TO MAKE US HOLY MORE THAN TO MAKE US HAPPY?

That's the subtitle of Gary Thomas's book. Not our idea of romance, once again. If life is all about God, knowing Him and make Him known, then it would make sense that part of what God has designed marriage for is to help us know Him better. Thomas writes, "We need to be called out of ourselves because, in truth, we are incomplete. God made us to find our fulfillment in Him—the Totally Other. Marriage shows us that we are not all there is; it calls us to give way to another, but also to find joy, happiness, and even ecstasy in another." Thomas's book explores how marriage teaches us to love, to respect others, to have a servant's heart, to persevere, and to forgive. It also exposes our sin, builds our character, and makes us aware of God's presence.

You may have experienced some of that from just having a roommate. Living with someone else tends to reveal "areas of growth," a.k.a. annoying weaknesses or—let's just call it what it is—sin. In the context of marriage, where you are committed to living with each other for life, there is a much higher motivation to push through those areas and help each other grow. You might be surprised how selfish you really are when it comes to stupid things that reveal your heart—like which side of the bed you normally sleep on or what temperature the thermostat should be set at. You might not realize your need for control until you have to include someone else in your decision-making process. You might not realize how angry you can be until someone you love as much as your husband really disappoints you. Frankly, it's painful to see yourself—the good, the bad, and the ugly—so clearly through the eyes of someone you love dearly. But someone knowing your every weakness, scar, and broken place, and still loving and accepting you, is a rich reflection of God's unconditional love for us.

A few years ago, my husband and I packed up our four small children and moved overseas for two years. My husband loves change. He thrives on it. I hate change, and suddenly I found almost everything in my life different. I missed things I never knew I appreciated, such as my super-capacity washing machine. (Try doing laundry for two adults, two preschoolers, one toddler, and a baby in a tiny European washer. Be prepared to take all week and then start all over again!) We learned a lot about ourselves and our marriage during those two years. We became acutely aware of some differences in our natures that we hadn't discovered in our previous years of marriage. Through some hard conversations and hard work, we learned to respect those differences and improved our relationships both with each other and with God.

THE BRIDE

Marriage is more than this, though. It is also, as mentioned before, a powerful symbol (when done right) of Christ's love for believers, His bride. Revelation describes the new Jerusalem, inhabited by all the saints forever, as "the bride, the wife of the lamb" (21:9). Paul speaks of this relationship

> Husbands, love your wives just as Christ also loved the church and gave Himself up for her; that He might sanctify her, having cleansed her by the washing of water with the word, that He might present to Himself the church in all her glory, having no spot or wrinkle or any such thing; but that she should be holy and blameless. So husbands ought also to love their own wives as their own bodies. He who loves his own wife loves himself; for no one ever hated his own flesh, but nourishes and cherishes it, just as Christ also does the Church. (Ephesians 5:25-29)

Women, does this not sound romantic? Who doesn't want to be sacrificially loved, to be nourished and cherished, to have someone pour his life into helping make us holy and blameless? No man is capable of this without Jesus. God has not only designed this relationship; He has also provided the power through His Holy Spirit for it to be accomplished.

What is my role in this? My husband can be following Christ and empowered by the Holy Spirit to work in my life to make me holy, and it will never work unless I am subject to my own husband as to the Lord (Ephesians 5:22). Most of us have heard that the Bible says we need to submit to our husbands. That verse is certainly more palatable when we understand why. When marriage is rightly done, my husband is serving me, and I need to swallow my pride and allow him to do that, in order that I may know God better.

I confess that I hate to submit. I come from a long line of take-charge women. And I just know that I know that I know I am right, even when I am wrong. It is annoying when my husband doesn't agree with me. I can choose to insist on my way and cause discord to my whole family (cuz if momma ain't happy…) or I can submit to my husband (and dang it if he's not right a lot of the time) and in doing so allow God to work through my spouse to defeat and "untrain" my pride and selfishness.

AND THEN THERE'S THE "BE FRUITFUL AND MULTIPLY" THING

Certainly with all stated above, a marriage without children is a complete and whole marriage, but doesn't it seem right that God ordained that new and vulnerable souls should enter into existence within the protection of a godly, biblical marriage—that they should grow up with the example of Christ and His love for them played out constantly between their mother and father? Aren't we glad that we are not in a Matrix, plugged in to some cold and uncaring machine that nourishes us and sustains us for its own selfish reasons? God's picture is so much better. How will my five children know unless I tell them? And how will they believe that it is true if my husband and I are not living it out daily in front of them?

These words, which I am commanding you today, shall be on your heart; and you shall teach them diligently to your sons and shall talk of them when you sit in your house and when you walk by the way and when you lie down and when you rise up. (Deuteronomy 6:6-8)

For He established a testimony in Jacob and appointed a law in Israel, which He commanded our fathers, that they should teach them to their children, that the generation to come might know, even the children yet to be born, that they may arise and tell them to their children, that they should put their confidence in God, and not forget the works of God, but keep His commandments. (Psalm 78:5-7)

That is quite a responsibility—overwhelming at times. So few parents are intentional about that. No wonder we are so screwed up. I had a friend growing up named Kris whose father was the pastor of our church. I was a little scared to go over to her house. Her mom spent most of her time locked in her bedroom and her dad in his study. He was gruff, joyless, and unkind. One time when I was out with Kris her old VW Beetle broke down and she called her dad for help. He came, griping and complaining the whole time that this was his day off and he didn't appreciate it being interrupted to come and help out his daughter. And what did he spend his time doing in that study? Reading the Bible and prepping sermons about God's love and compassion. People who think Christians are hypocritical probably came by that opinion honestly.

I'm a sinner. I mess up daily, sometimes hourly, in front of my children. I pray that God would continually reveal my mistakes to me so that I can make it right. I apologize all the time, although still not nearly enough. I want to be real in front of my children. I never want to present myself to them as something other than what I am, a woman who loves God and who is trying to know Him more and more and walk in His way and who is failing and repenting often. It is okay that they know life is messy. It is not okay if they see me accepting that messiness while making no effort to clean it up.

THE SEX
Finally, speaking of children, let's talk about sex.

When I was in freshman English at the University of Texas, I was assigned to a random partner to work on a paper. My partner's name was Aaron. He was good looking, wealthy, popular, and really smart. I mean really smart. He was at the University of Texas on a full-ride academic scholarship. So I was a little astonished when he asked me what my spiritual beliefs were, and when I replied that I was a Christian, he said, "I could never be a Christian. They believe in sex only for procreation. That's ridiculous."

You're right, Aaron, that does seem ridiculous. What surprised me was how such an educated and savvy guy acquired such a belief. He was Jewish, after all. We have the same God; two-thirds of our Bible is the same. Where did that come from? Unfortunately, I think it came from our own ranks. Historically, the church has been confused over this issue of sex and its intention. Certainly our society has made a huge mess of it. Perhaps the church has had a tendency to overreact in its defense of biblical virtue and move the line way back from where God placed it.

Consider this bit of history:

In the second century, Clement of Alexandria, one of our church fathers, taught that only procreative sex was allowable and only during twelve hours of the twenty-four (at night). By the Middle Ages, preposterous as it now seems, the Church forbade sex forty days before the important festival of Christmas, forty days before and eight days after the more important festival of Easter, eight days after Pentecost, the eves of feast days, on Sundays in honor of the resurrection, on Wednesdays to call to mind the beginning of Lent, Fridays in memory of the crucifixion, during pregnancy and thirty days after birth (forty if the child is female), during menstruation, and five days before Communion! This all adds up to 252 excluded days, not counting feast days. If there were thirty feast days (a guess that may, in fact, be on the conservative side), there would have been eighty-three remaining days in the year when (provided, of course, that the woman did not happen to be menstruating or pregnant or in a postnatal period, and provided that they intended procreation) couples could with the permission of the Church have indulged in (but not enjoyed) sexual intercourse! (from Oliver's *Conjugal Spirituality*, as quoted in Sacred Marriage).

I'm pretty sure that's far from what God intended.

God's idea of sex is yet another symbol of the deepest, most intimate type of connection—two becoming one—physically, spiritually, and emotionally. When done right, it is truly the most intimate connection humanly possible. It's just a taste of the intimacy he longs to have with each of us. We, too, long to be known that intimately.

There are clearly defined parameters for sex in the Bible. In a nutshell, sex is to take place only within a marriage between a man and a woman. Not before the marriage, and not within a marriage but with a different partner, and never man with man or woman with woman or solo. But within those biblical parameters (and remember God sets parameters to protect and to preserve), sex is intended for pleasure. Consider for a moment God's design of the female body. He purposefully made woman with a clitoris, which has one function, and that is sexual pleasure. Author Betsy Ricucci says, "Within the context of covenant love and mutual service, no amount of passion is excessive. Scripture says our sexual intimacy should be exhilarating (Proverbs 5:19). Believe it or not, we glorify God by cultivating a sexual desire for our husbands and by welcoming their sexual desire for us."

I attended a marriage conference recently where the speaker said that physical union between a man and wife is a symbol of oneness between Christ and the believer. He went so far as to say (and the whole room squirmed) that orgasm may be God's way of saying, "If you think this is good, wait until you are in my presence eternally in heaven—I am so much more pleasurable." What if that's true? I used to think God intended that sex be within marriage only to protect us from STDs and unwanted pregnancies and unhealthy emotional entanglements, etc. But what if the bigger picture is that He wants to protect us from such a cheap, unfulfilling counterfeit of the real thing so that when we experience it in the right context we can understand Him more and have just a taste of His glory?

But sex isn't just a physical and spiritual connection; it is an emotional one as well. And while pleasurable, it isn't always initiated just for pleasure. Sometimes it's about comfort, oneness, and strengthening an emotional bond. I recently woke up in the middle of the night with my head spinning, full of details and tasks I needed to complete and couldn't find the time to do. I was just anxious. I prayed. I got a drink of water. I tried for three hours to go back to sleep and not toss and turn and disturb my husband. But I felt like the Lord was telling me to seek comfort in my spouse. So I woke him, and the oneness (not passion) that ensued brought calmness to my anxious mind. I went back to sleep with a peaceful heart. That kind of deep, emotional connection happens only in the context of a committed, trusting marriage. I am completely comfortable with my husband in bed. I don't have to hide parts of my body (those stretch marks and "altered" abs are the results of five babies we made together, after all) or my emotions or any part of me.

DESIRES NOT TOO STRONG BUT TOO WEAK

C. S. Lewis sums all of this up best by saying, "We are half hearted creatures, fooling around with drink and sex and ambition when infinite joy is offered us. ... We are far too easily pleased. ... Our Lord finds our desires not too strong but too weak."

Women, don't be too easily pleased. Don't settle for a counterfeit (i.e., marriage as an end in itself). Know Him as fully as you can, whether single or married. Experience His riches for you. You are worth it. As a wife, as a mom, as a single person, strive to know Him and make Him known. "If we embrace—not just accept, but actively embrace—these two missions, we will have a full life, a rich life, a meaningful life, and a successful life. The irony is, we will probably also have a happy marriage (if married); but that will come as a blessed by-product of putting everything else in order" (Thomas, *Sacred Marriage*).

PAULA KEELS has been on staff with Campus Crusade for Christ for sixteen years in Waco, TX, Southern France, and currently in Austin, TX. She and her husband, Jeff, have five children.

Blind Spot

"I slept on the floor by my sister's bed, thinking if there were two of us, he'd leave us alone. It didn't matter.

"I told my mama he came into my room, but she told me I was a lyin' fool because he'd been in her bed the whole night long. I never told anybody else ever again.

"Sometimes I feel like those images are burned on the inside of my eyelids. I can't close my eyes without reliving every one. It's been eight years.

"I could not believe this was the same guy. I kept thinking he was kidding around and was going to stop any minute and we'd laugh about it. But he didn't. I told him he was scaring me, then he laughed and just kept pushing … and ripping. It was as if he was a totally different person.

"I took two or three showers a day after it first happened. But after about a month or so, I figured out that didn't really help. I was never going to be clean—really clean—again. So I just quit taking care of myself altogether."

"It's sort of like when you have a blind spot in your eye. You can't ever look away from it. It's always there, no matter which direction you look, because the problem is with your vision. It's like that. It's always part of your perspective. It warps how you see everything else. Now I've become a different person."

You can't read far into the history of humankind before you run into sexual abuse—people using sex to control, to hurt, to get what they want, to manipulate. Things haven't changed.

Genesis begins with a beautiful picture of man and woman being naked and unashamed, being joined together, becoming one flesh as man and wife. In the same way that the Father is three in one with Jesus and the Holy Spirit, so God became one with the first husband and the first wife as well. It was an ideal picture of community. But with sin came shame and guilt. The humans suddenly knew they were naked, and they were ashamed.

Not much further into Genesis you've got Abraham and Sarah using sex to force the birth of an heir through Hagar the maidservant. Then you've got harlotry coming into the scene with Judah. Next there's Pharaoh's wife chasing Joseph and making false accusations of rape. The Ten Commandments and the rest of the law include several sexual prohibitions, so there's no doubt these things were going on.

Then you get to 2 Samuel and there's the story of Tamar, the beautiful daughter of King David. Her half brother Amnon literally made himself sick with lust for her. So much so that he took his cousin's suggestion and tricked her into caring for him while he was faking illness. As she was feeding him, he took advantage of her and, in spite of her pleading, raped her and then abandoned her with hate. Tamar was devastated. She covered herself with ashes in the tradition of mourning and ripped her beautiful garment, the token of her virginity.

The real tragedy of the story is that neither her brother Absalom nor her father the king rose in her defense. Neither could or would restore her dignity. We don't know what happened to Tamar in the end. She's never mentioned again. We can only assumed she lived out her days in isolation and brokenness.

We, too, are daughters of a King. And we, too, are living in an age when the victimization of women is prevalent. Whether we've experienced it in a personal way or just vicariously through the assaults of the culture—objectification in media and advertising, being measured against airbrushed models, being told we should be more like men when it comes to sex and business—we are all victims to some extent. Our womanhood, our sexuality, our self-worth have all been abused.

However, our Father the King can and will restore us if we let Him into those broken places. He wants to restore our virtue and dignity and honor. Beth Moore, in her study *Breaking Free*,[1] writes a different ending to Tamar's story: Beauty from Ashes. I cannot begin to tell it as powerfully as she does; this is only my abbreviated version of her story.

Imagine Tamar in her grief and heartache sobbing in a heap on the cold stone floor. The door slowly opens. Her heart stops with fear. She's never seen this man before, but He seems familiar. He speaks her name with warmth and familiarity as He takes her face into His hands. As He wipes the tears from her face, she sees the filthy ashes on His hands. Her filth. He draws back and she senses weight on her head. Suddenly she's standing, trembling, looking into the mirror. She hardly recognizes her now clean and beautiful, bright-eyed face. A crown sits on her head and a veil flows to her shoulders. Her torn garment has been replaced with beautiful white linen. He turns her face and lifts her chin to look into His eyes. She's been restored— the pure, undefiled daughter of the King.

He bestows His glory on us and is the lifter of our heads (Psalm 3:3).

HOPE

I cannot write this book without acknowledging that one in four women has been sexually abused. Such abuse comes in all sorts of forms and degrees—everything from being exposed to pornography at a young age to date rape to things more heinous than I can imagine. It is all tragic evidence of how this thing that God intended to be a good gift has been twisted into self-serving destruction. Sexual abuse is one of the most grievous ramifications of sin in the world.

Many of you have tragic and heartbreaking stories of how your innocence was taken from you. Some of you have never told your story to anyone. Some of you think it's over and done with and has no effect on your life now. And thankfully, some of you have talked about it, have sought wise counsel, and have experienced God's healing.

One of the main reasons I was motivated to write this book is that all of us, to some degree, have warped views of sex, men, and marriage—a blind spot, so to speak. These views are based on our experiences, our sexual history, our upbringing, and the things we've been exposed to in movies, TV, magazines, and the Web. There are so few voices that talk about sex as God intended it.

If you have abuse in your background, there is no doubt that experience has influenced your perspective. Fears, anger, bitterness, brokenness, and lies about you and your sexuality taint your view and haunt your heart. It may be more difficult for you to hear or believe the truth about God and His desire for you to experience a rich relationship with Him, as well as marriage and sex as He intended it. My hope is that this book at least brings some of those things to light.

I am not a counselor and not the one to walk you through a healing process. But it is my prayer that I could motivate you to consider the events and influences in your life that have shaped your views of sex, men, and marriage. If there is abuse in your past and you are living with brokenness, I pray that you would pursue hope and healing. I want to at least point you in the right direction. There are some great resources listed in the back of this book; those are a good place to start. But I also recommend that you find someone to process your story with. Seeking out good counseling can be tricky, so I suggest that you ask the staff at your church for a list of counselors they recommend.

Our Father, the King, longs for all of us to see clearly. He knows and has seen everything that you've seen and experienced. His heart grieves that what He intended for good has been so misused and abused and that you suffer the consequences. Can you trust Him to restore your heart, your self-worth, and a right and true perspective?

[1] *Breaking Free: Making Liberty in Christ a Reality in Life* (Nashville, TN: LifeWay Press, 1999) p. 120

Caught in the Web

By Marnie C. Ferree, M.A.

"I can't believe I really called, much less got you on the phone. Oh my gosh, now I don't know what to say. I don't know if I can say it. I'm so embarrassed and ashamed, and I don't want anyone to find out. I know it's wrong and I should just stop, and I've tried. I really have. But I keep going back and I don't know what to do. Someone gave me your name and said you'd be a good person to talk to. Do you get many calls like this just out of the blue? Do you have any idea what I'm talking about?"

Amy's words tumbled out almost without a breath, and her anxiety was evident, even though we weren't talking in person. I could picture her sitting at her desk behind a locked door, her heart beating wildly as she cradled the phone. Although she believes otherwise, Amy is a typical coed on any campus across the country—smart, serious about her studies (most of the time), active in campus life and in her church, attractive,

surrounded by friends, hoping to marry one day, trying to walk faithfully with the Lord. She participates in a regular Bible study and disciples another girl. She has plans and dreams and long talks with God.

Deep inside, though, Amy also has a secret. One she hates and protects and wrestles with in the night. Until now, she never thought she'd tell anyone, but the poison is choking her and finally comes vomiting out when she connects on the phone. Her secret? Amy regularly surfs the dark side of the Web.

If you identify with Amy, you understand her struggle. You're probably afraid to be seen reading this chapter. You can't imagine placing a call to a stranger to ask for help. You feel ashamed and dirty and worried. You especially feel like you're all alone. None of your friends ever talk about this, and you wouldn't dream of bringing it up. Like Amy, you've tried to stop doing what you readily admit is wrong, but also like Amy, you find you can't stop. Or at least you can't stay stopped.

I understand your fear and am well acquainted with your shame. I know what it's like to feel out of control in my sexual behavior, to have the good girl others saw on the outside fighting the bad girl within. My personal struggle predated the Internet

(by a whole lot), but the rest of the story is pretty much the same.

The problem of pornography is, of course, well known. It's occasionally mentioned by some guest speaker or a daring minister, usually along with a list of other pervasive problems, such as date rape or alcohol or drug use. Everybody knows the culture is sex crazy and Christians need to stay away from all that. Purity or pornography—it's an easy call, right?

The reality is that pornography is the most abused "drug" in our country and sexual addiction is the addiction of choice among Christians. Based on surveys conducted by *Christianity Today*, 47 percent say porn is a "major problem" in their homes and 51 percent of ministers say it's their biggest temptation. For 37 percent, it's a current struggle.[1] People of faith aren't exempt from the dark side of the Web or other forms of sexual sin.

WOMEN LIKE SEX, TOO

"But aren't all those people men?" Amy whispers, her question fueled by the stereotype of bleary-eyed men clicking on lookatsex.com in the middle of the night. Categorically, sexual acting out is largely considered a male phenomenon, much like it was first thought that alcoholism primarily affected men and not women. Even cultural standards for feminine behavior limit women's expressions of sexuality more than men's practices. After all, boys will be boys. Women's participation in Internet sex is far outside the stereotypical boundaries.

Women themselves are reluctant to expose their battle with problematic sexual behavior. The enormous shame that surrounds sexual sin is experienced exponentially by female strugglers. Madonna or whore—society allows for little room in between. Few women, especially Christian women, speak openly about their involvement with online pornography or sexual chat rooms. No wonder Amy feels like no one else has a problem with sexual sin.

In contrast to general perception, the reality is that women indeed participate in Internet sexual activity, often to a surprising degree. One in three visitors to an adult Web site is female, and nearly 10 million U.S. women access such sites each month.[2] Although women are online significantly less than men, according to a study done in early 2000 (14 percent females as opposed to 86 percent males), women are over-represented among those who progress beyond "recreational use" to the realm of addiction.[3]

And it's not just "those" women—the Paris Hilton types, the ones who wear their low-riders well below their thong and their crop top well above their belly button ring. Regular women like Amy struggle, too. Students and teachers, doctors and soccer moms, divas and athletes, and every other category imaginable. Does she have a computer? Then she's possibly counted among the growing number of women who act out online.

INTERNET INTERACTION
Typically, women are more likely to want romance and relationship as part of their sexual activities, and this pattern translates intact to the Internet. Female users strongly prefer chat rooms, where they can "relate," instead of solitary activity such as accessing pornography. A major study found women were disproportionately represented in the interactive media such as chat rooms, which were preferred by 70 percent.[4] Simply put, women's online sexual behavior mirrors their offline behavior: females most often favor relationally oriented activity. Even those women who want the same thing as most male users—the casual sexual encounter—tend to couch their activity in some semblance of a relationship (however fleeting) instead of anonymous sex.

A growing number of women, though, are looking online at the more traditional kind of pornography. Generally speaking, most women who choose visual material are younger females, ages eighteen to thirty-four. This generation was raised in a media-oriented culture and is more accustomed to visual stimuli. Advances in neuroscience indicate that our media-driven culture is literally altering the human brain—and not just men's. Today's young women seem equally visually oriented. It's no surprise, then, that females are drawn to pornographic pictures.

What they're looking at, though, may be surprising. Women who prefer visual pornography often access lesbian activity instead of heterosexual images. Though most women deny being sexually attracted to other women, they nonetheless frequently surf for female images, if only to play the comparison game. On any college computer, then, a female may be looking at the same kinds of pictures as her boyfriend is. Women, though, in general are more economical in their online pursuits. Maybe because they're more used to bargain shopping, girls differ from guys by usually taking advantage of free sexual material, while men (especially those out of college with paying jobs) are more prone to paying for online sexual images.

A key difference surfaces in the way women progress in their Internet sexual activity. According to an early study, females who frequent sexual chat rooms are more likely than men to seek real-life meetings with their online sexual partners. In fact, an astounding 80 percent of female cybersex users admitted to this behavior.[5] This escalation of sexual activity clearly has enormous implications and risks. Once a woman steps offline, she's increasingly vulnerable to dangerous interactions.

THE ALLURE

The World Wide Web is the great accelerator of sexual activity because of its "triple-A engine": anonymity, accessibility, and affordability. Without much risk of getting caught, women can get into any kind of pornography imaginable for about the cost of a cup of coffee a day. The lure of illicit sex is no longer "out there" somewhere; it's across the room.

Cyberspace technology allows for an immediate (though artificial) sense of connection with another person, which provides the rocket fuel for females' participation in Internet sex. As an added boost, women can eliminate the challenges associated with face-to-face interaction. Without the relationship hurdle of physical attractiveness, users may believe they're making a connection based on real factors, which is especially appealing. In reality, many users report that they falsely describe themselves, doctor their electronic images, or even substitute someone else's picture altogether.

The Internet also allows a woman to be in total control of her sexual activity and relationships. Without the element of physical dominance, the playing field is level online and women possess equal clout, which they lack in most real-world stadiums. This power component is a huge draw for women, who often stage a power struggle through use of their sexuality. The Internet provides the perfect arena for females to exert their power, both sexually and relationally. Even if a woman is disappointed by an Internet partner, other possibilities are only a click away. The hope for the perfect romantic connection lures women around the next cyber corner.

TRUTH AND CONSEQUENCES

Women who use Web pornography decline in their positive image of themselves as physical and sexual beings. The fantasy world of pornographic material can't be matched by typical women marred by normal physical flaws. In this contest, a woman will always lose. Females who use pornography themselves, as well as women whose partners use pornography, suffer from comparing their bodies to online images.

Internet communication fosters pseudo-intimacy, in which people perceive that they know each other well because the anonymous environment prompts them to quickly reveal themselves beyond what they would do in a real-life relationship. On the other hand, the Internet prevents physical touch, which is essential in all relationships, not just for the purpose of sexual activity. Because of their lack of authenticity and genuine intimacy, online relationships lack the true commitment necessary for meaningful human bonding.

Women, perhaps because of their relational wiring, find it easy to overlook these flaws of courtship in the compelling environment of the Internet. As hard as it is to hear, the truth is that the Web is often a draw for psychologically or emotionally unhealthy women. Females who are unsure of themselves, needy, insecure about their physical attractiveness, lacking in communication or relationship skills, or looking for another person to make them feel whole can compensate for their deficiencies in the Internet environment of illusion. This medium offers the perfect breeding ground for fantasy-based interactions, which in turn feeds the potential of "romance" addiction, to which women are particularly susceptible. The Web transforms fantasy sexual activity and relationships into reality—at least virtual reality.

BEYOND THE WEB

Amy's phone confession described being unable to stop looking at online pornography. That description raises a red flag that she might be *sexually addicted*. What a horrible label! Exactly what does it mean to be addicted to sex? When does a woman cross the line from engaging in sexual sin to being addicted? First, a woman is a sex addict when her behavior is out of control. When she keeps doing what she knows is wrong, and she can't stop despite her best efforts, she's clearly an addict. Second, when a woman keeps doing these things despite experiencing negative consequences—that is, she doesn't learn from her past sexual mistakes—that's another indicator of addiction. Addictive behavior is also progressive, meaning that it gets worse over time.

In reality, almost any kind of sin has an addictive element. For Christian women, the problem isn't ignorance about right and wrong. Sinful choices are a heart problem, not an intellectual one, so many of us continue doing things we know are wrong. It's easy to use the idea of addiction as a false measuring stick. On the one end, a woman sees that she's not a full-blown addict and so discounts her sexual behavior as being "not that bad." On the other end, she may recognize that she's truly caught in an addiction and may despair about there being any hope for change. Both approaches miss the point that women's struggle with sexual behavior is a common problem that needs to be addressed, no matter where it may fall on the continuum of acting out or addiction. Amy is a member of a growing group of women whose involvement with Internet-based sexuality ranges from casual interest to full-blown addiction and whose ability to stop ranges from the challenging to the nearly impossible.

Other sexual activities can be problematic, even addictive, besides Internet pornography. Indeed, most women who struggle with their sexual behavior tend to think of themselves as relationship addicts or love addicts, not sex addicts. (Those descriptions don't sound quite so awful.) In fact, one of the main presentations of sexual acting out in women involves relationships, which may take the form of promiscuity for a single woman, affairs for a married woman, or a pattern of one-after-another romantic and/or sexual relationships. This "love addict" may believe her behavior is normal, which is a view society reinforces. She may be a romance junkie who fuels her fantasies with romance novels or movies, and she may not realize that her thought life takes precedence over building genuine relationships. This romantic preoccupation is especially prevalent on college campuses, and most women are oblivious to the destructiveness of their behavior, as well as their inability to stop.

DEEPER ISSUES

To describe women's behavior as struggling with "sexual issues," including leading to the point of sexual addiction, misrepresents the truth, because this problem isn't about sex at all. It's about a longing for acceptance, affirmation, and self-worth. These underlying issues are a common denominator for problematic sexual behavior, whatever its form and level. These are legitimate needs, but many women don't know how to meet them in healthy ways. The roots of using sex to get love are found in certain unhealthy family dynamics and in our sex-saturated culture. For example, females today compare their bodies to those of cover girls and see themselves as inferior, so they act out sexually to prove their attractiveness. Many families don't understand how to affirm daughters as precious children of God and instead (perhaps unconsciously) only reward performance. When the woman isn't perfect, she feels worthless.

Sometimes girls aren't encouraged to think independently and they allow others to think for them, including rationalizing unholy behavior. Families (and sadly the church) often fail to teach emotional language, so it's not okay for females to feel angry or sad. Women, then, don't know healthy ways of dealing with difficult feelings, so they medicate their internal pain with external distractions. Parents may not model genuine intimacy, so females don't have a standard for measuring relationships and are easily deceived into believing that sex equals love.

For many women who act out sexually, the common denominator driving their behavior is sexual abuse. Conservatively, one out of four girls is sexually abused by the time she is eighteen.[6] Like nothing else, sexual abuse hijacks healthy relationships and healthy sexuality. These women are more susceptible to the false allure of counterfeit connection, whether it's in person or online. Illogically, they find that the best way to medicate the shame of sexual abuse is to prove their attractiveness through sexual activity.

For Amy and countless other Christian women, sexual addiction is the false solution for problems that are much deeper than sexual behavior. The obvious acting out is just the tip of the iceberg, the way a woman attempts to deal with her feelings, fears, and unmet needs.

BECOMING UNTANGLED

The first—and hardest step—toward freedom from sexually or relationally sinful behavior is to admit the problem. As Amy experienced, however, confessing is easier said than done. Fear of being honest about their secret activities is an enormous obstacle for most women. As Amy explained, "I couldn't imagine anyone would still love me if she knew the truth." Sexual strugglers live in isolation, at least emotionally, and the first step toward healing is to let someone into their dark places. Remember, the problem of Internet pornography is epidemic among women, and when a woman dares to tell the truth about her secret, she's likely to find other women who relate to her struggle.

Equally important, a woman must invite accountability into her life. No woman can win the sexual struggle alone, especially if her Internet sexual issues go beyond "recreational." It's crucial to establish a network of accountability partners, not just rely on an individual or two. Ideally, the women in a network will have personally struggled with similar behavior and can come alongside as fellow travelers in the journey. These sisters can provide practical advice about breaking free of the behavior, but they also can offer support and fellowship, which are the antidote to the loneliness that drives the acting out in the first place.

A woman must also commit to some practical changes in her life. If her acting out involves the Internet, she can install a Internet filtering software and go online only when someone else is present. If necessary, she may have to disconnect from the Web completely for a while. If she's involved in an addictive pattern with another person, she must end that relationship. Period. No exceptions and no fudging. The standard for healing is being willing to do whatever it takes.

Often women also need to connect with a counselor who understands sexual struggles. Remember, this problem isn't really about the behavior; it's about medicating pain and attempting to fulfill needs. Most women need help to work through these core issues. If the roots of the problem aren't addressed, a woman is at high risk to return to her old solutions or to substitute equally unhealthy ones.

HOPE FOR HEALING

Like Amy, when I first started my journey of recovery from a pattern of sexual sin, I couldn't imagine I'd ever be free from my addictive behaviors, much less be free from the shame. Today I'm at peace with myself, with my sexual behavior, with my relationships, and with God. I know that only God can meet my deepest needs, and I trust Him to do that one day at a time.

If you're struggling with similar issues, you're not alone! On college campuses everywhere, countless thousands of young women wage similar battles daily. Refuse to believe Satan's lie that you're uniquely perverted or that you'll never stop acting out. Wherever you are on the spectrum of Internet involvement, you can be free through confession and community. When you courageously face your underlying issues, you can learn to meet legitimate needs in healthy ways.

By God's grace, it is possible to be transformed from a life of sexual sin into a new walk of purity. A woman can't do it in her own strength, but with help from loving sisters who have gone before, and other sisters who simply love her, she can find grace to step out of her dark secret and into the light.

MARNIE C. FERREE, M.A., is a licensed marriage and family therapist in Nashville, Tennessee, where she directs Bethesda Workshops. Established in 1997, the Bethesda Workshops became the first program in the country to provide treatment for female sex addicts. Ferree is also an author and frequent lecturer. Her book No Stones: Women Redeemed from Sexual Shame is unique in addressing sexual addiction in women. She may be contacted through www.BethesdaWorkshops.org or toll-free at 866-464-HEAL.

ENDNOTES

[1] Leadership Journal, "The Leadership Survey: Pastors Viewing Internet Pornography," Leadership Journal 22, no. 1 (2001): 87–89.

[2] Nielson/Net Ratings, Sept. ember 2003, www.nielson-netratings.com.

[3] A. Cooper, D. Demonico, and R. Burg, "Cybersex Uusers, Aabusers, and Compulsives: New Findings and Iimplications," Sexual Addiction and Compulsivity (2000): 5–30.

[4] Ibid.

[5] J. Schneider, "A Qualitative Study of Cybersex Participants: Gender Differences, Recovery Issues, and Implications for Therapists," Sexual Addiction and Compulsivity (2000): 249–278.

[6] N. Kellogg and the Committee on Child Abuse and Neglect, "Evaluation of Sexual Abuse in Children," Pediatrics 116 (2005): 506–512.

Another Way
By Tanya Walker

KATE'S STORY

Kate[1] and I sat across from each other in the café, talking. The topic of conversation had turned to rejection—the kind we'd faced from those closest to us. Although I'd known Kate for a couple of years now and had figured from her life that she was living as a lesbian, she'd never before shared her story with me.

As Kate described a family who had not expressed a lot of affection and acceptance during her childhood, a sense of the pain of emotional distance and the struggle to meet impossible expectations became all too palpable. But the year she went away to summer camp, Kate encountered women who loved her and expressed the affection and acceptance she was so desperately hungry for—a hunger that had been growing for years. The continuing struggle to sort out conflicting desires and feelings culminated in a discovery Kate made on the Internet. A Web site she'd come

across had (almost psychically) described so many of her feelings and desires. At the end of the long list of "If you feel this way …" the conclusion came: "You are a lesbian."

I left the café, hugged Kate, and headed home sad and angry. Not angry at Kate—how could I not feel compassion for her struggle?—but mad at the reality of a world that had given her only one way to sort through real needs and desires. It had offered her only one explanation and only one solution—embrace lesbianism.

Kate took a courageous step in telling me her story. After experiencing so much rejection from her family, how could she know that I wouldn't reject her as a friend?

Talking about our sexuality, especially homosexuality, seems to hit so many hot buttons. It's a mess of complex feelings—pride, anger, relief, fear, confusion. … Often there seem to be more questions than answers and no place to safely talk about them.

Does it have to be wrong in God's eyes—can't it just be an alternative lifestyle as long as it's filled with love? How can someone change if she has always felt this way? What am I supposed to do with the feelings I have for other women? Did God

make me this way? What will people say or think about me?

Kate's certainly not alone in her story. I don't have enough fingers to count the women I've known over the years who have felt the pain of rejection by society and family as they've sorted through their own issues of sexual identity. As public acceptance of homosexuality has grown in our culture, the conversation has unfortunately grown more heated and polarized. Sexual identity is complex and personal. If you (or a friend) are sorting through your own feelings and thoughts about sexual identity, this is simply a place to start, a few foundational thoughts to illuminate your path as you come to understand who you are.

I DIDN'T DECIDE TO BE A LESBIAN

Perhaps you are a woman who has feelings and desires for other women.[2] What do you do with that? They are real feelings and desires. Is it possible that the heart of those feelings is not really a desire for a sexual relationship but instead a need to be known and accepted? To be exposed, warts and all, and still be loved? A desire for intimacy?

As children and teenagers growing into adulthood, we go through universal emotional and sexual stages of development. As girls, our sense of our own gender identity hinges on identification with our same-sex parent, our mother. It's from her that we first get our sense of what it means to be feminine and how relationships between the sexes work. (In an age of conflicting messages about what it means to be feminine and masculine, you can imagine how hard this is.) Our fathers, and other male and female figures, also reinforce our gender identity. And the kids at school, by their acceptance or rejection, influence what we conclude.

What if my mother is emotionally distant and unaffirming? What if my mother smothers me with her expectations and control? What if my father or uncle or baby-sitter sexually abuses me? What if the girls at school call me a "boy" because I prefer playing with trucks rather than dolls?

If our same-sex affection, affirmation, and acceptance needs aren't met, they don't just go away. We try to have those legitimate needs met some other way. While we had no control over what was done to us by family and others early on in life, we continually make decisions (often unconsciously) about how to deal with those hurts and unmet needs. Often we'll settle for substitutes that mask the pain but prevent the healing process. When we reach puberty, those unmet desires are all set up to become eroticized.

Enter confusion, rejection, experimentation.

IT FEELS NATURAL

It's not surprising that over time we can't imagine being any other way. The behavior choices we make reinforce and authenticate our feelings. It becomes normal—the way it seems we've always been.

What's normal has to do a lot with how often something happens (e.g. it's normal for cars to cut me off in traffic). But what's natural is intrinsically linked to design (e.g. it's natural for the follicles of curly-haired people produce curly hair every time). Of course, something can be both. But even as a society, we recognize that our normal (usual) desires are not necessarily what they are supposed to be. We have to teach children to play fair and share—being selfish comes naturally to them. Left to their own devices, they'd always take the bigger piece of cake instead of letting their sibling have it. (In fact, to ensure fairness, my mom would give one sister the task of cutting the two pieces of cake and the other the task of choosing first. I never found a way around her foolproof method.)

WHAT IS NORMAL, ANYWAY?

For a number of years, I lived in a small Massachusetts town where the uncommon and the unusual became the norm. Due to the high number of those who practiced pagan religions, such as goddess worship and Wicca, it always remained a point of confusion for some when Halloween came—is this how he usually dresses, or is it a costume? It also wasn't unusual to walk down the street and see women who were virtually indistinguishable in appearance from the men in the town. My favorite coffee shop was home to teens, college students, and adults who pursued and experimented with alternative lifestyles of various kinds.

So it wasn't surprising when a pregnant man crossed in front of my car one day as I drove down Main Street. At the first of two pedestrian crosswalks, I stopped to let him cross and thought, *He looks almost nine months along, about ready to give birth.* When I reached the end of Main Street, my nonplussed reaction became a startled realization of *Hello, wait a minute! A man can't be pregnant!* (The mystery was solved later when I saw the man again, one of the town's homeless, and concluded that his nine-month basketball-like belly must be some kind of tumor growth that was strangely pregnancy shaped.)

The point of this story is the fact that it took me until the *end* of Main Street to recognize the inherent problem with a man's being pregnant. Even though intellectually I knew the truth about how pregnancy works (middle-school sex ed was not wasted on me), I had become desensitized by my environment to anything out of the ordinary. Everything had become possible and normal.

Normal: "conforming with or constituting an accepted standard, model, or pattern; esp., corresponding to the median or average of a large group in type, appearance, achievement, function, development, etc.

Normal implies conformity with the establishment norm or standard for its kind.

Natural implies behavior, operation, etc., that conforms with the nature or innate character of the person or thing.[3]

BACK TO THE BEGINNING

So, how do you sort out what's natural? Sometimes there seem to be so many cultural and religious voices saying so many different things that it's hard to know which end is up. When the ground beneath my feet feels shaky, I've found some advice from *The Princess Bride* to be particularly helpful.

Do you remember the scene in *The Princess Bride* after the Man in Black has defeated the giant Fezzik, the "You killed my father …" master swordsman Inigo, and the (now dead) Sicilian genius Vizzini? Fezzik is separated from the others in the confusion, and so not knowing what to do next, he joins the King's Brute Squad. Inigo … well, Inigo drowns his confusion in alcohol and waits for Vizzini to come and tell him what to do now.

I am waiting for you, Vizzini. You told me to go back to the beginning. So I have. This is where I am, and this is where I'll stay. I will not be moved. … When a job went wrong, you went back to the beginning. And this is where we got the job. So it's the beginning, and I'm staying till Vizzini comes.[4]

If we're going to say anything in the midst of the confusing messages about our sexuality, we've got to go back to the beginning. You've got to have a starting point; otherwise, you might as well shift your thinking to whatever happens to be trendy and culturally acceptable at the moment. Past fashion trends have already left us with photos we'd rather burn, so let's not go down that route. (If you haven't experienced that feeling yet, wait a few years—you will.)

As a Christian, I've got to go back to the one place where I can get it sorted out: the Bible. Never one to leave us hanging, God lays out what He's thinking in the Bible. It conveniently begins, "In the beginning …" Let's start there.

"In the beginning God created …" (Genesis 1:1).[5] God's the originator of it all, the Designer who has an incredible creative masterpiece in mind. An artist with a plan.

"God created man in his own image, … male and female he created them" (Genesis 1:27). God makes us, specifically two kinds of us, men and women. Similar, yet different. But both of us bear the marks of the unique character of God.

"Then the Lord God made a woman from the rib he had taken out of the man" (Genesis 2:22). "For this reason a man will leave his father and mother and be united to his wife, and they will become one flesh. The man and his wife were both naked, and they felt no shame" (verses 24-25). The relationship between men and women—it's a closely connected one. Adam, the first man, describes Eve, the first woman, as "bone of my bones and flesh of my flesh" (verse 23). You can't get more intimately connected than that.

Consider what it was like to be Eve at the very beginning (before everything got messed up). Naked and without shame. No demeaning comments from Adam. No "I wish you'd lose a little weight." No *Sports Illustrated* swimsuit edition defining the perfect woman. No wondering if Adam was being faithful. No jealousy. No lusty catcalls that reduced her to an object. No rape. No fear. Imagine if you'd been their daughter.

PARADISE LOST

Doesn't the story of Adam and Eve's relationship strike you as nothing more than an idyllic fairy tale? Last I checked, divorce lawyers and talk-show hosts were making a killing off our relationship and family problems.

Everything was paradise. That is, until Adam and Eve listened to Satan and decided that they wanted to usurp the Designer and make up their own rules about how things should be. Cut to reality. Now shame, fear, and selfishness mar God's perfect design. That's a lot closer to my reality in the twenty-first century. A reality where "Adam" treats me as a sexual object, where my brain is still seen as less intelligent than a man's, where a toolbox belongs to the dominion of guys, and where I can't walk down streets at night without fearing for my safety.

SOLID GROUND

Here's the foundational point that will bring clarity to the confusion of "fairy tale" versus "real life." It's the bottom line that I come back to time and

again. In Genesis we get God's picture of how this relationship design is going to play itself out. Biologically, societally, socially, emotionally, and relationally, God designs marriage (the two become one)—a sexual, emotional, relational union between a man and a woman for as long as they both are living. Out of that relationship comes children, and the whole process continues as the children grow up and marry. It's an intimate, secure, loving, enduring design that provides for and protects us as we live in this world.

God hasn't changed His design even through people distorted and dismantled it and tried their own hand at redesigning relationships.

When we go outside God's original design, we call ourselves god. We deny His right to decide how we should have been made. Since this is God's perfect design, any sexual activity outside a lifelong marriage between a man and woman—adultery, premarital sex, homosexuality, bestiality, pedophilia, and incest—messes with His intended design.

Okay, you may be feeling pretty angry with me right now. "Are you telling me that the way that I feel about women is rebellion against God?" Stay with me for a just a bit longer. Remember, this is

our starting point. It's the firm ground we need to start from. There's a whole lot more to the story.

WILL THE REAL ME PLEASE STAND UP?

If you've been struggling with same-sex feelings for some time now, it's probably pretty hard not to say, "This is the way God made me: I'm a lesbian. This is normal." There's probably a lot of relief in finally being able to have an honest cultural identity that matches your feelings and desires. *This is who I am.*

In society our sexuality has become our identity. The gay community, as it works for public acceptance of homosexuality, has elevated this label to the forefront of its members' identities. Lesbian tennis player. Gay mayor.

But if you're a Christian, your primary identity (no matter what you struggled with in the past or in the future) is that you are "in Christ" and Christ is "in you." Satan wants you to believe that your essential identity is lesbian or bisexual. He wants to reduce your identity to sexuality. That's like reducing your identity to your shoe or bra size. We get enough of that kind of objectification from the world, thank you.

But you are a new creation in Christ (1 Corinthians 5:17). God can transform all aspects of your life (not just your sexuality) into the wholeness of your identity in Christ. That's why the apostle Paul, himself a former killer of Christians, urged believers from Corinth to live out the true freedom of their new identity in Christ. He reminded the Corinthians that they once were "homosexual offenders"— among a long list of other things—*but* that they "were washed, … were sanctified [made holy], … were justified [made right with God] in the name of the Lord Jesus Christ and by the Spirit of our God" (1 Corinthians 6:9-11).

Jesus asks you, as His child, to live out your new identity so as to reflect the ways of His kingdom, even when they look nothing like the ways of the world around you. A child of this kingdom seeks her love and acceptance from the One who gave His life for her. In her human relationships she lives out sexual intimacy within the boundaries God has set up (a man and a woman within the context of a lifelong marriage). She practices sexual purity and celibacy outside that relationship.

KANSAS IS FAR, FAR AWAY

When David Letterman hosted a lesbian stand-up comic, her routine about her relationship with her girlfriend didn't strike the audience or even the media as something out of the ordinary.[6] That's not surprising, considering the tremendous cultural shift that has taken place in just a few

years. Campuses across the nation offering LGBTA (Lesbian, Gay, Bisexual, Transgender Alliance) or similar groups are the norm. In 1991 the first lesbian kiss was shown on U.S. television.[7] The phenomena of LUGS (Lesbians Until Graduation) was launched by trendy experimentation. And in 2000 Showtime launched *The L Word*, the first television series devoted to the relationships of lesbian/bisexual women.[8] Advancement in lesbian visibility in media and cultural institutions has done much to normalize lesbian culture.

Because our culture is constantly changing, we've got to face the fact that our environment is not neutral territory as we seek to live out God's plan, design, and purpose. It presses in around us and defines our reality in subtle and not-so-subtle ways. Every day we hear messages defining "normal" for us. Some of the cultural change is good—women *are* just as smart as men—but our culture also wants us to accept and live lives that are not God's best for us. The phrase "alternative lifestyle" makes our sexual decisions seem no different than choosing our favorite flavor of ice cream. Do you prefer vanilla, chocolate, or Neapolitan?

We're in the midst of a tremendous cultural shift, especially in the area of our sexuality. While our culture accepts these cultural and moral changes

as signs of progress, we are called to not conform to our culture.

DON'T SQUEEZE ME IN

God had the apostle Paul write these words in Romans: "Do not conform any longer to the pattern of this world, but be transformed by the renewing of your mind. Then you will be able to test and approve what God's will in—his good, pleasing and perfect will" (Romans 12:2).

If you're struggling with your sexuality, the messages in our culture are increasingly telling you to pursue whatever feels right to you. In fact, each of us, because of our own unique life experiences so far, are particularly vulnerable to certain temptations that our culture will encourage. But lest any of us think ourselves immune, it not a bad idea to consider this folk wisdom: "Little drops of water wear down big stones" (Russian proverb).

If you put a frog in a pot of boiling water, it will jump out. It knows when it's in danger! But if you put that same frog in a pot of normal, pleasant water and slowly heat the pot until the water boils, the frog will not realize it's in danger until it's too late.

It always struck me as ironic that the teenagers in high school who most wanted to rebel against

the system and against conformity all dressed the same. If being a frog caught in boiling water isn't your idea of a good time, you might want to explore these questions:
• What are the environments that define "normal and acceptable" for me?
• How have I been influenced by my cultural environment?
• How am I using God's Word to renew my mind about my sexuality and the messages in my culture?

I WANT ANOTHER WAY
"I was really confused, and in despair. I was still going to church, but afraid to tell anyone about my secret struggles. I felt very much in love and happy with the person I was with. But, I also had a deep sense of the loss of my personal relationship with Jesus. I was really unhappy deep down. I was still hidden behind a wall of shame and denial about my sexual attractions and behaviors."
"I was very confused. I assumed all the old stuff from my past would just 'be gone' after I gave my life back to the Lord. I was wrong. Within the next year, I met yet another woman, and ended up in a similar relationship."

Even our desire for God—the key relationship for which we were created—waxes and wanes. Sometimes the desire to stay in bed on a Sunday

morning or the endless entertainment distractions win out.

But desires can change. Women who have known only attraction to other women have found complete freedom from their same-sex orientation. Others have learned to identify the triggers that push them toward meeting their needs through lesbian or bisexual relationships and have found appropriate and healthy ways of meeting those needs. There is hope.

Change is possible. You can know the transforming power of God in this area of your life. But God often does this over time. Even the apostle Paul talked with hope about his own transformation process (Philippians 3:12-14) because he knew that God finishes what he starts in a person's life (1:6). God doesn't necessarily take away our desires for other women overnight, for essential to long-term growth is the process of understanding how we got to be where we are. It is only then that we learn to meet the needs behind those desires in appropriate ways. After all, a desire for relationship and intimacy is a desires He created us with. But what all the research (and I suppose common sense) highlights are two critical factors: (1) You have to want to change. (2) Change usually involves a process and a community.

There are complex reasons why attraction to other women is something you deal with. You've formed habits and paths of thinking over the years that need redirection. And you need other people who love and accept you right where you are as you seek to live out your true identity in Christ. The church hasn't always been a safe place, but there are people who are filling that gap. There are many others who have walked this path before and have found healing and wholeness. Their stories and help for your journey are found in these resources. I wish my friend Kate had discovered these Web sites during her search. Her story might have taken a different path. But the story's not finished yet. … You might want to check them out.

Appendix: A Word about Women in Lab Coats

You can't get far in the conversation about homosexuality before the topic of science comes up. "Isn't there a gay gene or something?" "Aren't people born that way?" Not being a scientist myself, I'll defer to the experts. (See the resource list at the end of this chapter.)

Nothing I have read points that way. No "gay gene" determining behavior has been found. The statistics about homosexuality don't bear out the claims that are being made. Instead, the facts seem to be a lot more complex than what can be contained in a media sound bite. (How can you accurately condense pages and pages from scientific journals into a three-word phrase?)

But urban science, like Internet urban legends (they're harvesting kidneys from unsuspecting travelers!), gets passed around our culture until most of us have a vague "Haven't they proven that?" kind of scientific knowledge floating around our brains. We've ingested all sorts of ideas about what science has proven to be "true," but unless our degree is in something like genetics or biology, our knowledge about science and sexuality is really only the sum total of what we remember from eighth-grade science (not much) and attention-getting media sound bites.

By all means, read the scientific research. But even the scientists don't have it all figured out. (Just look at the conflicting diet advice.) Science, by its nature, is always changing as scientists learn and discover more about the world God created. And all of us—me included—are biased by our own assumptions about the world and the way we want it to be. (I always pay close attention to any scientific study that tells me that chocolate is good for me.) So again we're still left with a choice of where to sink our foundations. I'd suggest that the design God has revealed to us in the Bible is the safest way to go. Today's science news (the earth is flat) may be tomorrow's myth. (Though I sure hope the chocolate one isn't proved wrong.)

TANYA WALKER has been a staff member with Campus Crusade for Christ for the past fourteen years. She's helped in giving leadership to the ministries at Smith College, the University of Massachusetts, Brown University, the Rhode Island School of Design, and Oxford University. Currently she works in Orlando, Florida, with the campus ministry research & development team.

Judy's Story
By Judy Dolhof

As a little girl growing up, I felt twinges of things being not quite right with my interests. Dolls seemed lifeless and boring, as did playing house. My best friends were the boys in the neighborhood, and we played all kinds of sports and exciting cops-and-robbers games. On the other hand, I enjoyed learning to cook and playing jump rope with the girls at school. *Who am I, really*, I wondered, *a girl or a boy*? When feelings of being

different would surface, I'd just push them back down, because they made me feel badly.

As I continued to grow up, I was more and more aware of how different I seemed from my sisters. I couldn't imagine myself being a teenager who would giggle and read magazines about boys like they did. In the neighborhood, I was sometimes made fun of for playing sports or for acting or saying something goofy. And it felt like my dad pulled away from me the older I got; it seemed to me that he liked my sisters better. But mostly I loved being a child and enjoyed being outside and being active. So if I felt badly about myself, I'd just push it aside. But, because of these confusing feelings, I put up a wall to keep from being hurt by other people. Unfortunately, the wall also kept out the love I needed.

During my first year of high school, I was mortified—and yet fascinated—by my attractions to two different girls at school. It didn't make sense, but I felt drawn to something about each of them. I was very confused. I dealt with it, of course, by pushing it down and trying to ignore it. I even allowed myself to become sexually involved with an older man during that period, perhaps partly out of a desire to seem somehow more normal to myself.

About this time, one of my sisters shared the gospel with me and I became a Christian. When she went back to college, however, I didn't have others to help me grow or understand what my new commitment meant. And being a Christian did not magically change how I felt about my gender identity. So I was glad when I finally went off to college, imagining the freedom I'd have. I thought, *If I get a good job, I'll be independent, people won't hurt me, and I'll be happy!*

I was surprised to meet a girl at college who became a good friend. It seemed like she got past the wall I had built, and it really felt good to be "known" by someone. Our close relationship turned sexual over time. As much as I loved her, we went our separate ways after graduation, and I headed off to become "happy." I was jolted by the reality of how much I missed my friend and how the world of work was not all it was cracked up to be. I was "successful" but depressed. Fortunately, I met a nice young Christian couple at my job. They had me over for dinner several times, and we would talk about the Bible and our lives. But I never told them about my past, because I was too ashamed. Because of them, though, I again hungered for a real relationship with God.

But then I was transferred to a new city, where I met a woman at work who was a lesbian. Eventually we grew close and ended up in a secret sexual and emotional relationship. Again I was

very confused. I assumed all the old stuff from my past would just be gone after I gave my life back to the Lord. I was wrong. Within the next year, I met yet another woman and ended up in a similar relationship. Now I was really confused and in despair. I was still going to church, but I was afraid to tell anyone about my secret struggles. I felt very much in love and happy with the person I was with, but I also had a deep sense of the loss of my personal relationship with Jesus. I was really unhappy, deep down. I was still hidden behind a wall of shame and denial about my sexual attractions and behaviors.

I had an opportunity to move to new city again, and I knew I needed to do that. This time, though, it was painful to leave my latest friend. But in my heart, I truly knew that I needed to get away from that relationship. As much as I felt for her, I knew I was putting her above God. I was also discouraged about my ability to live a Christian life. This time I decided that I'd be obedient no matter what. I didn't care if I ever had friends again or even if I was happy.

This was much harder than I thought it would be. During the first few months, I cried and cried and felt so much sadness. I almost chose to come out as a lesbian during one particularly dark stretch, but in the end I could not convince myself that God

didn't care what I did. And I could not get away from the truth I saw in the Scriptures. Looking back, I see that this major step of obedience changed the pattern of failure in my life. I did not decide based on feelings but simply on what I believed to be truth. Again, I had to make the same choice—I would do my best to live as a Christian, regardless of what I felt.

From then on, I felt God leading me, and I started to understand how to follow Him better. I learned that I needed to be open and honest with the Lord about what I was feeling. I started talking to Him about my past girlfriends and my current sadness. God used Psalm 51:6 to open my eyes more:

> You desire truth in the innermost being,
> And in the hidden part You will make me
> know wisdom. (NASB)

That was it! God wanted access to my "hidden part"—my heart. God wanted to reveal to me why I felt like I did, and He did just that. I was amazed at the sense of His love I felt as I came out of denial, talked to Him honestly about my attraction to women, and read my Bible.

I began attending a church that majored in excellent Bible teaching, with an equal amount of grace, mercy, and love. The pastor was like a father figure, and I felt protected by him, even if it was from behind the pulpit. I also realized that there were other things in my life besides my sexual identity, and I loved receiving that knowledge. I actually looked forward to going to church—something I never would have imagined.

Finally, I had to learn how to be comfortable with other Christians. My "wall" had kept others out over the years, until my inner needs were so great that I latched on to any woman who seemed like me. This changed for me when I met a group of young Christians who loved God and were very "real." I became good friends with one of the women who was not gay but who had her own sexual issues. At first I wrote her off because she hadn't dealt with homosexuality, but she was kind and pursued a friendship with me. Over time, we were surprised to learn just how many core issues we shared: fear of people, lack of confidence, anxiety in new situations, and so on.

I was amazed at how rich a same-sex friendship could be with someone who loved God and who was willing to be gut-level honest about her shortcomings. So much better than any of the sexual relationships I'd had with women! I had not known that I was really looking for a close friend, not a lover. I also came to trust the guys in our group, who loved God and were kind and

respectful. Now, through obedience, honesty, and good friends, I was armed with an understanding of how to live out my Christian life. I could more easily resist temptation and grow from it, rather than be shipwrecked by it.

For the last twenty years, I have continued to grow as a person and as a Christian, and I have been involved with several ex-gay ministries. However, this time has not been without trials. Several years ago, during a particularly stressful time, I gave in to sexual temptation with another woman. Fortunately, my church had a Living Waters program. It was a place where I could talk freely about my sin, the pain I felt, and the anger I was experiencing. The group leader was not condemning, nor did she condone what I had done. Instead, I received grace from her to again be honest before God and fellow believers. I received prayer from the group, not advice, and was restored in my soul.

Living Waters is a great program for anyone on the road to sexual and relational wholeness. It is for the person just starting on her healing journey or the person (like me) who finds that she blew it after many years on that road. Today I am part of a Living Waters leadership team, and I continue to receive God's grace through teammates and

others within the body of Christ. (Find Living Waters at www.desertstream.org.)

ENDNOTES

[1] Not her real name
[2] Thoughts gathered from interview with Beth Geary, from *My Genes Made Me Do It! A Scientific Look at Sexual Orientation* by Neil and Briar Whitehead (esp. p. 72), and from NARTH (National Association of Research and Therapy of Homosexuality) articles.
[3] Webster's New World Dictionary, 2nd college edition, s.v. normal.
[4] The Princess Bride, 1987, directed by Rob Reiner
[5] All Scripture references in this chapter are from the New International Version.
[6] See www.afterellen.com.
[7] Ibid.
[8] See www.afterellen.comIbid.

God Fathers

By Katie James

One of the most potent memories I have of my father is in a canoe. Our family tended to go on wild, educational, death defying vacations, usually initiated by my father. For many years we canoed in the Boundary Waters, an enormous area of upper Minnesota and Canada with thousands upon thousands of lakes and no electricity or running water. We'd set off in two canoes, packed with supplies, and head off to nowhere land, my father in the back of one boat with a waterproof map spread out across his knees and his bright red compass tied around his neck. He would dip his paddle silently and evenly into the water, pull it back out, feather it perfectly, and then back in to let it pause in the water as a tiller, readjusting the bow of the canoe.

He would keep his chin up as he looked at the horizon and I remember thinking that his face was aristocratic looking with its straight nose and deep set eyes, not particularly suited for the wild white water and pine trees of Minnesota's thousands of lakes. His shoulders weren't broad, any virility he was missing on the athletic field he made up for in technical knowledge – how to sharpen a knife in the woods, how to rope a pack of food high in the trees away from bears, the best way to make coffee over an open fire. When he talked to my brothers and me, it was usually to instruct us on flipping a canoe on our shoulder for portage, or to explain, once again, the ice age to us – how ice a mile thick had slipped down from the top of the world and melted into the legion of puddles we were so faithfully dipping our paddles into. Later on in my childhood he purchased a series of larger and larger sailboats. He loved the way a sailboat was dependant on his understanding of the natural world. Navigation: the sun, the moon, the stars. Power: the wind and the sails. I pictured him at night with a sextant at his face - a metal hook of a thing - pressing it towards the black dome of infinity like a surgeon at an incision. But I remember him mostly in the canoe with the map and his compass. He would pause, laying his paddle across the canoe, and focus again on the map - aligning his compass, looking up at the horizon, ready to guide our family to the next portage or campsite for the night. He would navigate us through thunderstorms and slice bug-eyed walleye into fillets for dinner. Once, he performed a rudimentary operation on my brother when a fish hook became embedded in the muscle of his hand.

At home, in between vacations, he read. History mostly. Big books with titles like *Churchill*, or *The Napoleonic Age*. Or the New York Times. If I asked him a question he might utter a yea or a nay from behind the noisy, crumpling newsprint, not bothering to look up.

My father never told me he loved me. He never lifted me up on his knee to talk, or on his shoulders to look at a parade. But I always knew there would be food on the table, that if the powers of the age we lived in were to turn against us, we'd be okay. I always knew we would get where we needed to go.

Flash forward. I went to college and through a series of what I can only describe as divine interventions, I began to understand that God loved me and had a design for my life – that he cared about my infinitesimally small and insignificant soul, and had every intention, if I would let Him, to draw me close to himself. I committed my life to him, felt the massive, copious love of a God who forgives, and began to spend time each morning in prayer and reading the Bible. It felt as though I was a newlywed. I loved God and he loved me. Nothing, it seemed, could pollute this precious new life that I had found with Him.

After a few years, however, I began to experience a vague distance in my walk with God. It was as though ever so slowly God was turning his back on me. He seemed more interested in other things, like the tilt of the universe and black holes and exploding nebula - that sort of thing. I continued to do what I was supposed to do – praying, reading the Bible, asking for forgiveness, but it felt dry. I felt, quite honestly, like I bored him, like I was bothering God. On my best days, I felt I was doing pretty well if I got a glance above the New York Times.

In case you haven't made the connection, I'll make it for you. Our earthly fathers, whether affectionate and loving, unpredictable and violent, absent or even nonexistent, affect in almost an intrinsic way, how we perceive our Father in Heaven and his feelings towards us. Because of growing up with a father who always provided for me, kept me from physical harm, and understood sometimes complicated things about this world, It is very easy for me to believe that God will always provide food for the table and get me out of sticky situations if necessary. I haven't, however, found it easy to experience the love and affection that the Bible is so clear God has 'lavished' on me. It has taken a long time for me to understand, at a heart level, that God desires for me to be close to him. I've had to put some work into understanding and really believing that my Father in Heaven actually loves me, and is not just taking care of me out of duty – that he is a father who wants me to climb up on his lap and tell him about my day, about my fears, my desires, my hopes.

THE GRAVITY OF FATHERHOOD

Earthly men, I'm afraid, are the ones who demonstrate fatherhood for us. God has packed the scriptures full of earthly metaphors to help us understand the mysteries of the spiritual world. Rocky soil represents a heart that is reluctant to grow, a vine represents a life that with pruning and care, will grow, flourish, and produce more fruit. Earthly fathers, in their deep and persistent love for their daughters, represent the lavish and joyful love that our Father in Heaven has for us as his children.

Metaphors, more often than not however, fall apart. Our earthly fathers will always fail us in one way or another. Understanding God as our Father in Heaven by understanding the father/daughter relationship here on earth, is a lot like explaining a three dimensional character by two dimensional means. John Singer Sargent, arguably the best portrait artist the world has ever known, painted Teddy Roosevelt in a way that captures not only his physical features, but hints at the very soul beneath astute and vested chest. None of us, however, if we were to meet the living, breathing Roosevelt pressing his round wire rimmed glasses higher on his nose as he shifted his weight from one leg to the other, would argue that Sargent showed us Roosevelt in a way that made actually meeting the real Roosevelt obsolete.

In fact, God makes a point of telling us that the metaphor falls short, that the fathers we have here on earth are ultimately a pretty limited representation of His own love and care for us. Matthew 7:9-10 says, "Which of you, if his son asks for bread, will give him a stone? Or if he asks for a fish, will give him a snake? If you, then, though you are evil, know how to give good gifts to your children, how much more will your Father in heaven give good gifts to those who ask him!" Focus here on the *how much more*. God, your father, wants you to understand that his gifts are far more complete and full and lavish and sincere than even the best father's are here on earth.

The need for a loving, responsible, guiding father here on earth is a valid one. There is a real loss that's experienced when this need is not met. If your father was the type who would dangle candy in front of your face and then snatch it away at the last minute, chuckling under his breath as you went to grab at the air, well, that pretty much rots. And it should. You've been wronged, and it'll take some work to believe God when he says, "For I know the plans I have for you, plans to prosper you and not to harm you, plans to give you hope and a future." (Jer 29:11)

There are so many ways that our earthly fathers can warp our perspective of God. If you never had your father's approval or affection, it can lead to a tendency to look for that missing approval and affection in men and unhealthy relationships. An abusive father can lead to a mistrust of men and God. An emotionally absent father can lead, as it did in my case, to seeing God as disinterested and bothered by you. A father who shows up every now and then with gifts and then apparently vanishes, can lead to difficulty in connecting with God. We all have these sort of visceral images that we attach to God whether we mean to or not, and it affects the way that we respond to him. It affects how we view certain passages of scripture and how even the quality of our prayer times.

A REAL DADDY

It is important, as you begin to understand the ways that your earthly father has influenced the way that you view God, to take the time and do your homework. Without a true understanding of who God is as your father, it will be tempting to try to meet those needs that God himself put in your heart, in unhealthy ways. It will be tempting to go

to men, or working for people's approval, or mint chocolate chip ice cream to meet those natural needs you have for love and approval. Take the time to work on realigning your perspective of God with what is really true of him. If your earthly father was verbally abusive, for example, think of some words that express the opposite of abuse — love, gentleness, kindness, goodness - and look them up in scripture. Look up love in a concordance - there's like a bazillion entries. Psalm 136 says, *His love endures forever,* I don't know, like 26 times. Picture God saying this to you, looking you in the eye and saying, "My love endures forever." He wants you to know him as the perfect father.

Jesus in the flesh, in his living, breathing, personality of love, came to earth with the express purpose of showing God as Father to us. As Christians we often forget, in our gratefulness to Christ for His sacrifice for us, that he came to show us the Father. He is God in the flesh. When you see a pastel picture hanging on a Sunday school wall of Jesus surrounded by little children, perhaps cupping the face of a particular little girl and looking into her eyes, you are seeing God your Father.

DEEP BLUE SOMETHING

God desires that you see Him this way. He himself created in you a deep desire and need for Himself as your Father. Any longing that you have for a father, any desires that you feel for a powerful, loving, intimate relationship, were put there by God, himself. He created the need and then whistles for your attention. Romans 8: 15 says, "For you did not receive a spirit that makes you a slave again to fear, but you received the Spirit of sonship. And by him we cry, "Abba, Father." Abba is Aramaic for Daddy, or Papa, or dear Father. It speaks of intimacy, tenderness, and a complete absence of fear or anxiety. The God of the universe wants you to call him Daddy. The God of the universe wants to take your face in his hands, look into your eyes, and tell you he loves you.

Sometimes I picture what it would have been like to have a perfect father. In my mind I keep some of the fuzzy background memories I have of my real father — I keep the bookshelves with the history books, the *Churchill,* and *Napoleonic Age,* and I remember his big leather chair he used to sit in and I think back to some of the conversations we had in different locations about how things were made. I remember standing in a cavernous cathedral, St. John the Divine, and feeling like I was in the belly of a whale as he pointed up to the elongated windows, describing to me in detail how buttresses were designed. I keep some of the good stuff. But then I focus on scripture and what I know intellectually is true of my Father in Heaven to take the place of the ways that my own father let me down. I think about the ways that Christ showed us the father – telling the disciples he wanted the children to come to him, and I think about what a father who is everything good and excellent looks like. It's not a pipe dream. Our Father in Heaven is this for us. Not only that, but he wants us to understand this more and more as we grow in him. He is approving and affectionate, he is faithful and gentle and loving, he is present – always – and never leaves us. He is emotionally interested in us. Work on getting to know him as he really is.

I recently went through a Bible study on relating to God as Father. In the study there was a section that had a line that was a continuum of blue color – a deep blue at one end to a pale, almost white at the other. There was a sentence in bold type above the line that read something like, *place an X on the line to express how well you feel you know God as your Heavenly Father.* At the dark blue end of the line, it read, *not very well*, and at the light blue end of the line, it read, *very well.* I remember thinking that they had the colors wrong, that someone had messed up – they'd gotten the colors backwards. Intuitively, the deep blue, it seemed to me, should represent *very well*, and the

light, almost white color should represent, *not very well.* When I have felt the closest to my Father in Heaven, when I have felt the kinship of being his daughter and the privilege of inheriting a life full of his very being, it can be described as nothing less than full and deep and rich – in a word, "colorful." It has been during the dry times, when I have had difficulty grasping those things that he so wants me to grasp – when I see Him with his face behind the paper – that I have felt weak and pale and almost overwhelmed with the insignificance of who I am.

J.I. Packer writes, "To know God as our father – as our almighty, loving Father – is the highest, richest, and most rewarding aspect of our whole relationship with him."

JUST ONE DROP

My father was great with a canoe. Every dip of his paddle into the cool lake water was purposeful and precise. I remember sitting in the front of the canoe with my own paddle, trying to feather it perfectly like he did, looking at the expanse of rippling lake water and the horizon of pine trees, wondering where we'd end up for the night. I've since learned to see God, not only as the sure navigator, but also as loving and kind and interested in me.

This morning I got a letter from my dad in the mail. It was an article from a page of the New York Times, folded into small squares with a post-it note stuck to it on which he had written, "Something to think about -Dad." I never got to crawl up on his lap and tell him about my day when I was a kid, but I can appreciate his love of knowledge. My dad, in all of his earthly, faultiness is one drop in an ocean of true things about God and I've learned over the years to take that one drop, that element of truth, and through the Holy Spirits' work in my life, through discipline and an increasing understanding of scripture, discover more and more the completeness, the perfectly sufficient Father that I have in Heaven.

KATIE JAMES has been on staff with Campus Crusade for Christ for seventeen years. She is currently pursuing a masters degree in creative writing from Columbia University. She and her husband, Rick, and three children live in West Chester, PA.

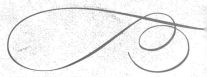

Soulnaked
By Ladonna Witmer

It ambushes me often in the middle of a thought,
Creeping up behind to snatch at my sanity.
And then it stays,
clinging to my psyche like a soft sucking leech
Draining the peace from my soul.

It reminds me of my loneliness and tells me
I'm too tired.
It weighs at my feet so I don't want to run away.
I don't want to move.

So I succumb. I sit.
Let it tangle me in its bleakness,
squeeze me in its emptiness.
And I should want to exorcise it but I never hear its
name.

It lurks in the hollow of my heart in the aching of
my head in the hunger of my soul.
It taunts the emptiness of my bed
And the dryness of my lips.
Echoes the screams lodged inside my throat.

Flaunts elusive satiation in the corner of my eye.
I pace my world, restless I stare through its bars.
I am walled in a cage for which I have no key
And I cannot find a door.
My body feels cracked. I'm thirsty.

Jonesing for a taste of anything to stifle the
oneness.
For I am one.
Alone.

And I'm addicted to Two.
I call it jealousy
I name it envy
love is heat
and I want it, too.
I dabble in lust.

I wish
I could *blind* myself with desire.
Drench myself with passion.
Swallow the moment.
Stop thinking. Drown.

But I'm too scared or too smart.
And I like the color of white.
Besides, the water goes deeper.
Past the gridlock of throbbing bodies and the
burning of my flesh
Beyond the longing
For even in the moment it is not enough.
The ache still calls.
It grinds in the pit of my belly.

I never asked for happiness.
I do not pursue ecstasy.
That is not where The End is.
No fairytale ever after.

I want Reality.
I need the real thing.

I am suffused with this homesickness, but I have
never been home.
I groan for resolution in a language

I cannot understand.
I yearn for what I have never seen.

because I know
There Must Be More.

www.ladonnawitmer.com

The Beauty of Forgiveness

By Shellie R. Warren

I had my fourth abortion on a Saturday. For me, that is the seventh-day Sabbath—a day when I am usually in church (if not in spirit, then at least in body). But on this particular winter day, I was on a road trip with my baby's daddy to terminate my pregnancy.

Looking back, almost six years later, I see more clearly how much of that three-hour drive on I-65 was a battlefield just waiting to take all the casualties in that blue Isuzu SUV. I can't speak for what the father was going through (although I do know that a year later he impregnated someone else and currently he is raising his daughter and two children that his wife had with two other men). Nor, unfortunately, can I speak for my child, because that child's voice was silenced before he or she could even speak. But I can tell you

that I was a wreck. I hated needles, pap smears, and the suffocating wait time it took in those abortion clinics, let alone the wooziness, cramps, and emotional roller-coaster rides I rode after every single procedure. And so I chalked up the butterflies in my stomach (which felt more like fear than morning sickness) to my personal anxiety rather than to my conscience begging me to make an immediate U-turn for the sake of all parties involved.

I did make a U-turn … some five hours later. But one of the passengers was missing on the return home: my fourth child. The one who had two parents who were brilliantly gifted. The one who had paternal grandparents who begged me to ignore their son's selfish agenda and go full term. The one with whom I had the most challenging time (in every way) even getting through the abortion doors. The one who, within weeks of my discovering I was pregnant, I felt was a son and would be named Solomon and called "Solo" for short.

I was still coming down from my anesthesia high on that evening, and so I can recall only snapshots of memories. I remember the father of my former child asking me if I needed anything and my hating him for trying to be so nice. I remember trying to watch television in hopes that the volume would

drown out my internal conflict. And I remember waking up in the middle of the night with a half-chewed french fry in my mouth. Even my mouth and stomach were mad at me, it seemed, because no matter how much I tried, I couldn't chew and could barely swallow.

I tried reciting that cliché garbage about "the past being the past" and about how "I couldn't do anything about it now even if I wanted to" just so I could get through the rest of the night. But it wasn't working. I tried to seek comfort by burying myself under the arms of the man who I believed I loved, but I started resenting him just as much for not wanting me to be the mother of his child. It wasn't working. I tried asking God to assure me that the ache in my heart was all in my head and not the sign of an impending heart attack. That wasn't working either. It's amazing how, when you make choices in sin's favor, the solutions initially seem so simple but the aftermath is always so much more complicated than you had bargained for or are prepared to handle alone.

It was weird. Usually when my boyfriend came to spend the night, I didn't want to be anywhere else the following day for as long as he would stay. This time, though, I jumped up at the first sight of sunlight and announced that I was going to church (sometimes I went on both Saturday and Sunday).

The announcement startled him and shocked me, but I knew that sooner or later he was going to be leaving my home and my heart, probably for good (that's what happened with my other pregnancies, and so I came to expect it), and I couldn't bear the thought of being in my own space all alone … again.

So I got into the shower and tried to wash away at least one layer of residual guilt, did my hair and makeup in hopes of covering up my shame, and put on a pair of festive gold, open-toed stilettos. Those shoes weren't the best for my physical health—you are supposed to stay low to the ground for a few days following an abortion to reduce the risk of hemorrhage. But they did do a little something for my ever-ailing self-image. And so I went to church.

I don't know who I thought I'd find there. I'm sure I'm supposed to say God, but to be honest, I felt that He had left me a long time ago. All I knew was that my home was no longer a safe place for me because there were too many memories of what used to be with my soon-to-be ex and what could have been with my former baby. At church there were so many other people who had mastered the art of masking their own pain that I would be in good company. Their matching suits, hats, and gloves would serve as a great distraction,

at least for a few hours. I would deal with the rest of my life later.

FORGIVE OR FORGET ABOUT IT?

I wish I could tell you that December of 1999 was the last time I had premarital sex—or even unprotected sex, for that matter. I wish I could tell you that was the last time I got into a relationship with a man who was not good for me. (Aside from a few rebounds with a couple of guys, I actually slept with someone's fiancé for several months, and I dated a guy whose sexuality was in question for almost a year following this experience.) I wish I could tell you that every time the personal condemnation was too much to bear I went down to the altar for forgiveness and that all became right and spiritually bright in my world. But that's just not the truth.

Even after all I had been through, it took *years* to come to a place where I believed that God really loved me, had a plan for my life, and wanted me to have faith in His promises of grace, mercy, and forgiveness. In church school I was taught that if you do what God requires of you, you will be embraced as one of His children. In church, many of the sermons I heard were about following the letter of the law so you could avoid going to hell (known as "H-E-double-hockey-sticks" to all those

who felt that saying the word would grant them a one-way ticket for there on the spot).

My family life made things even worse. My biological father was someone I saw only during the summer months, and by this time, memories of my stepfather were bittersweet. I knew that the Bible encouraged me to see God as my spiritual Daddy, so to speak, but my experiences with earthly ones were so dysfunctional that I just wasn't interested in taking the risk. For this reason, I think I feared God more than I loved Him, which is no way to have a healthy relationship with anyone.

I'm sure some cynics would even question whether I feared God, given that I was promiscuous and had four abortions under my belt. But one of the biggest tricks of the enemy is getting you to a place where you think that hell is your destiny, that no good can come out of your circumstances, and so you might as well prepare yourself for the inevitable and take matters into your own hands on the ride. When preachers preach on the passage about the devil coming to steal, kill, and destroy, I wish they would focus more on the fact that if he steals your self-esteem, everything else that follows is par for the course. If you don't know your worth, you won't value much of anything else either.

But I think the most damaging element in my previous relationship with God was the experience I had with forgiveness as it related to my parents, my friends, and my exes. Because my mother and father were also raised in homes that had Bibles, as well as iron fists and wandering hands, I was accustomed to abuse being followed by "Can you forgive me?" even though my abuser had asked the same thing earlier that week. And because most of my friends were just as religion-without-relationship based as I was, I knew that "I'm sorry" really meant "I will probably do again what I just did to make you mad at me, but can we deal with it later so that we can hang out now?" It's sad, but I can't recall one time when someone apologized to me and then did not repeat the action for which he or she had "repented."

Since this was how forgiveness was modeled to me, I followed suit—with my parents, with my family members, with my friends, with my exes, and yes, even with God. I never thought about what asking forgiveness really meant. I just knew that it was something my parents did after hurting me and something my friends asked so that "we could be cool and hang out again."

Many people who are on the outside looking in on the one who is caught up in a cycle of sexual suicide don't see or understand that person's bondage. For many of us (both in and out of the church), falling down in regret of sexual sin, only to get back up and repeat it again, is not about not wanting to do right or not being remorseful for doing wrong. It's about not understanding whose we are and what forgiveness can do to return us to our intended purpose.

AT THE END OF ME
God never intended for any of His children to be in a place where another human being would set the tone for their self-worth. He never wanted us to be so wounded by lust that we would lose the capacity to love. God never designed sex to be treated as the "dirty three-letter word." Nor did He want the emotions that followed the act to leave two people broken, confused, angry, and alone. Godly sex is to be a wonderful experience that brings a man and a woman in covenant closer together; it was never meant to tear the hearts of two uncommitted people apart.

But if healthy intimacy has never been modeled to you, if a high sense of self-esteem was not taught to you, or if "I'm sorry" only seemed to buy the offender more time to hurt you again, it's

challenging to understand true repentance and godly forgiveness. Trust me, I know.

I shared the story of my fourth abortion because I wanted you to see something about how I processed God and spirituality at the time. Of all of the emotions I experienced—fear, regret, resentment, shame, anger, physical and emotional pain, confusion, and on some levels, even denial—what I did not feel, and yet what was pivotal to my spiritual progression, was humility. I was so embarrassed by the habits I was caught up in, and so disillusioned about God's total awareness of all that I had done and was going through, that I was too proud to run to Him and say, "I don't know what I am doing with my life anymore. But I know I messed up, and I need You to help me fix it."

Feeling bad is not what changes your life. Wishing you had more is not how you get it. And running back to what's familiar is not what will move you forward to all that God has in store for you. I am a living and breathing testament to the fact that it is only when you go to God with all of your baggage (past and present), all of your R-rated and at times even XXX filth, all of your preconceived or even misconceived notions about who you thought He was versus who He really is, all of your "I really don't want to give this up, God, so help me to want to" confessions—it is only when you go to God with *all of you* that your life can be restored.

One of the biggest mistakes I made on that cold Saturday in December was relying on my baby's father's limited insight when it came to the destiny of our child. He's just a human; what does he know? It took years for me to *really* forgive him and release all the bitterness, anger, and at times even pure hatred I had for him when it came to that day. The pure, unadulterated fact was that elevating him above my spiritual health is what got me into having sex, having an abortion, and hating him for it all in the first place. That's not his fault; it's mine. And I take full responsibility for that. No person should have enough power to determine my happiness, my decisions, my emotional stability, or my fate.

But it took humility to get me to that point. In time, I came to really realize, believe and accept the fact that God loved me enough to pick me up and clean me off, and in spite of all of my sexual memoirs He was able to restore me to the spiritual state of being His innocent and pure little girl. No matter how rebellious I was in my past, I have a promising future and that makes the scripture "All things work together for good" a very real thing in my life.

The fact that my sordid tales are saving the lives of other unborn children whose mothers are also sexually broken shows the beauty in true repentance and forgiveness. How dare I not extend to someone else what God freely gives to me each time I humble myself enough to ask for it—even when what I've done has hurt Him and even when He knows I may do it again?

The awesome thing about God is that He's always ready and willing to forgive. There's nothing we can do that will make God not love us enough to extend grace and mercy our way each and every morning if we chose to accept it. It's when we don't understand the authentic place that repentance should hold in our lives that we trip ourselves up. We have to be willing to admit that we can't do it alone and that, when we do, things never work out right. We have to be willing to face the cold, hard fact that God's way is *the only way*. We have to be less concerned with the earthly consequences than we are with our eternal fate. Only *then* can our heart be in a state of repentance.

That doesn't mean things will change overnight. In the wise words of a man by the name of Jim Rohn, "You cannot change your destination overnight, but you can change your direction overnight." Repenting to God and receiving His forgiveness is not some magic potion that will change all of our circumstances in one breath, but it will change our heart toward them. This is key, because some of us run back to our strongholds as we treat forgiveness like fairy dust. Those of us who did not have forgiveness properly modeled to us think that it buys us time to stay bound to our mess. But repenting to God is not a "courtesy call" that we are taught to say, like "Please" and "Thank you"; it's a crying out to our heavenly Father to meet us at our lowest place so that He can lift us up toward something better. It's the only way we can find hope in doing what's right and becoming a better person. When we repent, we are no longer looking at things from the way we see them but rather from the way He designed and desires for them to be. Forgiveness doesn't make us perfect, but it aids in making us whole.

HEIGHTS UNKNOWN

At thirty-one years of age, I stand here a new woman. Why? Not because I do everything right. Not because the memories of my past do not haunt me from time to time. Not because the road to sexual purity is an easy (or even a fun) one. And not because I am at a place where I don't need the things that place me on the path of spiritual growth and revelation in the first place—mercy, grace, and forgiveness.

For me, the cycle of sexual suicide has been broken because accepting God's forgiveness, and forgiving others in return, has restored me to a state, not of perfection, but of royalty, as a child of the King. In knowing that God loves me unconditionally, I am no longer afraid of messing up; instead, I now focus on making Him proud of me. In knowing that there's nothing I can do to make Him want me any less, I have no real desire to see how far I can go to prove Him wrong (God's never wrong). In believing that with all the mistakes I have made, He can turn my personal lemons into spiritual lemonade through my testimonies, I am no longer bitter. And in knowing that only He holds my future, I am no longer at a place in my platonic, professional, romantic, or family relationships where I expect them to be more than what they are—human.

There's a new freedom that comes in living a life knowing that you are loved and forgiven. You become more sensitive to doing anything that would cause anyone harm, including (and especially) yourself. You become more receptive to any instruction that God gives you. And you become more aware of your purpose in life—one that is meant to be without fear, regret, resentment, shame, anger, physical and emotional pain, confusion, and on some levels, even denial (all the things that come in relying on self). Instead, you begin living out a life of humility. And this life is one that God promises (1 Peter 5:6), should you put your total trust and faith in Him, will exalt you to heights unknown—in every area of your life … in His time … in His way.

SHELLIE R. WARREN is a full-time freelance writer living in Nashville, TN. She's been published in over 40 publications and is the author of Inside of Me: Lessons of Love, Lust, and Redemption. (Relevant Books)

Dr. Henry Cloud & Dr. John Townsend

Making Dating Work

BOUNDARIES
in Dating

BOUNDARIES IN DATING
By Dr. Henry Cloud and Dr. John Townsend

Boundaries in Dating helps singles of all ages to think, solve problems and enjoy the benefits of dating to the fullest, increasing their abilities to find and commit to a marriage partner.

Zondervan Publishing House

The Place of Faith

By Rick James

In his book *Not Even a Hint*, Joshua Harris states, "I've come to believe that lust may be the defining struggle for this generation." Purity is perhaps the hardest battle we will ever fight in our quest for holiness. That being the case, it requires the employment of all our spiritual weapons, not just one or two. The focus of this article is the role that faith plays in this struggle. As just stated, it is one of many weapons, though our tendency is to look for a silver bullet that will make the struggle simply go away. Some would say that faith is that silver bullet. It is believed by some that if you have enough faith, you'll be healed of sexual sin. We do not believe this to be the case.

While faith plays a critical role in our struggle, so do other spiritual components, such as prayer, community, the Holy Spirit, and discipline. None of these weapons, no matter how powerful, was meant to bear the entire brunt of the battle. God wants us to mature in all these areas. He will use our struggle with sexual purity to help us, without resorting to a silver-bullet approach to spiritual growth.

In the book of James, the author makes a strong argument that faith and works go together. His point is that faith is not simply a state of mind but is expressed by our choices. To believe God is to act on His promises. To cave in to lies is to act in unbelief.

Faith is trust, and the better you know God, the more you will trust Him. Faith actually grows by exercise. So as you exercise faith in God for the following promises, you will find Him faithful and worthy of trust. This will encourage you to trust His promises even more. With that said, here are some truths and promises.

FAITH AND FORGIVENESS

Few of the great battles in life are ever won overnight, so it is safe to assume that in your relational and sexual struggles, you will see failure before you finally see the flag raised, hear the national anthem, and take your place on the winner's platform. It might be a small failure or a stunningly gross one (please, I don't want to know details!), but in either case, you will need—desperately need—to experience God's forgiveness. The problem with sexual sin is that even after we've confessed it, it is difficult to feel cleansed, to not berate ourselves and not suspect that God is still fuming over the incident ("How many times have I told her … ?"). It's like the annoying detergent commercials where a guy accidentally spills a quart of engine grease and a bucket of blueberries on his white shirt (what are the odds?). Some stains just don't come out as easily as others. To help us obtain that which we crave—forgiveness—we often employ several psychological tactics, as opposed to exercising faith.

The first tactic is some form of self-crucifixion. You've sinned and somehow you feel that you need to pay for what you've done, so you inflict mental torment on yourself. In essence, rather than trusting in Christ's death to pay for your sin, you've decided to pay the tab yourself. (A nice gesture on your part, but rather pointless.) Jesus has paid for that sin, and it makes Him sad, as well as negates His suffering, when you will not receive it (by faith). I truly wonder if God is more sad about our sin or our refusal to accept His payment.

The second tack we take to feeling forgiven is to make some form of vow or commitment. Somehow you feel better about your sin if you can convince yourself that it will never happen again. Your mind says, "You pathetic, weak-willed, desperate ditz.

How could you do that?" You say back to yourself, "I promise, I'll never do it again!" Then your mind responds back to you, "Okay, I won't beat you up, but I'd better never see that nonsense again." The effectiveness of this strategy lies in how good you are at convincing yourself that this time you *really* mean it. I'm pretty gullible, so I usually believe me. But the basis of this feeling of forgiveness is really faith in ourselves—faith that we will be more obedient in the future. Yet faith in future obedience is neither reliable nor the true basis of forgiveness. You must simply trust that, no matter how bad your sin, what God has done for you has paid for your immorality. You must believe that His grace is beyond measure and that His mercies are new every morning. The object of your faith must be Christ. Thankfully, He is far more gracious with you than you are with yourself.

The third approach is some form of rationalization or justification. This is an attempt to procure the feeling of forgiveness by minimizing the offense. If it wasn't that bad, your mind reasons, then it will be easier for God to forgive. This expresses a belief that Jesus forgives but that He has limits. This is not what God wants you to trust about His nature, because it's simply not true. He is much happier with our complete truthfulness and robust faith that chooses to count on the depth of His mercy.

The fourth approach is an attempt to shift blame. How can you feel guilty for something that really wasn't your fault? And if you think about it, it really wasn't, was it? You were in a vulnerable state; you were lonely because God hadn't provided for you; and frankly, you were taken advantage of. See, I can shovel it almost as good as your mind can. But because you know yourself so well, your justifications and blame shifting will border on genius. Sin has occurred, so someone must pay, and it sure as heck ain't gonna be you. So what address can we forward it on to for safe delivery?

Of course, what makes this all unnecessary is that someone has already paid the price: Christ. What is needed is confession. The problem is that we can confess our sins while failing to employ faith. Faith involves a choice of the will to believe that God has forgiven us through Christ's death, while turning a deaf ear to doubts. We reckon that God is more merciful than we can imagine and believe that through Christ's death we are completely forgiven, and "as far as the east is from the west, so far has he removed our transgressions from us" (Psalm 103:12).

There is an old ministry exercise in which you write a list of your sins on a piece of paper and then write 1 John 1:9 across the list, afterward tearing up the list. I see no expiration date on this exercise. It is effective because it develops the faith component of confession—it's a visual aid to undergird a young and underdeveloped faith muscle.

FAITH THAT GOD CAN MAKE YOU HOLY
In many of Jesus' healings we note that the miracle transaction often has faith as a contingency clause.

As Jesus went on from there, two blind men followed him, calling out, "Have mercy on us, Son of David!"
When he had gone indoors, the blind men came to him, and he asked them, "Do you believe that I am able to do this?"
"Yes, Lord," they replied.
Then he touched their eyes and said, "According to your faith will it be done to you." (Matthew 9:27-29)

The story has a happy and poetic ending, until we apply it to our lives, where it becomes somewhat haunting—I will receive, but only in measure to my faith. There are three truths concerning God giving us ultimate victory in our sexual and relational battles that faith must cling to and never release. Most of the great heroes of the Bible have two things in common: they all wore sandals and they were all required to persevere in their faith, though final victory was often years in the future. We, too, no matter how many setbacks we encounter, must never waver in our belief that God can make us sexually and relationally holy and, if we persevere, will ultimately lead us in triumph. We must participate, and it may take time, but we can trust that God can and will give us victory.

Here is the second truth into which the teeth of faith must sink: you must choose to believe that your temptations and struggles are not unique and therefore are not insurmountable, unfixable, or unforgivable.

> No temptation has seized you except what is common to man. And God is faithful; he will not let you be tempted beyond what you can bear. But when you are tempted, he will also provide a way out so that you can stand up under it. (1 Corinthians 10:13)

You are not the exception. It is also a lie to believe that any temptation is irresistible. God always provides what we need to remain holy, even if it is an escape from a situation that might overpower us.

> His divine power has given us everything we need for life and godliness through our knowledge of him who called us by his own glory and goodness. (2 Peter 1:3)

Last, we must never believe that sexual purity is not possible for us. I was speaking at a conference some years ago on the topic of sexual purity. The title of my message was "Feeling Forgiven." Before the talk, a student came up to me and said he had something he thought God wanted him to share with the other men. His message was simple: he had been immersed in lust, but now he was living a holy life and he wanted everyone to know it was possible for every person there to do the same. I let his message replace mine. I had planned to prepare the men for failure. But God wanted them to plan for victory and believe that holiness in the sexual area was not only possible but exactly what He wanted for them.

A small way in which we develop along these lines is how we talk about our sin. With both God and others, it's important to affirm your responsibility for poor and sinful choices and to not speak of yourself as a victim or your circumstances as determinative of your actions.

FAITH THAT ALL THINGS WORK FOR THE GOOD

> We know that in all things God works for the good of those who love him, who have been called according to his purpose. (Romans 8:28)

The next battle of faith is for all those who have in one way or another experienced damage and scarring in their lives, or within themselves, due to sin. As 2 + 2 will always equal 4, so this equation is always true: God can take any manure and out of it grow a garden, as you participate in this promise by faith. While it may be impossible for you to imagine how God can bring good out of your past and present circumstances, injuries or failures, this is hardly a limiting factor. God can do "immeasurably more than all we ask or imagine" (Ephesians 3:20).

There is no limit to His capacity to redeem evil. Everything in your past (like Mary Magdalene's past) can be taken and used for good. Every failure (like Peter's failures) can be transformed by God's mercy. Every weakness (like Paul's weaknesses) is a vehicle for God to demonstrate His strength. Though we must persevere in faith, sometimes for years, the equation will always be true, provided we hold to it in faith.

Like in a game of cards, everyone is dealt a certain hand in life, over which they have little or no control. It does not matter even remotely what cards you are looking at, for any hand with the right tradeoff of cards can become unbeatable. God's promise is that it will become a winning hand as you persevere in faith.

If you were to have known nothing of God and simply picked up the Bible and read it, you could only walk away with the following conclusion: God delights in redeeming, healing, and using that which is bent, broken, and battered.

FAITH IN GOD'S GOODNESS

"I know the plans I have for you," declares the LORD, "plans to prosper you and not to harm you, plans to give you hope and a future." (Jeremiah 29:11)

If you go back to the Garden of Eden (which is probably now a parking lot somewhere in Baghdad), you will notice that the first sin was a distrust of God's goodness. Adam and Eve became convinced that God was holding out on them and that in keeping them from the tree He did not have their best interests at heart. The foundation of most sin is a lack of faith in God's goodness, along with disbelief that His plans for us are really best.

When things do not work out in a relationship, or when we have no relationship or even the prospect of one, it is terribly easy to embrace the lie that God doesn't care. Swallowing the pill of unbelief is the spiritual equivalent of Extacy, making one utterly vulnerable to the allure of all manner of sin and temptation.

You must fight the battle against denying God's goodness, using your faith in the battle and not giving an inch. Everything God does in your life is motivated by love. Any minor deconstruction of that truth is a lie and will lead to sin.

When we don't get what we want or think we need, we are vulnerable to disbelieving God's incomparable goodness. But also, when life gets hard and trials press in on us from all sides, our minds reason, *God must really be ticked off. He must be punishing me.* The following verses carry an important message.

If you are not disciplined (and everyone undergoes discipline), then you are illegitimate children and not true sons. Moreover, we have all had human fathers who disciplined us and we respected them for it. How much more should we submit to the Father of our spirits and live! Our fathers disciplined us for a little while as they thought best; but God disciplines us for our good, that we may share in his holiness. No discipline seems pleasant at the time, but painful. Later on, however, it produces a harvest of righteousness and peace for those who have been trained by it. (Hebrews 12:8-11)

The passage says that, unlike earthly parents, who do in fact discipline out of anger, God does not. Because most of us have been disciplined in anger, God wants us to know that He is not like our earthly parents. His discipline comes from His heart, not His fist. His discipline is not an exercise of His judgment upon our sin. Christ has already assumed that judgment. Rather, it is for our good, done in love. The writer of Hebrews is concerned that those enduring painful trials will doubt God's goodness and graciousness toward them.

As the exercise of writing out our sin and writing out 1 John 1:9 over it can instruct our faith, journaling can be a helpful exercise for the same reason, as can memorizing passages of Scripture. Fueled by our emotions, our minds channel-surf constantly and we easily find ourselves glued in to episodes of doubt and worry. The discipline of journaling our faith convictions ("Lord, I trust You in this!"), identifying lies, and memorizing and meditating on the truths of God's goodness can ground us and keep us from drifting. These techniques bring us back to channel 38 (the worship channel on my TV).

OUR SALVATION

We'll conclude with the most important and fundamental truth—ground zero—for faith. All things build upon this.

To all who received him, to those who believed in his name, he gave the right to become children of God. (John 1:12)

I write these things to you who believe in the name of the Son of God so that you may know that you have eternal life. (1 John 5:13)

In describing our spiritual armor, Paul describes the truth of our salvation as a helmet—that which protects the mind. No matter how often you have failed or how gross the sin, if you have received Christ, you can know that you have eternal life. You can doubt that Iraq had weapons of mass destruction. You can doubt that the Cubs will ever win a World Series. But never release this truth from your grip of faith.

HOW FAITH GROWS

Faith is like a muscle; it grows by lifting weights. Weights are the resistance: the doubts, mental whispers, and circumstances that tell us the opposite of what faith must believe. When God seems to be absent and horrible circumstances swirl around us, everything seems to shout, "God isn't here! Or if He is, He certainly doesn't care." In those circumstances, faith curls truth toward your heart and says, "No, God is good. He is for me. He has a plan." Thus, circumstances adverse to our faith become the vehicle for our growth.

Like all disciples, we are periodically tossed into a boat and a raging storm, and God feels absent. As we lift the weight and exercise faith, we don't feel very spiritual, because our thoughts are filled with doubt. But when the storm stops and God's presence once again becomes acute, we notice that through the process, our faith muscles have become firm.

Your struggle with sex and relationships at times will form a great resistance to the truths mentioned above. But as you perseveringly lift these truths like a weight, God will redeem your struggle and turn it into a powerful faith.

END NOTE

The greatest enemy of faith can be contrary circumstances and emotions. An old expression says, "Perception is reality." For many of us, emotions are reality. Because emotions can so loudly tell us the opposite of what faith is whispering, I have suggested enlisting certain aids, such as journaling.

If you want to be a woman controlled by faith and not feelings, I cannot underscore enough the need to be in the truth of Scripture constantly, to make use of pen and keyboard, and to have relationships within which you can be completely transparent about what lies you are listening to and what truths you are struggling to believe. They provide an anchor of objectivity, strengthening faith against emotional storms.

every young woman's battle

by Shannon Ethridge & Steven Arterburn

Guys aren't the only ones
fighting a battle for purity.
The counterpart to the award-winning
"Every Young Man's Battle."

WaterBrook Press
Visit www.waterbrookpress.com for information on Every Woman's series

MAC and the Knife

I wonder what Adam and Eve looked like when they were freshly created—just out of the oven, so to speak. I mean, if they were God's original creation, without the ramifications of sin in their gene pool just yet, they must have been perfect, God's idea of beauty in the flesh. I wonder if they looked anything remotely like our idea of beauty. Was Eve the buxom, smooth-skinned magazine model with exotic eyes? Was Adam tall, dark, and ripped? Or were they maybe short and a little pudgy, as some artists have rendered them over the years? Hard to know, really.

You know they had to be disappointed after they were kicked out of the garden and they started to notice signs of aging. Eve was probably freaked out the first time she noticed a bit of cellulite, a few gray hairs, or varicose veins. Then again, they lived for a few hundred years back then, so who knows at what point that all kicked in ("You don't look a day over 234"). Not to mention the uncorrupted ozone and organic diet. I'm guessing they held up pretty well.

I think it's interesting that we aren't told anything about Adam and Eve's physical appearance, other than the fact that they were naked. In fact, there are few people in the Bible about whom we're told the specifics of what they looked like. We know Esau was "red and hairy" even from birth—"like a hairy garment."[1] ¡Ay caramba! ("He's precious, so cute in a … rodentlike way.") David was "ruddy, with a fine appearance and handsome features."[2] Esther was "lovely to look at."[3] Zacchaeus "was a wee little man and a wee little man was he" (see the vacation Bible school version of the story in Luke). But ironically, the prophet Isaiah describes the Messiah as having "no beauty or majesty to attract us to him, nothing in his appearance that we should desire him."[4] Satan, on the other hand, is described as a beautiful angel of light, at least before he made some poor choices.[5]

God created the idea of beauty, yet He never defines it in Scripture. The closest thing we get is the Song of Solomon—a comparison of teeth to newly shorn sheep and hair like goats descending a mountain. Lovely.

PLUMP WHITE GIRLS AND LONG-NECKED WOMEN

It's intriguing to observe the changes in the perception of beauty throughout history, cultures, and fashion. Just a few hundred years ago in Europe, plump, pale women were the models of the day. (I could have been their Heidi Klum.) Even in our own country and recent history, the iconic sex symbol of the twentieth century, Marilyn Monroe, vacillated between sizes 14 and 16. Weight didn't seem to be an issue for her. We've all looked at National Geographic enough to know that some cultures value things we find blatantly unattractive, even freakish—women with really long necks or lips stretched over saucers. Future anthropologists may say the same about our own subculture of those who prefer body modification via tattoos and piercings. Or maybe they will be totally modified and they'll think the Sports Illustrated swimsuit issue is the equivalent of National Geographic for us. Okay, doubtful … but maybe.

Probably what is more consistent throughout history and cultures is what is considered unattractive—pretty much any sort of deformity or irregularity or asymmetry. All of us have our imperfections. Even model Cindy Crawford reportedly has different-sized wrists. (I know—how embarrassing for her.)

My point is not to talk so much about what is considered beautiful, though I do find that fascinating. Rather, I want to discuss to what the value of physical beauty is in the bigger scheme of things. As with most things, Satan has taken what

God created as good and corrupted it to mess up our heads and hearts.

VANITY FAIR

Our culture is obsessed with beauty. The recent wave of extreme-makeover shows on TV—*The Swan, Dr. 90210, Extreme Makeover,* and so on—prove that. Plastic surgery is not the norm just in Hollywood anymore but has moved into the mainstream, and it is no longer just for the middle-aged sector.

- According to research, last year there was a 400 percent increase from 2002 in the number of women eighteen years or younger getting breast augmentation. Apparently that's the graduation gift to covet these days. No longer the traditional set of luggage or trip to Cancún—"They're called boobs, Ed."
- Between 1997 and 2003, there was a 293 percent increase in cosmetic procedures overall, according to www.plasticsurgeryresearch.info.
- A recent news story on NBC reported that in 2004 there were 9 million plastic surgeries performed and $8.5 billion were spent on those surgeries. That is not including nonsurgical cosmetic procedures.
- One in four women on college campuses admits to binging and purging to control her weight.

The pressure to fit the mold is overwhelming. But I don't need to tell you any of that. You live smack dab in the middle of that pressure cooker.

We all suffer the ramifications. Those among us who are considered attractive experience great notice, value, and influence but often struggle with insecurity and fears to maintain that outward appearance, because truly that is why the world values them. In January of 2003, Nicole Kidman, Julianne Moore, and Meryl Streep—three of the most beautiful and talented actresses in Hollywood—discussed their insecurities with Oprah. "The attention to how you look is so cruel and unrealistic," according to Meryl. Those of us who aren't so "blessed" struggle with insecurity because we are often overlooked, marginalized, underappreciated, and even blatantly rejected because we don't measure up to the magazine-model standard.

The truth is that in the world's economy beauty is a commodity, and if you have it, you're wealthy. You're treated differently, somehow made to feel more valuable and desirable. Studies have proven that point. One study published in April 2005 by the Federal Reserve Bank of St. Louis shows that beautiful people make more money than the not so beautiful—on average, 5 percent more. Less attractive people make 9 percent less than the average person.[6] Other studies propose that beautiful people are more intelligent. Also, beautiful people are more likely to get help from strangers and assistance in a crisis. And let's hope you don't end up in trouble with the law, but if you do, you're less likely to be convicted or will at least receive more leniency in the court if you're beautiful or handsome.[7] Attractive people are just that—attractive. People are drawn to them in general and want to please them, at least until their character or personality dispels the mist of beauty. Even then, some are so entranced that they fail to see a person objectively.

Eleanor Roosevelt, when asked if she had any regrets, she replied, "I wish I had been prettier."

Before she was first lady, she established and ran a school for the poor as well as a factory for the jobless. She was the first woman to speak in front of a national convention, to write a syndicated column, to earn money as a lecturer, to be a radio commentator, and to hold regular press conferences. She helped shape the New Deal social welfare program, helped found UNICEF and the Universal Declaration of Human Rights, and was asked to be a delegate at the first general assembly if the U.N.

Most of us bear wounds from being slighted or even rejected at some point for not measuring up to the standards. Even Jennifer Aniston admits in *Vanity Fair* of February 2004 that she still carries some hurt and insecurities from having been overweight while growing up.

IT'S A CONTEST

So, where do you fall on the scale of relative beauty? Admit it: in your head you have your own scale. Some supermodel, movie star, or sorority sister is at the top, and some slovenly creature who gives little concerted effort toward her outward appearance is at the bottom. Where you fall on any given day is a cumulative effect of multiple factors—menstrual cycle, humidity/hair ratio, past and recent comments made by friends/family/male interest(s), wardrobe selection, numbers on the scale, past self-perceptions about your own attractiveness, how attractive others in the room may be, and so on.

The overwhelming consequence is that we women struggle with constant comparison. Nancy Etcoff states the reality well in her book *Survival of the Prettiest*. "Why so much self-denigration and envy? Because every woman somehow finds herself, without her consent, entered into a beauty contest with every other woman. No matter how irrelevant to her goals, how inappropriate to her talents and

endeavors, or how ridiculous the comparison, women are always compared to one another and found wanting."[8] That last part is the kicker—we will always be found wanting. There will always be someone prettier, thinner, taller, funnier, smarter, more graceful, or whatever. Always.

In the same way that men look at beautiful women with lust, so we look at those same women and measure ourselves against them. We want to be them. We envy them. We catch ourselves thinking *Girl is cut* or *Those cannot be real* or *I could probably get my hair to do that with a little color and some serious product* or *If I had her money, I could look like that too*. We look at less attractive people and find comfort in the fact that at least we don't look like that; we judge and criticize them to make ourselves feel better. Confessions of my own thoughts this very week while grocery shopping: *At least my bum's not quite that flat* (I often speak with a British accent in my head—too much Jane Austen and the BBC). *Who told her she could wear leggings in public—really, leggings, period? So Sarah Jessica, circa 1988*. If my mother was in my head (and she often is), she'd say, "Don't be ugly!" referring to my evil thoughts, not the other person's appearance.

Comparison: it's a treacherous trap of discontent. It's one thing to appreciate another's beauty, gifts, or character, but when comparison turns into envy, criticism, and judgment, it leads only to self-consumption, insecurity, and heartache, not to mention sin.

13021 LEGENDARY DR.

I moved into a fabulous home about a year ago, one that I rent. Finally, I have a place where I can unpack and decorate like I want to decorate. The plan is for me to buy my own house in a couple of years, but in the meantime I take great delight in sewing drapes and bedding, buying artwork and accessories, rearranging the furniture, and so forth. I did put some minimal effort and money into paint, and I do certainly keep it clean and maintained, but for the most part I'm not investing much time or energy in the home itself as far as tearing down walls, replacing carpet or cabinets, or landscaping goes. It makes no sense to invest in things I won't be able to take with me when I move into my own more permanent home.

The Bible says that beauty is sort of like that. "Beauty is fleeting, but a woman who fears the Lord, she shall be praised," according to Proverbs.[9] The thirty-first chapter describes the qualities of a godly woman, much of her character, and little or nothing of her outward appearance. Investing in this temporal body has a limited and short-lived return—it's fleeting, it's not going to last. Certainly

we can care for our bodies and present ourselves as attractively as possible, but we're aging regardless of how many products we use and how many procedures we submit to. Instead, it seems wiser to focus on what's on the inside, the things we can take with us. Our character is a much wiser investment and offers an eternal return. Paul says it well when he talks about the fact that our outward bodies are "wasting away" but our inner self is being renewed daily (2 Corinthians 4:16, NIV).

However, that's not to say there's no value in outward beauty. Peter says, "Your adornment must not be merely external—braiding the hair, and wearing gold jewelry or putting on dresses, but let it be the person of the heart, with the imperishable quality of a gentle and quiet spirit, this is precious in the sight of God."[10] He says let it not be *merely* external, meaning there is value in external beauty. We are to add to external beauty a heart attractiveness—in personality, attitude, and character—which has far more value in God's economy.

If a person has a strong and mature character, then she will have an appropriate and balanced perspective of outward beauty. Her beauty becomes more of a reflection of who she is than an attempt to become someone she isn't.

AN OLD RED BLANKET

Once again I'm risking my credibility with you, the hip college chick, but I confess to watching *Antique Roadshow* on a regular basis. (I promise, PBS and public radio are on the rise as far as the hipness scale—you just wait.) Everyone who comes on that show hopes to be the next old man from Oklahoma. This guy brought in the blanket he's kept on the back of his sofa (or "divan," as his generation calls it) for the past fifty years and finds out it's worth half a million dollars because it's some rare Indian relic. I confess I still get weepy every time I see that episode. (I can't stand to see an old man cry, even if it is tears of joy. "Why, we're just dirt farmers.") The blanket itself is not remarkable or beautiful. In fact, it is pretty simple, really, with its wide red and white stripes and a few black V's woven in. But the value lies in who made it: our Indian predecessors. You're just like that. You may be that blanket or a painting by a famous artist or a rare coin issued by a now-defunct government—your value lies not in how beautiful you are but in who made you.

One of the Bible poets wonders at being God's creation:

> You created my inmost being;
> you knit me together in my mother's womb.
> I praise you because I am fearfully and
> wonderfully made;
> your works are wonderful,
> I know that full well. (Psalm 139:13-14)

It's interesting to note what the passage does and does not say. It does say God was intentional: there is design and purpose in each person. It also says that anything created by God is wonderful. The word translated "fearfully" literally means "with awe, astonishment, and reverence." You are an awesome creation—a masterpiece, if you will—that deserves respect because of who created you.

If you showed up at the roadshow with some wacky painting you've kept in a cheap plastic frame hanging in your bathroom and then found out it was a Picasso, I guarantee you would give it more respect. It may be described more as "interesting" than as "beautiful," but once you got the insurance taken care of, you would be quick to frame it well and display it with pride and prominence, not so much because of the painting itself as because of who created it. The passage does not say that God

made everyone beautiful by the current standards, but it clearly says you are created wonderfully.

HAMMERTOES AND ACNE

Everyone is knit together with some "imperfections" that make us unique, ranging from big ears, astigmatism, or a flat chest to deformities and disease. Does God have a purpose in all this?

Yep.

Not because He's cruel and heartless but because He has your best interest in mind. Like any good parent, He's far more concerned with your heart and character than with your shallow and momentary happiness. I truly believe He has a purpose and plan for you that fits into the bigger plan of history and for which you are perfectly designed.

I don't want to make light of serious health issues. All of it, from acne to serious birth defects, is the ramification of sin in the world. The problem of ugliness and deformity is, in fact, the problem of evil, and the reasons for it are not always easy to discern and are certainly not fully disclosed to us. But Scripture does affirm this: God, in His wisdom (that's admittedly hard for us to understand at times), does often choose to allow sin to run its course. But even when it includes tragic

consequences, He can still bring His good and glory from it.

Ephesians 2:10 gives me great confidence at times when I feel the pressure to conform or measure up to someone else's standard. "For we are God's workmanship, created in Christ Jesus to do good works, which God prepared in advance for us to do."

He made Esther beautiful because He knew she would have to please the king to save her people, the nation of Israel. But He made a man blind from birth because he would bring glory to God when he was healed (Luke 18:43). Everything about you is for a purpose and a plan—your physical appearance, your family, your life experiences, your gifts and weaknesses. Though tainted and warped by sin, all of it is ordained by God to conform you to Christ, to help others, and to bring glory to the Father.

WHERE THE PLASTIC MEETS THE KNIFE

So, if that's the case, then it seems I should embrace who God made me to be. Does that mean it's wrong for me to try to fix my imperfections? Well, pass me the can opener (best read with a Dolly Parton twang). There are all sorts of worms in this can—contentment, vanity, identity, control, idolatry, insecurity, confidence, stewardship, self-consumption, and health. And then, if you start bashing plastic surgery, where do you stop? Waxing? Coloring your hair? Using Crest White Strips? Getting manis and pedis? Using makeup? You see how this is a slippery slope and you can quickly end up with your hair in a bun, no makeup, unshaven legs, old sweats, and $2 flip-flops (not to be confused with me doing a little late-night shopping at the Wal-Mart).

So there's this guy—"Catman." Maybe you've seen the show about him and others like him on the Discovery Channel. "Catman" wants to become a cat. He has had cheek implants, a brow implant, lip clefting, teeth sharpening, ear pointing, all sorts of tattooing, and next on the list—whisker implants. Well, I don't know exactly where the line is for any individual, but I do know this—that's way past it. If God meant him to be a cat, he'd have been born in a litter.

On the other end of the spectrum, in the not too distant past, I was in a room with four or five women in ministry leadership planning a women's conference. It came out through our discussion that only two of us in the room had not had plastic surgery. I confess the option had never crossed my mind, but it certainly led to some interesting "what if's." Now that we are all well versed in the lingo, thanks to *Extreme Makeover*, I'd go for some microderm abrasion, Lasik eye surgery, varicose vein laser treatment, breast lift, liposuction, and tummy tuck. And throw in a little Botox while we're at it. But would that really make me happy?

Actually, yes, it probably would. It would be nice to feel better about myself and more confident and perhaps have the attention of men and reap the benefits of the more beautiful people. But is my circumstantial happiness the point? Is that really the goal or purpose in life?

There is a web of tensions to consider in making such decisions. Whether it's plastic surgery or just a cut 'n' color over at the Curl Up & Dye, it's an opportunity to examine your heart. As all sorts of procedures become more accessible and more the cultural norm, I can only imagine we're going to have many options and opportunities. In fact, maybe you already have—you may have already

gotten that graduation gift. But here are some things to think about when the time comes.

1. MOST OBVIOUSLY, WHY DO YOU WANT TO DO IT?

Heart motive and expectations are big concerns. Any good plastic surgeon is going to ask you about your expectations and hopes before he or she takes you on as a client. If you have unrealistic expectations of how this will change your life, solve all your problems, or turn you into a completely new person, they are not going to put you under (or at least they shouldn't).

2. CAN YOU AFFORD THIS, AND IS IT REALLY A WISE FINANCIAL STEWARDSHIP OF WHAT YOU'VE BEEN ENTRUSTED WITH?

This is probably the greatest concern. Contrary to popular belief, debt is not a wise option, and though plastic surgery has become more affordable, few people have that kind of discretionary income. And even if you do, is it wise to invest gross amounts of money in the temporal and fleeting? I know this whole area is relative to individual values, lifestyle, and experience. But before you decide to make an investment, do me this favor: read through some passages about stewardship and then make a decision (Matthew 6:19-24; 25:14-30). This is not just about the $10,000 boob job. This is an issue I have to wrestle with when it comes to buying my $20 shampoo rather than the generic wholesale knockoff. The money thing is a bigger area of your life that you're going to have to process sooner or later. You might as well start here.

3. IF YOU HAVE THIS DONE, WHAT'S THE NEXT THING?

Is this going to start you down a path of pursuing perfection? Once you fix this one thing, are you going to feel compelled to fix the next thing and the next? Oprah and others have certainly done enough shows about those addicted to plastic surgery—those in pursuit of ever-evasive youth. You've seen the sixty-five-year-olds with taut, wrinkle-free faces, swollen lips locked in a perpetual smile, and eyes oddly unable to blink. I know you're only twenty-something, but you're just as susceptible. Perfection is a futile pursuit and only spirals down the rabbit hole of the discontent.

4. IS THIS ABOUT GAINING THE ATTENTION OF MEN OR THE RIGHT MAN?

I know that it seems every guy out there is in pursuit of a woman with a perfect body. And unfortunately, that's mostly true. (Oops—is my cynicism showing?) However, are you motivated to catch a wink and a whistle from the general population of red-blooded men in order to feel good about yourself for the moment? Or is it really your desire to capture the heart of the man whom God has created as His good and perfect provision for you?

5. ARE YOU STEALING GOD'S GLORY, OR IS HE USING YOUR IMPERFECTION TO BRING GLORY TO HIMSELF?

Whatever your area of physical self-dissatisfaction is—your thorn in the flesh, so to speak—is the enduring of it something that is building your character or enabling you to connect with or help others? Or could it be that God, in His kindness, is providing a means of fixing it in a way that is bringing glory to Himself?

6. IS THE PURSUIT OF BEAUTY AN IDOL IN YOUR LIFE?

Okay, so maybe you don't have a little shrine in your room with pictures from *In Style* and *Cosmo* surrounded by your MAC makeup and Bed Head hair products, with candles and incense. But then again, you may actually have some version of this. Anyway, the point is, does how you spend your time, energy, and money, or your words or your heart attitude, reflect a higher value placed on outward appearance as compared to honoring and obeying God?

7. WHAT ARE THE HEALTH RISKS?

This is just plain common sense. Weigh the risks involved. Do the research. Don't just take your doctor's word for it. I'm sure *People* magazine has an archive of procedures gone awry to make anyone think twice, but you probably want to consider some more reliable sources. That's what the Web is for.

8. ARE YOU VALUING THE WORLD'S ECONOMY OVER GOD'S?

What have you done to focus on your heart and character lately? How do you see your outward appearance as a reflection of your inner self? What are the issues that connect the two for you? For me, it's certainly issues of discipline and self-control. There are issues of insecurity and choosing to find my confidence in who I am in Christ rather than what the world thinks about my outward appearance. What's on your list?

HEY, PINNOCHHIO!

"Go ask that big-nose girl over there." Out of the mouths of babes, such cruel words. Bambi (obvious fake name, though I went to High School with a Bambi) endured all sorts of cuts about the size of her nose when growing up, and her mom was the first to remind her that she could have that problem fixed one day when she had the money. In fact, for a long time that was the first thing on her list for "one day." In the meantime, however, she became a Christian. One of the things she wrestled with the Lord over was the size of her nose. But she came to terms with the fact that God had created her that way on purpose and trusted that He must have had a plan for it, so she let it go.

A few years later her sister, a local news anchor, called and asked if Bambi would have her nose fixed if it was paid for. As she prayed about it, she sensed this was a gift from the Lord (via WIS-TV, the news station, and the doctor who would provide her surgery if they could do a news story about the surgery). So Bambi did it and had her fifteen minutes of fame.

She would admit that, had she not become a believer, she would have had the surgery as soon as she could have—and for all the wrong reasons. What before would have only given her a false sense of security, built up her pride and ego, and further convinced her to look for affirmation from men now didn't really change her life at all. She'd already found her security and contentment in Christ. It was much more like a sweet gift that reminds her of a Father who delights in giving good gifts to his children—just for fun.

The truth is that I have several friends who have had procedures done. Several of these procedures I would even say have been a miraculous provision and gift from the Lord Himself, like Bambi's—a testimony of His kindness. And I wouldn't be telling the truth if I denied spending my fair share of time, money, and energy fighting the ravages of time and searching for the next miracle product. So I am in no way saying that all cosmetic procedures or products are wrong or evil. God does care about our outward appearance, especially as it relates to our character and relationship with Him. I think it's important for you and me to wrestle with the related heart issues and pray for God's wisdom and insight to have a true perspective, holding this issue of personal beauty in balance.

SIZE 8 FOREVER AND EVER, AMEN

For those of us who have a relationship with God, we're promised that one day we will have a perfect and beautiful body for eternity (1 Corinthians 15:42). For me, that means life without the wobbly bits, without the hideous scar on my ankle, without astigmatism, without turkey wings or crow's feet—a body without the ramifications of sin (not to mention a character without sin). That's what we all long for and, frankly, what we were created for. No wonder we're ever in pursuit of it.

The truth is that God, in His wisdom, has allowed the ramifications of sin to take their toll on my body. I don't like it anymore than I like the ramifications of sin in my character. Blick! And I do want to take care of my body, but rather than at the expense of my character, to do so in a way that can build my character and draw me closer to Christ.

Like my current home, I think I'll do the best I can with what I have for a body. I'll make it as attractive as possible in a way that gives honor and respect to its God. And then I'll spend my time and energy on what goes inside—the heart and character and relationship with its Creator. I can take those things with me to that new and perfect size-8 body I'll have for eternity.

REAL BEAUTY

Beauty, by the world's standard, is an elusive concept—always changing from era to culture to fad. It's mildly humiliating to think that we obsess over something so fickle, comparing ourselves with others in a contest that doesn't really exist. Someday we'll see how the term "Vanity Fair" was quite an appropriate commentary on our lives.

The truth is we haven't seen or experienced real beauty. It's not just that our perspective has been so skewed; it's that our perspective is so finite to begin with. Because no one has seen God, no one can begin to imagine the depth and mystery of infinite beauty. Our sense of beauty is just a taste, really, of what is truly beautiful—God Himself. The value of beauty lies in the fact that it is a reflection of Him. He created us in His image as a means of pointing people toward Himself. The value is shortchanged when beauty becomes an end in itself.

The beauty that God values is the reflection of a godly heart that manifests itself outwardly—in your demeanor, in how you carry yourself and how you care for and present your body, as well as in your words and actions. With the Spirit of God within, anyone can have that kind of beauty.

[1] Genesis 25:25
[2] 1 Samuel 16:12
[3] Esther 1:11
[4] Isaiah 53:2
[5] Isaiah 14:12
[6] http://money.cnn.com/2005/04/08/news/funny/beautiful_money/?cnn=yes
[7] all statistics in this paragraph http://weattract.com/ASPhysBeautyHaveEasy.html
[8] *Survival of the Prettiest* by Nancy Etcoff (New York, NY: Anchor Books, 2000)
[9] Proverbs 31:30
[10] 1 Peter 3:3

COSM

CONFESS!
fueling the fantasy

5 ARTICLES!
to help lower
your standards

Famous Lives
and why you should
loathe your own

**ANATOMICALLY
IMPOSSIBLE!**
and you thought
you were <u>already</u>
self-concious!

SHARON KEYS
attorney...
swimsuit model...
mother of 12.

**COMPARE YOUR WORST
DATES TO THESE**

ENCOUNTERS WITH
THE SLEAZIEST, CHEAPEST,
CHEESIEST LOSERS **YET!**

FIVE MINUTE TRICKS
WHAT TO WEAR TO MAKE
THE GUYS GO GAGA

9 781563 992506

- Fifty thousand of the cells in your body will die and be replaced with new cells, all while you have been reading this sentence.
- If you cut your skin, within ten seconds it will begin to replace itself.
- Placed end to end, your body's blood vessels would measure about sixty-two thousand miles in length.
- Your stomach has to produce a new layer of mucus every two weeks; otherwise, it would digest itself.
- The average human produces a quart of saliva a day, or ten thousand gallons in a lifetime.
- Every human spent about half an hour as a single cell.
- A fetus acquires fingerprints at the age of three months.
- It takes seventy-two muscles to say a one-syllable word.
- One human brain generates more electrical impulses in a single day than do all of the world's telephones put together.
- Human thighbones are stronger than concrete.
- Every person has a unique tongue print.
- The nervous system transmits messages to the brain at speeds of 180 miles per hour.
- The human eye can detect more than ten million different colors.

Body Temple

Your body truly is a wonderland, and not just in the John Mayer sense. The Psalmist's idea that God "knit" you together in your mother's womb takes on a whole new meaning (seems a bit more complex than your basic knit one, purl two stitch).

It is nothing less than miraculous that six billion human beings walk this earth right this minute—each one more complicated than the most complex computer network, the space shuttle, or the New York City infrastructure.

And I treat my body so flippantly. I take it for granted.

I lop off toenails here and there with reckless abandon. I pick off a scab with little regard to the miraculous regeneration that just took place. I move around constantly and effortlessly, for the most part, often without purpose or intent. I speak words as they come to me, without any measure of economy. I go out in the sun without sunscreen in spite of the once-freckles-now-age-spots-soon-

to-be-cancer risk. I feed it "chemolicious" treats like Dr. Pepper, Fudge-Covered Mint Oreos, and Cheetos. I pay no attention to 99 percent of my bodily functions and trust they will carry on without my conscious instruction. Really, my own sanity and clarity of mind are only assumed. (For all I know, they've long since left me.)

God created your body, and it's good—really good. True, we are spiritual beings, but we are so much more than that. It is through our physical body that we interact with God. With our eyes, ears, mouth, and nose, we experience His creation. With our voice, we pray and praise Him. With our hands and feet, we serve Him. With our arms, we embrace and love for Him. With our mind, we comprehend and learn about Him. In one sense, our every word and action is some manifestation of our relationship with Him.

God created this masterpiece of flesh and then gave some specific rules about how to take care of it. Leviticus is chock-full o' rules about personal hygiene, grooming, diet, and rest. Crazy stuff like if a man throws up, he's unclean and everything he touches is unclean. Well, science and experience have certainly shown the wisdom in that. You won't catch me riding in his saddle (Leviticus 15:9). Then there's stuff like not eating shellfish (probably a good rule in the days before refrigeration) or things that swarm (not a temptation, really). There are a whole lot of disturbingly descriptive things about leprosy in there. Fascinating. Thankfully, not so much of an issue for us.

God's heart is obviously to protect and provide for this body He created and entrusted to you and me. It is stewardship. Which brings us to this point: "Do you not know that your body is a temple of the Holy Spirit, who is in you, whom you have received from God? You are not your own; you were bought at a price. Therefore honor God with your body" (1 Corinthians 6:19-20, NIV).

The word translated "temple" does not refer just to the physical building of the temple; it's the same word used for the holy of holies, the place where God resided among the people, where the ark of the covenant was kept. Only one priest was allowed to go into the holy of holies, only once a year, to make an offering. They tied a rope to his leg in case he was struck dead while he was in there, so they could pull him out without having to go in themselves.

If you've ever seen *Raiders of the Lost Ark*, you know what happens if the wrong person opens the ark. I know the whole face-melting thing seems very Hollywood, but that might actually be an underestimation of the true gravity of being in the

presence of God. No one can see or touch God and survive. It's written that after Moses received the law from God on Mount Sinai, he glowed—sort of radioactive like, I'd imagine. Very sci-fi.[2]

Then there was this poor guy named Uzzah who stumbled while transporting the ark of the covenant. He grabbed a corner of the ark to keep it from touching the ground—a slight error in judgment. He was struck dead upon contact. (2 Samuel 6:7) Apparently he was less holy than the earth it would have fallen upon. It's hard to understand the gravity of holiness and what that means to us.

But all of this is to say that, in God's eyes, our bodies are just as holy as the ark of the covenant in the holy of holies. Fortunately, people aren't struck dead when they touch us, but that may be one form of sexual purity accountability to consider and pray for. Truly, if you are a believer, then in the way that the ark of the covenant was the physical representation of the presence of God to His people at that time, so your body is the physical representation—the dwelling place of God—now.

The statement that we've been "bought at a price" (v. 20) is a reference to the slave market. We were once slaves to our sinful appetites, but now we have been purchased by the blood of Christ, and the Holy Spirit living within us is His mark to show to whom we belong. I know that's a lot of churchspeak, but I don't know how to say it any other way. It's profound truth, and I am a good Baptist at heart.

EVICTION NOTICE

I'm guessing you live in a dorm, a sorority house, an apartment, or your parents' house—the point being, you probably don't own the place where you live. You're under the authority of the owner or the landlord. You abide by house rules because the house doesn't belong to you; you've just been entrusted with living there and caring for it. You might think of your body in the same way—as rented space. You don't own it; you've just been entrusted to care for it, to use it, and to enjoy it but not to abuse it. The landlord would be most disappointed.

Have you ever read the story in Matthew about Jesus going to the temple in Jerusalem and getting angry at the money changers and the marketing going on in the temple (Matthew 21:12-13)? It was a misuse of His Father's house. He had righteous anger for the abusive and self-serving people taking advantage of those who came there to worship. They were treating the dwelling place of the Father with great disrespect. He literally threw them out, physically turned over the tables, and tossed stuff out.

Now there's something to think about the next time you're tempted to misuse or abuse your body.

WHAT DOES HONOR LOOK LIKE?

So, what is a balanced perspective on all of this? What does it mean to honor God with your body? Well, consider the context of 1 Corinthians 6. That passage is right smack in the middle of a discussion about sexual immorality. Surprise, surprise. Like you haven't read enough about that topic so far.

Verse 18, right before the verses we've already looked at, says, "Flee from sexual immorality. All other sins a man commits are outside his body, but he who sins sexually sins against his own body."

Every sin has consequences for you and for others, but sexual sin has consequences for the body itself. Not only can it lead to disease, but in light of all the other things you've read in this book, by now you should understand that sex is like gluing two pieces of paper together. When you pull them apart, there are bits and scraps of each piece stuck to the other. They will never be the same whole, untorn pieces of paper again. When you have sex outside marriage and then the two of you go your separate ways, there are consequences, physically, emotionally, and spiritually.

Paul understands the power of sexual temptation. He says to flee. Don't try to stand your ground and fight off the temptation—break into a sprint in the other direction.

But sexual immorality is not the only area we need to consider in honoring God with our bodies.

ST. BASIL'S, ST, PETER'S, ST. OLAF'S …

Have you ever been to Europe and visited any of the great cathedrals? Or have you at least watched Rick Steves on PBS or the Travel Channel touring the cathedrals of Europe? (Okay—long shot on the Rick Steves, I know.) It is amazing the amount of time, energy, and money that went into building these great churches—these places in the center of every town where people came to worship and meet with God. Unfortunately, they have become monuments unto themselves and to those who built them, much more so than to the God they were intended to honor. They are valued for their beauty and art, not for what they represent or for their intended use. The actual church services, if held at all, are usually in a small corner of these massive monuments. Tourists come to gawk at the building, not to worship or meet with their Maker. Sometimes we, too, can become so focused on the body itself and its appearance that we neglect its purpose. The body, rather than the Spirit of God within us, becomes our object of worship.

We've already addressed some of these issues in the previous chapter, but let me reiterate here that to be consumed with one's outward appearance is nothing short of idolatry. Depriving your body of what it needs to function well, controlling your weight with binging and purging, or exercising addictively is not honoring God with your body. Allow me a slight but serious tangent: food.

The truth is that most women err on one side or the other when it comes to how we view food. That's one of the ramifications of the wealth of our culture. Food is not just about eating to live and providing nutrition for our body. Food has become an experience, a drug, a social event, something to control and conquer. It's either our enemy or our lover, rarely a friend.

I know that issues surrounding eating habits are far more complicated than just saying that it's wrong—stop it. They're often rooted in issues not related to your body at all. This book is not about eating disorders, but we would be naive to not acknowledge that about 25 percent of you reading this book fall somewhere on the spectrum of unhealthy views of food and eating, and many of you don't even recognize it. The root issues are often tied to topics we've discussed—the need to be loved, wanted, and known. We don't have the space required to address all the issues that lead to such disorders or all the ramifications of it. But I do know that healing starts with recognition of the problem. Let me ask you a few questions:

• Do you think about food often—when, what, and where you're going to eat next?
• Do you have feelings of guilt and remorse after you eat?
• Do you look forward to times when you can eat alone and/or plan secret binges?
• Have you ever forced yourself to throw up after eating or taken a laxative, diet pills, or diuretics?
• Do you constantly count fat grams, calories, and carbs?
• Do you think you'd be happier and better liked if you were thinner?
• Do you exercise more than once a day or five times a week?
• Do you skip meals in hope of losing weight?
• Do you weigh yourself more than once or twice a week?
• Do you think you're overweight, though others have said otherwise?
• Do you hide or lie about your eating behavior?
• Are you fearful of being out of control of your eating?

There's no magic number here, but if you answered yes to more than a couple of those questions, I'd say it's worth having conversations about your relationship to food with some good friends or family member. See what they think. Also, check out some of the books and Web sites listed in the resource section.

Honoring God with your body has everything to do with keeping your body healthy and little or nothing to do with an irrational pursuit of attractiveness and beauty.

TWO DOORS DOWN FROM THE GET 'N' GO

Here in the U.S. we don't do the giant cathedral thing so much. In our era of the nondenominational church, we focus on the church being the people and not the building. We don't think about our church buildings as being "temples"—dwelling places for God. Instead, in the modern evangelical world, we often rent strip-center space; throw in some folding chairs, a fake ficus on either side of a music stand, a screen, and a VPU; and have church. Not quite the same as a "temple," is it? Ironically, that is often how we treat our body temples as well. Whatever. It's not worth the time and effort to maintain them well. There are other more important things to do. We consider the body to be purely utilitarian while we focus on the inside—how we feel, what we're experiencing. But can you really do one without the other?

Here we find those of us who err on the side of overeating or just eating poorly or not giving the body the rest it needs or even drinking too much or using drugs or just being plain lazy. We give in to the appetites of our flesh—what feels good in the moment. We focus on whatever we need to do to feel better on the inside, or make it work for us in the moment, giving little thought to the long-term consequences, much less to the God who resides within us.

I realize you are at an age when your body is forgiving and can quickly recover from just about anything. You can keep it awake for hours on end with a never-ending supply of Starbucks Double Shots. You can feed it only cereal and pizza for weeks with limited repercussions. You can go days with little more movement than is required to shift from the computer to the bathroom. You can give it large doses of alcohol for several weekends in a row and be unaffected during the week. It's amazing the level of tolerance you have right now. But at the risk of sounding like my Great Aunt Eura, "It's not going to last, dearie" (pinching of the cheek).

The heavy drinker and the glutton will come to poverty, and drowsiness will clothe one with rags. (Proverbs 23:21, NASB).

I'm going to wager that the hope of poverty and rags is not why you and/or your parents are spending tens of thousands of dollars to educate you. This season of life is not just about gaining head knowledge and a piece of paper with a seal on it; it's about becoming a responsible adult. This is when you are determining who you are going to be, what habits you're going to make or break. This is when your decisions and actions begin to have some long-term consequences and benefits. Credit card and beer companies know that if they can gain your allegiance at this age, they most likely will have you for a lifetime. Why else would they spend billions of dollars blanketing your campus with their propaganda? Developing healthy habits and a strong character at this stage in the game can determine your whole trajectory in life.

Remember back in fourth grade when you had that plastic half-circle thing called a *protractor*? (Engineering majors, please do not take offense—I'm trying to communicate with the broader audience.) Do you remember how to draw angles? It's crazy to me that if you start at one point and draw one line, and then draw a line from the same

starting point but just one degree to the right or the left, those two lines will end up with miles between them if you kept drawing them out infinitely. If you make even the most minor adjustments in your habits, character, and/or spiritual life at this point in your life, you will end up in a completely different place years down the road than where you would otherwise have been. Believe me, from this point, just fifteen years down the line, I can tell you that the decisions you're making and habits you're developing now will make a difference when you're thirty-eight and beyond.

EATING FOR ONE

I know this might seem far-fetched as you look around your local sorority house, but 60 percent of Americans are overweight. If you question that, take a trip to your local Wal-Mart and observe. (Those sorority sisters make up a good percentage of that 40 percent who aren't.) In America we eat because the food is there, not because we're hungry. We eat what's convenient and tasty, not for the nutrition our body needs. If you can develop a habit now of honoring God with what you eat—eating for health—it will save you heartache, pain, and money down the road when your body begins to age and your metabolism changes. The benefits are truly priceless.

There are more than 130,000 health and diet book titles currently in print. Amazing how many ways you can say what is basically common sense. Eat lots of fruits and vegetables—the more raw and organic, the better. Eat some lean meat and fish for protein—the more hormone free, the better. Avoid chemicals and processed foods. (I know, like you have control over these things when you're on the meal plan. But you do have some choices.) If it's such common sense, why is health and diet publishing a multimillion-dollar business? Human nature. God knows human nature and addresses the real issue—lack of self-control. Gluttony, in a word. We all know what we should do, but we don't do it. That's where the Spirit of God is vital. Relying upon His help to develop discipline with your eating habits now will serve you well over your lifetime.

COME TO ME, ALL WHO ARE WEARY

Americans get an average of 6.9 hours of sleep per night. For college students, I'm guessing that average skews to extremes, based on the day of the week and the time in the semester. You may not feel it now, when you're young and your schedule is more flexible, but sometimes the most spiritual thing you can do is take a nap. The idea of the Sabbath being a day of rest is not optional; it's a biblical command. But in our work-to-get-ahead culture, we seldom take the time. Sunday is usually a plan-for-the-next-week-and-catch-up-on-what-I-didn't-get-done-last-week kind of day. Getting a good night's sleep and scheduling time for rest and doing the things that re-energize you are all godly habits that will serve you well and honor God.

DOS EQUIS AND X

Alcohol and drugs are prevalent on every campus, even my good ol' Baptist alma mater. On the one hand, I know that the party scene is a huge part of the college experience and you've already made some choices and decisions about it. There's so much I could and want to say. But on the other hand, that's not the focus of this book. So I'm going to limit my thoughts to Paul's: "'Everything is permissible for me'—but not everything is beneficial. 'Everything is permissible for me'—but

I will not be mastered by anything" (1 Corinthians 6:12, NIV).

Depending on your age, drinking may not even be permissible for you, which answers that question. (Paul was referencing permission under the fulfillment of the Old Testament law.) I'm also assuming you know that drunkenness is not a biblical recommendation—or even an option, really. (See Romans 13:13, Galatians 5:21, and 1 Peter 4:3.) Given that drinking (though not drugs, of course) is legal for you, is it beneficial? Is it a controlling factor in your life?

Those two questions get to the heart issues. If you can answer them honestly, then you can figure out how to honor God with this area of your life.

"AS THE DOOR TURNS ON ITS HINGES SO THE SLUGGARD TURNS IN HIS BED"

Proverbs has nothing good to say about sluggards—the lazy. Several verses talk about their foolishness. One of my particular favorites is this: "The sluggard buries his hand in the dish; he is too lazy to bring it back to his mouth" (Proverbs 26:15, NIV). Now, that's lazy. I envision a guy at the kitchen table with his hand in a bowl of Froot Loops and his head resting on his elbow, drool dripping down his sleeve.

Laziness has always been a popular vice, but I think we've reached new heights of sluggishness in our convenience- and comfort-driven culture. There are so few activities that require an expenditure of energy anymore. Maybe walking to class, but then you sit when you get there. You sit in front of your computer to study or work. You put forth no effort in attaining food or water—it's handed to you in a bag or on a tray. You're entertained by TV, movies, Xbox, or the Internet—more sitting. Most of us drive if we have to go more than three blocks away. To exert energy requires being intentional.

There is some truth in the idea that you have to expend energy to gain energy. I don't have to convince you that exercise is good for your body. But I'm not sure you know how much it can impact the rest of your life—your overall energy level, your immune system, your ability to concentrate. It's just a good habit.

Believe it or not, your college years afford you the luxury of laziness more than does almost any other time in life. You're free from dependents and have relatively minimal responsibilities. For the first time, you determine how you will spend your time. You've got your schedule; you know your deadlines; but inevitably you'll be pulling an all-nighter before the test. It's almost a rite of passage. Most people chalk up their procrastination to personality type, but really it's just human nature. Habits of being diligent, exercising consistently, working hard, pursuing excellence in your work, and using your time wisely are all a reflection of the character of God and give Him honor.

INSEPARABLE
We can buy into the idea that our spiritual life is all about our soul and our spirit, but the inescapable truth is that our body and our soul are organically tied together, and while we're here on this earth, one greatly affects the other. It doesn't take long to figure that out. When I'm living a chaotic life, eating poorly, and not taking care of my body, then my spiritual life and relationship with God are just as stressed. Often, when I'm tired, my time with the Lord becomes the first casualty. But when I'm choosing to be more disciplined with my eating, rest, and exercise, it's reflected in my connection with Him.

Our body is a temple—the dwelling place of the ever-living, ever-loving God of the universe. We can't really get our finite minds around that concept, but I have to say that if Jesus were coming over for a slumber party, I'm pretty sure I'd clean my toilets, scrub the kitchen floor, clean out the fridge, and put clean sheets on the bed. Take this as an opportunity to do a little housecleaning inventory. Is your temple worthy of its resident?

[1] Psalm 139:13
[2] Exodus 34:29

Waiting Room

None of you wants to be me. I mean, sure, I can understand that you might want to have my sharp wit and profound insight and be highly sought after by the publishing world. But take my word for it, you do not want to be me. No one says, "I hope I'm thirty-eight and single and not having to deal with men calling me all the time ... or ever. It would be so nice to go for decades without a date. Maybe I could have just a couple of dysfunctional 'relationships' along the way, just for kicks. But then, to just be able to settle into waiting." No one is fantasizing about my life, that's for dang sure.

Sometimes when I try to explain to non-churched people what I do for a living—full-time ministry—people respond with "I see. So you're sort of like a nun." I used to try to explain, but frankly, I've gotten to the point where I just say, "Yeah, for all practical purposes, I am a nun."

(As an aside, I realize, having revealed this truth about my relationship/dating life, you may be wondering why the heck am I writing this book.

Me, too. It sort of landed on my plate, and I said yes before I thought it through. I'll be going to counseling as soon as this thing goes to print. However, what I lack in credibility by participation, I excel in by observation. I like to think it's sort of like Jesus talking about sin.)

Anyway, my situation is in no way due to lack of longing and wanting and praying on my part. I'm just like the rest of you—just a little more jaded by that insight and hindsight that come with age. And I hate to say it, but some of you are going to be me. Actually, in some way, *all* of you will be me. Let me explain.

THE BAD NEWS

This in no way will be encouraging to you, but I'm going to say it anyway. Elongated periods of waiting, staring at the horizon for God to deliver and provide, are a key theme of Scripture and the Christian life. It is the theme of most of the Psalms. Waiting for redemption that takes forever to arrive is a major theme of the Old Testament. The Hebrews Hall of Fame lists those who are strong in faith because they waited for God's promises. There is, in fact, a whole theology of waiting. (I don't really know what it is; I just thought that sounded impressive.)

The thing is, we only wait, or are conscious of waiting, for things we really want, and as relationships are one of the major things that women want, relationships will no doubt be one of the objects of waiting in our lives—waiting for a date, waiting for a husband, waiting for children, waiting for a husband to change, waiting for a child to return to the Lord. Waiting is one of the main crucibles of growth described in the Bible. How we wait, what we wait for, how we feel as we wait, and how we respond to God and His truth while we're waiting for Him to show up are all parts of the process. Waiting is a vehicle to move you toward mature faith. The only two givens are that you will find yourself waiting and that you do not get to choose what you will be waiting for.

THE REAL CHALLENGE

Delayed gratification is not my forte. I'm the annoying person who takes a bite out of the pan of brownies while they're still hot. If dessert is on the table, I have a bite before dinner. I've been known to unwrap a gift, rewrap it, and put it back under the Christmas tree. I'm no good at secrets or surprises. I have to tell someone. As you might imagine, waiting is a challenge for me, especially when I have no control. And like most women, I love to be in control. I just want to know if and when. I'm willing to go with God's timetable; I just want to know what it is.

But the challenge is not the waiting itself, because really you have no choice about that. You have to wait it out regardless. The challenge is in waiting well. I waited for over two months for my diamond matelasse porcelain blue duvet to arrive, but had a few choice words for the customer service department in the process. I did not wait well. The difference between waiting and waiting well can be summarized in one word: *discontentment*.

Discontentment is a polyester blend, meaning it is woven from several different fibers.

Envy: This first thread is often subtle. It builds slowly and then one day it sneaks up on you in the craziest places. For example, at the mailbox when there's another check from Daddy—your roommate's daddy, that is, and you're having mac 'n' cheese for dinner again. Or at the party when the guy you've liked all semester shows up with your sorority sister. Or when you're walking down the aisle in a bridesmaid's dress … again. It makes you mad at the people who have what you want. One of the Big Ten is "Do not covet." Hard rule to follow when there is always something that would make your life just a little better, if not perfect.

Cynicism: This thread develops over time, with disappointment after disappointment. You know you're there when your faith has lost its sense of expectancy. It's often disguised as sarcasm. "Yeah, right! Like I would ever … [Insert your lack of expectancy here—"get to go there," "have that job," "be asked out"]." The Pessimist club is right around the corner, Eeyore. (See the intro to this article as a prime example—for the sake of humor, of course.)

Bitterness: This is an interesting one because it's usually rooted in believing that you had a right to something you didn't get or that you got something you didn't deserve. True, there are some real losses, hurts, and disappointments—and grief is entirely valid. But when disappointment crosses the line to bitterness, there is some wrong thinking involved.

This is going to sound harsh—*really* harsh—but I'm saying it for your own good. (And I guarantee you're going to say it to your kids one day.) The concept of having a right to something is not biblical. Just because we're human does not mean we have rights, in spite of what our Founding Fathers had to say. The truth is, we deserve hell. It's not just that we don't deserve anything good; we do deserve the absence of anything good. So when that soaks in, you realize that anything and everything better than hell that you get is gravy. Anything good in my life is God's grace, and anything I've been spared is His mercy. That'll pull out your roots of bitterness. Sometimes we think we're more like my friend's three year old singing, "Amazing grace that saved a wretch like me"—seems preciously paradoxical. But sadly, the beautiful little angel is a wretch, just like you and me. Praise God for His amazing grace and mercy.

Sin: It's been defined as meeting a legitimate need in an illegitimate way. Basically, meeting your needs how you want to meet them because you're either tired of waiting for God to meet them or you don't like His provision. Classic example: Abraham and Sarah. (Genesis 16) They were promised a child, but they were getting up there in years and thus far, no tots. So they thought they'd help God out a bit by having Abraham sleep with Hagar, the maidservant. She gave birth to Ishmael. Even though it was her plan to begin with, Sarah was just livid—bitter, envious, the whole bit. However, she did get pregnant as God had planned all along, in His timing. When she was ninety-seven Isaac was born. As it turns out, there have been quite the consequences for this couple's sinful impatience. The descendants of Isaac are the Jews and the descendants of Ishmael are other Middle Eastern peoples making up much of the Muslim population. They've been fighting ever since. You can turn on CNN right now and hear all about it. Imagine if Sarah and Abraham had waited just a little while longer.

For women waiting for a date or a relationship or a husband, it can be tempting to go out and get yourself one. We all could. I could be married, really. There is always someone who is just as desperate, if you know where to find him. Women do it all the time, and they settle for their first catch. Relationships are hard enough between two people who do try to follow Christ. Trying to have a healthy relationship with someone who does not share that priority, is … well, I've never seen it happen without some really challenging circumstances. In spite of my previous sarcasm, I do actually love my single life and am grateful for God's protection from the choices I would have made in the past out of my own impatience or poor judgment. It is far better to be single and waiting with the hope of God's good provision than to be trapped in a marriage of my own making.

Envy, cynicism, bitterness, and sin—weave all of that into one fabric and that's one ugly, heavy blanket of discontentment. Interestingly, Paul says in Philippians that he has "learned" to be content in all circumstances—wealthy or poor, full or hungry. Basically, whether his needs are met or not, he's learned to find satisfaction in Christ, who gives him strength.[1] That all sounds well and good. We want to be like Paul—until we realize that part of his learning curve was being thrown in jail a few times, being shipwrecked three times, floating at sea for a day and night, being beaten with rods, and even being stoned once. Hopefully, you and I can figure it out with a much easier curriculum.

A GOOD WAITER

So, what is the anatomy of contentment? It's hard to just decide to be content. It's like saying, "Stop worrying." Emotions are not easily turned on and off. We can't just fix it, but we can change our focus.

Focus on Christ. A lot of times people come to Jesus and want to try Him out. See if He works for them. Basically, just date Him with little or no commitment. *The first time He doesn't come through for me in a way that I want Him to when I want Him to—that's it, I am out of here.* It doesn't work that way. As in a relationship with anyone, you certainly grow in your understanding and connection with Jesus over time, but it requires commitment, a marriage commitment. "For better or for worse, in sickness and in health" forces you to wait and see God's hand over time. It requires some perseverance, some willingness to sit tight and focus on the character and nature of God.

I believe He has a perfect love for me. I believe He can only act in my best interests. I believe He is all powerful and can do whatever needs to be done. I believe He does not withhold good gifts from me. Focusing on these truths while I'm waiting guards my mind from lies that would send me down the road to discontentment—lies like "He's punishing me"; "He doesn't love me"; "It's all my fault". When I am focusing on my relationship with Him, I can process my frustration, disappointment, longings, and fears with Him. What is it that is making me feel that way? Lies, sin, or wrong thinking? Or is it real heartache from valid unmet needs? Instead of letting my emotions separate me from Christ, I let them draw me nearer to Him.

Focus on thanksgiving. Remember that thing I said earlier about us all deserving hell and about every good thing we get being gravy? When you really get that, then every day is Thanksgiving. Turkey, dressing, pecan pie—bring it on. There is always a reason to celebrate.

What keeps going through my head right now is the image of an older lady at my church growing up. She has a high operatic voice and really tall hair and is singing the oh-so-popular number 354 in your hymnal: "Count your many blessings, name them one by one. Count your many blessings when the day is day is done. [Everybody now!] Cooooooouunt your blessings … see what the Lord hath done."

Pardon my flashback, but that, my friend, is some profound wisdom. Do it. Get out your journal and make a list right now of all the things you have to be thankful for. You'll be amazed at the number. If you can choose to give thanks in all things as you make your requests known to God (don't ignore your desires and longings—just bring them to Him), you're promised that "the peace of God, which surpasses all comprehension, will guard your hearts and your minds in Christ Jesus" (Philippians 4:6-7, NASB). Thanksgiving is a cloak of protection from anxiousness and bitterness. It is a path to joy.

Last, focus on community. People in general are not good at waiting alone. Our own mind, when it is left to its own devices and is in pain, can go down some crooked and depraved paths. A community of Christ followers helps you keep a right and true perspective.

I have a group friends who get together at least once a year, if not twice. We call it our "Waiting to Exhale" weekend. (The first time we met, that movie had just come out and we knew it was about a group of friends. However, we did not see the movie until years later and realized our mistake—bad movie. But it's too late now. We're stuck with the name.) Pretty much, for seventy-two hours straight, we talk—about everything. Literally, everything. (Guys cannot comprehend this.) No one else has been allowed to join our group, basically because of the stamina it requires. Our sleep is limited and we typically leave the house only once to eat out. Even then the talking continues. Three of us are single and one is married. Every year we talk about how much we *need* to be together—to be heard, understood, empathized with, encouraged, affirmed, prayed for, told truth to, cried with, laughed with. It is a *Lifetime* movie if ever there was one. Now, we do each have other communities and friends that we share life with on a more daily basis, and these are very important. But WTE, as we call it, is über-community, not for the faint of heart.

The other significant value of being connected in community is that it keeps you from self-consumption. On my own, I become overly introspective and egocentric. We were created to live in connection with others so that we would have to think about someone else for a change—to give and serve and love others. It's part of going on with life while you're waiting, instead of being paralyzed until you get an answer.

A CASE STUDY IN WAITING ... OF SORTS

Will and Debbie (actual names) are some friends of mine. They met in college and dated for a while, but as in many relationships, they reached the fish-or-cut-bait point and were not sure of which way to go. So they decided to break up for a time and wait—wait to see what God told them.

During this time, Debbie, of course, did what any woman would do. She obsessed. She analyzed, discussed, journaled, prayed, processed, and rode the emotional roller coaster.

Will, on the other hand, did nothing. He went on with life as usual—just without Debbie.

A few weeks later they got together for dinner, and Debbie finally worked up the nerve to ask, "So ... what are we, exactly?"

Will, mouth full of food, replied, "Nothin'."

Fortunately for him, a proposal covers a multitude of sins. Within a few days, he asked her to marry him.

It's hard to say who waited better or worse; they both did some things right and some things wrong. Certainly, in a period of waiting, there is a need to pursue knowing and understanding God's plan, as Debbie did. To be proactive. But it's also a good idea to continue moving ahead in life until you're directed otherwise, as Will did. But never—no, never—reply to a question like "What are we?" with "Nothin'." Even if you are nothing, make up something—a better way to say it.

AND LASTLY ...

This has probably not been the most encouraging article. I've had to hit you with several hard truths. Here's one more. Waiting is not an I've-got-that-down-so-let's-move-on sort of thing. As I have already said, waiting is a theme of God's kingdom. After you do see what you have been waiting for come to fruition, you will quickly find that something else will emerge in its place and you will once again be waiting—living day to day, hand to mouth on God, waiting for Him to provide and deliver. So... good luck with that.

[1] Philippians 4:11 -13

Conflicts of Interest

So I've been meeting with my friend Sabine (if I've got to use a fake name, I'm at least going to make it interesting). She's about your age. She grew up in church and knows all the Sunday school answers. But now she's decided that she's not sure if what she's been taught is true. She needs to figure it out for herself. So she's figuring it out with her boyfriend … Polaris, we'll call him. (That actually was the name of a guy who waited on me the other day.) Anyway, I'm all for her figuring it out and developing convictions and beliefs of her own. That's part of becoming an adult.

But part of Sabine's "figuring it out" involves sleeping with Polaris. Granted, this is not the first boyfriend she's slept with. But she does recognize the unhealthy consequences of her past relationships and will be quick to say that they were all an effort to fill a void that God should probably be filling. But of course, Polaris is different. This time she feels like she's separating herself from the guilt-evoking voices of her parents, pastors, and friends in the past, and she feels pretty good

about it. She's happy. This is different from any other relationship she's ever had, and she's pretty sure she's going to marry him. They've been dating three months. She turns twenty-two this Wednesday.

I'm sipping my mango chai latte and thinking, *For Pete's sake, I'm writing a book about this very stuff; I should I have something to say.* I don't, really. Nothing's coming to me. Nada. Zip. So I start asking questions.

"If you audibly heard from God and He said, 'Sabine, God here. Stop it.' Would you?"

She said she'd like to think she would. She loves God and everything. But then again, she admits to being stubborn.

I said, "Really, don't you mean 'rebellious' more than 'stubborn'? That would be a little closer to the truth." (I did laugh a little to soften the blow.)

A hesitant nod.

"So, basically, you're waiting for an experience or a feeling that is not guilt, but rather is conviction?"

"Exactly."

"Seeing God's word written out in Scripture is not convicting for you?"

"Not so much."

"Because?"

"I'm not sure what I think about the Bible."

"So, what you're saying is you want an experience that you know without a doubt is God telling you this is wrong—apart from the Bible?"

"Yep."

"Is this sex you're having so good that you are now questioning the whole Bible?"

"Mmm … not totally, but sort of."

"So, what do you expect conviction to be like?"

"I don't know. You tell me."

"Let me think about it and get back to you."

I'm wagering I could have this same conversation with at least half of you who are reading this right now. You trust your experiences and what feels right over just about anything else. So there are all sorts of things to think about here. I'll go ahead and admit, too, that I don't really expect anything I say to change Sabine's actions. Polaris is too tangible and comfortable and fun. And like she says, it's not so much the sex; it's the fun of waking up every morning with him. "It's like a fun surprise every day."

"So, really, it's the security of him?" I said.

"You could say that."

As I told her, I'm not so worried about her sleeping with him as I'm worried about her heart toward God.

GUILT VS. CONVICTION

Let's start here. How do you know the difference between your momma's voice and the Holy Spirit's? Could they ever be the same? Here's my verbal processing about that.

Voices/impressions/thoughts in your head—they're hard to sort out sometimes. Was that God or was that something I ate?

One of the roles of the Holy Spirit in your life is to convict you of sin. *Oh, joy.* Actually, it is a pretty good thing in the long run, though not always fun in the moment. If you've made a decision to follow

Christ, then you've got your own built-in alarm. God is not going to let you get away with much. Unfortunately, we all too quickly learn to use the snooze button. We'll "deal with it later" or we'll "stop next time."

Sometimes we confess our sin, but we still feel a nagging sense that all is not right. If we're still feeling guilty, that's when we might want to get suspicious.

If conviction is from God, guilt is diabolical. It's from the devil even if it is disguised in the voice of your mother or your preacher or your Sunday school teacher. (Before I have your momma calling me, let me say that the Holy Spirit can use those voices as well.)

Guilt: Its intent is to make you believe that you're a failure and all bad all the time—you are a bad, bad person.
Conviction: It's specific. When you did X, that was wrong. And often (especially when you ask Him to) God gives you a specific action point—a way to confess to others, repent, or make restitution.

Guilt: brings feelings of shame, disgust, and hopelessness.
Conviction: feeling of deep sorrow, yet also a sense of hope for change.

Guilt: driven by regret for personal consequences
Conviction: driven by remorse for an affront against God's holiness

Guilt: You feel like you've really messed up, so you don't want to go anywhere near God.
Conviction: You sense the power of God's holiness and your need to stay connected to Him so that you don't mess up again.

Both the devil and the Holy Spirit can put thoughts in my head, remind me of things people have said, or bring people into my life to speak lies or truth. However, there are some surefire things I know are of God. The Spirit clearly uses the power of Scripture to convict. Reminding me of verses, or as I read and study, often He brings areas to mind that I need to deal with. Also, He can use a recurring theme that keeps popping up in my thoughts, almost like a nagging e-mail reminder or a song I can't get rid of. That's usually how I know it's the Spirit—when it doesn't go away. I can't get away from dealing with it, making a choice, or acting on my repentance.

Most recently, it was an apology for a sarcastic e-mail I'd sent. Probably two or three times a week, I'd think about needing to apologize. But then I would think, *I'll do it later.* Finally he e-mailed me about something different (the guy I'd e-mailed, not the Holy Spirit). I replied, asking forgiveness, and he was very positive in return. To be honest, I think he's probably not a believer, and that e-mail may have made a difference in whether he stays at our church. There are so much more important things than my pride.

I think the best biblical example is in 2 Corinthians 7. God obviously used Paul's previous letter to convict his friends in Corinth. Paul basically says he is sorry that his letter upset them, but not really, because it brought them to repentance.

> Godly sorrow [conviction] brings repentance that leads to salvation ["salvation" can also mean "rescue" or "deliverance from sin," referring more to spiritual growth] and leaves no regret, but worldly sorrow [guilt] brings death. See what this godly sorrow has produced in you: what earnestness, what eagerness to clear yourselves, what indignation, what alarm, what longing, what concern, what readiness to see justice done. At every point you have proved yourselves to be innocent in this matter. (2 Corinthians 7:10-11, NIV)

As you can see …

Guilt: leads to depression, more sin, death.

Conviction: leads to a desire to make things right between you and God and all parties involved.

Then there's the situation where you feel nothing at all. That's probably what my friend Sabine would say about herself right now. All she feels is the lovin' from Polaris. You know, I think that kind of situation happens when you're not really willing to change. You hear what you want to hear. Repentance means turning from it, letting go of it. When we're not willing to repent, that's the beginning of a hard heart. The harder the heart, the less sensitive it is to conviction. The longer you refuse to deal with it, the easier it is to turn off the alarm. However, not so with guilt. It becomes much easier to warp your thoughts and lay it on thick.

Turns out, I had more to say about that than I thought.

HEAD VS. HEART
One of my past eighteen roommates was a basketball coach. (She would require that I say here, in exchange for printing this story, that she was one of my favorite roommates, if not my *most* favorite roommate of all time.) She spent one summer working at an inner-city Christian sports camp and had the privilege of doing the sex talk with the middle school girls. She was wrapping it

up with a poignant rhetorical question: "So, why then, ladies, if you know what kissing leads to, would you want to defraud your brothers in Christ that way?"

Before the room could appreciate the dramatic pause to reflect on that thought, a precious sixth grader in the front row shot her hand straight up, much like the ponytail sticking straight up on top of her head. Not waiting to be called on, she blurted out her response: " 'Cause, Coach Harris, sometimes you've got to have some of that sugar, 'cause that sugar is good!"

The room immediately erupted into "No, she didn't! No, she didn't! You've got to kick her out of here!" And the talk was over.

The sixth grader was on to something. That sugar is good, and bottom line, sometimes, in spite of everything we know, after having read all the Bible verses and worked through all the workbooks, we've still got to have some of that sugar.

I am just like the rest of you. Sometimes I just want what I want. Today is actually one of those days. I am under an intense deadline to finish this book *and* am having some intense PMS. In a few minutes I *will* be having some homemade peanut butter cups, because *that* sugar is good, too.

Premeditated sin. Okay, I don't know if it's sin, but it is over my caloric allotment for the day. (Look at me—trying to justify already.)

Anyway, here's what I'm getting at. We are emotional beings, and most of the time, if we're not allowing the Holy Spirit to guide us, we're being led by those emotions. Pretty much, in any given day, I do what I feel like doing. Now, granted, there is truth that shapes and directs those feelings, so it generally works out fine. However, what if what I *feel* like doing is contrary to what I *know* to be true, as in the case of Sabine? Her feelings are causing her to question everything she knows to be true—or at least thought was true. It gets messy.

This makes me think of the difference between King Saul and King David—fascinating story in the books of Samuel. Do read it on your own. But here's the greatly abridged version.

God chose Saul to be king and blessed him, but right off the bat, Saul only halfway obeyed God's command to wipe out every living thing among the Amalekites. Saul *felt* that was a bit extreme and *felt* there would probably be no problem with keeping some of the best oxen, sheep, and so on for himself. That was just the beginning of a pattern of selfish decisions followed by feigned repentance

out of fear of consequences. He was driven by an emotional heart, mostly jealousy and pride.

David, on the other hand, even when Saul was trying to kill him, chose to act out of faith—what he knew to be true—rather than anger. When he had the opportunity to kill Saul while he was somewhat indisposed (that is, going number one in a cave, or maybe number two—we don't really know). He knew that Saul was anointed king by God, though he was a poor one, so he spared his life.

Saul's consequence was the loss of the kingdom and death upon his own sword, with (ironically) an Amalekite to finish the job for him. David, on the other hand, was a man after God's own heart, and his kingdom was blessed. Jesus came from the line of David.

Someone once said there are only eighteen inches from your head to heart, but it may take years to travel the distance. To experience in your heart what you know to be true in your head is often a long road. My own addendum to that bit o' wisdom is this: going the other direction—getting your emotions to shape what's in your head—is a very short jaunt.

Emotions are certainly not all bad. We are created in God's image, emotions included. The danger

comes when we allow our emotions to rule our head. When the two are in conflict, I almost always put my money on the head.

It seems like a long jump from King David to getting some of that sugar. But really, both situations boil down to taking God at His word over what I feel in this moment.

I'm not saying we should set aside our emotions and discount their value. I think we need to enter into those emotions with the Lord. Be honest with Him. He understands and shares in our emotions. Sometimes our emotions are valid and based in genuine loss or grief or pain. Other times they're based on things that are not true—lies we've believed or warped thinking. Sometimes our emotions are based in our sinful desires—pride, selfishness, and so forth. Those are things you have to work through with the Lord, offering Him your heart for change.

My friend Margaret likes to say that all wise counsel comes back to Genesis 4:7. That's where God says to Cain, "If you do well, will not your countenance be lifted up? And if you do not do well, sin is crouching at the door" (NASB). Basically, if you act in faith and do the right thing, then you'll feel well and good. We want it to be the other way around: we want to feel good so that we'll be motivated to do good. It doesn't work that way so much. When you don't do well, sin awaits—you become trapped in a cycle. Like Saul, you are controlled by your emotions. All of this is closely tied to our next conflict …

TRUTH VS. LIES

Imagine what it was like to find out that the earth is not flat. Your whole life, you've lived in fear of one day taking a different way home from work and maybe taking a misstep in the dark, and lo and behold, you've done it—you've fallen off the edge into the abyss. What freedom to discover the truth. It's round! You can't fall off! And think of the ramifications. Okay, so maybe it didn't change the life of the workaday peasantry, but for the scientists and astrologers and wise men and such, it changed everything. A paradigm shift if ever there was one. It changed all the maps. It changed … well, their travel plans. It changed … some kind of math formulas … probably. … I'm sure it changed a bunch of stuff.

They didn't necessarily choose to believe the earth was flat—they didn't know there was an option. It's what they had been told. Sometimes I think there are lies like that, things we've just believed our whole lives, consciously or subconsciously—things we don't know to question. Like the fact that we landed on the moon in 1969. We've been told our

whole lives that we landed on the moon, but what if we really didn't? Then we would have to question everything else our government tells us. And maybe the moon really is made of cheese. And maybe … the food pyramid has been a lie all along. And maybe … Anyway, some lies are like that—so ingrained in our grid of reality that we don't recognize them. When we do, it makes us question and adjust all our beliefs, e.g. as "My value is based on my performance and/or my appearance" or "Men are not trustworthy."

Then there are some lies that sound true, and they are mostly true (about 90 percent), but they're just warped enough to mess things up. That's really Satan's best ploy. To take the truth and twist it just enough—just enough to tempt Eve to take a bite. He promised that, if she'd eat the forbidden fruit, her eyes would be opened and she'd be like God. She would know good and evil. (Genesis 3:5) There's some truth in that. Here eyes were opened and she did for the first time understand the difference between good and evil, and she was like God in that way. But she was not really like God at all. She was now susceptible to evil—just as Satan had planned.

The problem with lies is that we unwittingly make decisions and choices based on them, then take action in light of them, and the consequences can

be detrimental. What if the real lie were that the earth is round and then you didn't know to be careful and then one day you did take that misstep because you didn't know and … anyway. It's late.

Nancy Leigh DeMoss has written a book called *Lies Women Believe*.[1] Below is an excerpt of ten or so of the lies that I think women at your age in particular struggle with, followed by the truth.

Ten (or So) Lies Women Believe

For many women, there is a disconnect between what they know intellectually and what they feel to be true. And therein lies one of our problems: we trust what we *feel* to be true rather than what we *know* to be true.

1. God Doesn't Love Me

We look at our difficult circumstances and our feelings tell us, "Nobody loves me, not even God. He may love the world; He may love everyone else; but He really doesn't love me. If He did, I would not feel so lonely and unloved." We'd never say this aloud, but that is what we *feel* to be true. So the seed of a lie is planted in our minds. We dwell on the lie until we believe it to be true. Sooner or later, our behavior reflects what we truly believe, and we end up in bondage.

Truth: (Romans 8:32, 38 -39)
• God's love for me is infinite and unconditional.
• I don't have to perform to earn God's love or favor.
• God always has my best interests at heart.

2. God Should Fix My Problems

This way of thinking is deceptive on two counts. First, it reduces God to a cosmic genie who exists to please and serve us. This sets us up for disillusionment and disappointment with God. Second, it suggests that the goal in life is to be problem free—to get rid of everything that is difficult or unpleasant.

Truth: (Isaiah 46:10, Hebrews 5: 8)
• Life is hard.
• God is more concerned about glorifying Himself and changing me than about solving all my problems.
• God has an eternal purpose He is fulfilling in the midst of my problems.
• God wants to use my problems as part of His sanctifying process in my life.
• No matter what problem I am facing, God's grace is sufficient for me.

3. I Can't Help the Way I Am

This lie makes us into helpless victims of other people and outside circumstances. The suggestion is that someone or something else is responsible for who we are—that we have no more control over who we are and what we do than a marionette does. We somehow believe that we are destined to be controlled by whomever and whatever is pulling our strings. This lie leaves us without hope that we can ever be different.

Truth: (Romans 6:6-7, 1 Thessalonians 5:24)
• If I am a child of God, I can choose to obey God.
• I am responsible for my own choices.
• I can be changed through the power of God's Spirit.

4. I Should Not Have to Live with Unfulfilled Longings

We are encouraged to identify our longings and do whatever is necessary to get those "needs" met. Therefore, if you're hungry, eat. If you want something you can't afford, charge it. If you crave romance, dress or act in a way that will get men to notice you. If you're lonely, share your heart with a married man at work. At best, this way of thinking has left many women still unfulfilled, still groping, still searching for something to fill the inner emptiness.

Truth: (Luke 1:38, 1 Peter 5:7)
• I will always have unfulfilled longings this side of heaven.
• The deepest longings of my heart cannot be filled by any created person or thing.
• If I will accept them, unfulfilled longings will increase my longing for God and for heaven.

5. I Can Sin and Get Away with It

The enemy causes us to believe the following:
• "There will be no judgment on my sin."
• "I won't reap what I sow."
• "The choices I make today will not have consequences."
• "I can play with fire and not get burned."

Truth: (Galatians 6:7-8, Ezekiel 18:19-22)
• The choices I make today will have consequences; I will reap what I sow.
• Sin's pleasures last only for a season.
• Sin exacts a devastating toll. There are no exceptions.
• If I play with fire, I will get burned. I will not escape the consequences of my sin.

6. I Can Make It without Consistent Time in the Word and in Prayer

The essence of Satan's deception is that we can live our lives independently of God. The enemy doesn't care if we "believe" in God, if we are doctrinally orthodox, or if we fill our schedules with a lot of "spiritual activities," as long as he can get us to run on our own steam rather than living in conscious dependence upon the power of the Holy Spirit.

Truth: (Psalm 19:7,107:20,119:105)
• It is impossible for me to be the woman God wants me to be apart from spending consistent time cultivating a relationship with Him in the Word and prayer.

7. I Have to Have a Husband to Be Happy

Marriage is good and right, and it is God's plan for most people. There can be (and ought to be) great joy and blessing in the context of a God-centered marriage. However, Satan twists the truth about marriage by suggesting to women that the purpose of marriage is personal happiness and fulfillment, and they cannot be truly happy without a husband to love and meet their needs.

Truth: (Hebrews 13:5; Psalm 23:1)
• Happiness is not found in (or out of) marriage.
• There is no person who can meet my deepest needs. No one and nothing can make me truly happy apart from God.

• God has promised to provide everything I need. If He will receive more glory by my being married, then He will provide a husband for me.
• Those who wait on the Lord always get His best. Those who insist on getting what they want often end up with heartache.

8. If I Feel Something, It Must Be True

The enemy wants us to believe that if we *feel* unloved, we are unloved. If we *feel* we can't cope with the pressure, it must be true that we can't make it. If we *feel* God has deserted us or that He has acted unjustly in a manner that concerns us, then perhaps He has let us down. If we *feel* our situation is hopeless, then there must be no hope. If we don't *feel* saved, then maybe we aren't. If we don't *feel* forgiven, then we must not be.

The truth is that, due to our fallen condition, our feelings often have little to do with reality.

Truth: (Philippians 4:4, 6-9)
• My feelings cannot always be trusted. They often have little to do with reality and can easily deceive me into believing things that are not true.
• I must choose to reject any feelings that are not consistent with the Truth.

9. If My Circumstances Were Different, I Would Be Different

We are saying, "Someone or something made me the way I am." We feel that if our circumstance were different—our upbringing, our environment, the people around us—we would be different. If our circumstances make us what we are, then we are all victims. Because if we're victims, then we're not responsible—we can't help the way we are. But God says we are responsible, not for the failures of others, but for our own responses and lives.

Truth: (Philippians 4: 11-12)
• My circumstances do not make me what I am; they merely reveal what I am.
• If I am not content with my circumstances, I am not likely to be happy in any other set of circumstances.
• I may not be able to control my circumstances, but my circumstances do not have to control me.
• Every circumstance that touches my life has first been filtered through His fingers of love.

10. I Shouldn't Have to Suffer

Many modern-day evangelistic efforts have promised sinners unending peace and joy, a home in heaven, and a prosperous life in between here and there if they will simply come to Jesus. By convincing us that our sufferings are undeserved or unnecessary, the enemy succeeds in getting us to resent and resist the will and purposes of God.

Truth: (1 Peter 5:10, 2 Corinthians 4:17-18)
• It is impossible to be holy apart from suffering. There is a redemptive fruit that cannot be produced in our lives apart from suffering.
• We have been called to suffer.
• True joy is not the absence of pain but the presence of the Lord Jesus in the midst of the pain.
• Suffering is a pathway to sanctification, a doorway into greater intimacy with God.

11. It's All About Me

In spite of all the talk about poor self-image, our instinctive reaction to life is self-centered: How does this affect me? Will this make me happy? Why did this have to happen to me? What does she think about me? It's my turn. I need my space. It's not enough for us to be the center of our own universe. We want to be the center of everyone else's universe as well, including God's.

Truth: (Colossians 1:16-18, Revelation 4:11)
• God is the beginning and ending and center of all things. All things were created by Him and for Him. It's all about Him.
• My life is dispensable. I was created for His pleasure and glory.

I can almost guarantee that several things on this list are as ingrained in you every bit as much as the belief that the earth is round. But now that you've seen it on a list, it should be gone by the morning. A first step is always awareness. I would encourage you, as you locate something on the list, to pray about it and to journal some thoughts about it as well as about the ways it has shaped your life. As you become more aware of it in your day-to-day life, you can begin to weed it out. You can refuse to take actions predicated on the belief, and then your life will begin to align more with the truth, which backwashes into your thought processes and eventually reaches the emotional level.

Okay, so that's a lot to take in, admittedly. You could camp out there for the next week or two and look at each one of those individually. Not a bad idea, really.

UNRESOLVED CONFLICTS

So, back to my friend Sabine and the fabulous Polaris. I'll meet with her again next week, once I get this book to print. At least now I have some thoughts down on paper to discuss with her, some more questions to ask. My fear is that she will have to learn like most of us do—by experiencing the consequences of her own choices. She'll have to *feel* it to believe it. God does work that way sometimes, through our emotions, but it's usually a much harder path. She may not *feel* the consequences for a while, maybe not even for a long while, except maybe for the hardening of her heart toward God. Which is really the most serious consequence of all.

[1] *Lies Women Believe*, Nancy Leigh DeMoss (Moody; 2001)

The greatest danger could be your stupidity.

A nice cake waits for you.

A lifetime isn't long enough to figure out what it's all about.

Because of your melodic nature, the moonlight never misses an appointment

He who knows he has enough is rich

Clash of Doctrine is not a disaster. It's an opportunity

The greatest dan... your stupid...

Good to begin well. Better to end well

A lifetime isn't long enough to figure out what it's all about

✳ with God.

Spirit Filled
By Rick James

Pretty much everything about living the Christian life comes back to this one basic concept. This is the secret decoder ring that all too often is never passed on as a person begins their relationship with God and they end up living years of frustration trying to figure out how to really walk with God. The Bible is pretty clear in saying that the key to experiencing the Christian life as he intends is the filling, or empowering, of the Spirit of God. This is often referred to as living a "Spirit-filled life." If you have this sort of life, the Spirit indwells you and works in you "to will and to act" in accordance with God's will.

You have not been left on planet earth as an orphan to carry out the Christian life on your own initiative and by your own determination. The Holy Spirit separates the Christian life from frustrating self-effort and discipline—*Make good choices! Do the right thing! Just say no! Follow the commandments, and when you're done with that, take out the garbage!* The Spirit partners with you by motivating you to follow after Christ, and through a variety of means, He aids your choices.

Though you may be a disciplined person, living a life that is honoring to God is an impossibility apart from the Spirit, and therefore there can be nothing more relevant to the topic of purity than understanding the Spirit-filled life.

Ephesians 5:18 says, "Do not get drunk on wine, which leads to debauchery. Instead, be filled with the Spirit" (NIV). This is a commonly quoted verse in connection with the Spirit-filled life. But one is compelled to ask, what does getting drunk on wine have to do with being filled with the Spirit? Couldn't Paul just as easily have said, "Don't have the breakfast burrito at McDonald's, which leads to gas. Instead, be filled with the Spirit"? The link between drinking alcohol and being filled with the Holy Spirit seems to be the idea of control or influence. On this account, alcoholic spirits and the Holy Spirit are similar. (They are quite different in a lot of other ways, of course. The control exerted by alcohol can be considered a counterfeit of the control of the Spirit.)

Because the manner by which the Holy Spirit influences us is somewhat mysterious (or at least is not easily measurable), the metaphor of drinking alcohol might offer us a back door into a better understanding of how the Holy Spirit works in our lives.

WHAT IT LOOKS LIKE TO BE FILLED WITH THE SPIRIT

Interestingly, Ephesians 5 is not the only place in Scripture that puts drinking and the Spirit side by side. Acts 2 contains the story of the Holy Spirit's first descent upon the church. As onlookers witness the effects of the Spirit upon the believers in the crowd, they become convinced that the Christians are drunk. Peter stands up and explains, "These men are not drunk, as you suppose" (Acts 2:15).

So, what is it about being filled with the Spirit that would cause people to suspect that a keg party was underway? One manifestation would be the open display of love. Have you ever known someone under the influence of alcohol to say, in slurred speech, "I luf yooouuuu"? Actually, that's not so bad. It's the intoxicated "Will you marry me?" that you've got to watch out for. I haven't done a statistical analysis, but I'm betting few of these alcohol-induced marriages make it to their diamond anniversary. What we've all witnessed is that those intoxicated are much freer with their emotions and affections. Alcohol removes inhibitions. Likewise, a hallmark of the Holy Spirit's work in our lives is a greater capacity to love, demonstrated in both words and actions.

In addition, people turn to alcohol for comfort in difficult times. Country-and-western songs abound with laments about the difficulties of life: Mama's in prison; the bank owns the pickup; the dog had to be shot; and Jessica Simpson's boots were made for walking. These songs all seem to encourage finding solace in going to the local tavern, in drinking multiple alcoholic beverages, and in setting sail with Captain Morgan, because everyone knows that alcohol helps you cope with life's unpleasantries. In contrast, the Holy Spirit is referred to in Scripture as the "Great Comforter." (John 14:26) Life is hard, and the Holy Spirit promises comfort and the ability to live above life's circumstances.

Those who have been drinking alcohol also exhibit great boldness. They are liable to say anything to anyone for any reason. Similarly, after the Holy Spirit comes upon the disciples, we see the once shy and timid band of followers boldly proclaiming the good news of the gospel to anyone who will listen. When called before the religious leaders and ordered to stop, they proclaim, "We cannot help speaking about what we have seen and heard" (Acts 4:20). These men have been transformed by the influence of the Spirit, so they can't keep their mouths shut about Christ and the gospel.

It should now be clearer to you why onlookers thought the disciples were drunk at Pentecost. Besides the ones I have mentioned, there are other comparisons we could make between the influence of alcohol and the influence of the Spirit, but you get the picture. And while alcohol is a good example of an unhealthy influence affecting our wills and behavior, similar effects can be noted in states of rage, lust, or greed. Yet through all of these examples, we get a better idea of what it means to have a foreign influence affect our thoughts, feelings, and behavior while not eclipsing our individual personality.

THE CONTRAST

While in some ways the example of alcohol helps us to better understand the influence or empowerment by the Holy Spirit, we must also see that alcohol is a cheap counterfeit (or an expensive counterfeit, depending on the brand). What people are really thirsting for is the presence of God. Alcohol-induced states create the temporary illusion of a reality that only the Spirit can produce in our lives.

In fact, alcohol's control—as well as that of rage, lust, or greed—tends to be coercive, and it usually means a loss of our own will and control. In Matthew 20:25-26, Jesus says, "You know that the rulers of the Gentiles lord it over them. ... Not so with you." Jesus is telling the disciples that their leadership and influence should come through loving encouragement, not through coercion and domination, for such is the Spirit's influence. When we choose to listen to Him and desire to be directed by Him, the Holy Spirit leads and influences. But our desire and openness to being led are important to God and are essential for experiencing the Spirit's power.

HOW CAN WE BE MORE UNDER THE INFLUENCE OF THE HOLY SPIRIT?

Just as there are differing degrees of intoxication by alcohol, so there are differing degrees by which a person can be controlled or influenced by the Holy Spirit. Let's consider five things we can do to improve our sensitivity to the Spirit's leading and make His presence more acute in our lives.

1. Complete submission to the will of God.

How does one become more drunk (I confess that initially I wrote "drunkerer")? The answer, of course, is that one consumes more alcohol. But in the case of the Holy Spirit, we have all of Him that we will ever have. What determines how much influence the Spirit has in our lives is how much of us we let Him consume—we can't have more of Him, but He can have more of us. To put it more practically, how much of our lives are we willing to allow Him to control? Do we desire to live for His will above our own in every area of our life (dating, vocation, relationships, and so on)?

Sometimes the reason for withholding areas of our lives from God is fear. Romans 12:2 says that when we covenant with God to live entirely for His will and not our own, we will be able to know what God's will is—"his good, pleasing and perfect will." It is quite possible that this verse emphasizes "good, pleasing and perfect" to alleviate our fear. It reassures us that God's will in every area is always perfect, always motivated by His love, and always in our best interest. As one Christian put it, "There's no safer place than the center of God's will."

This decision to submit to the Lord is both critical and progressive. It is progressive in the sense that we are always becoming aware of areas into which we have never brought God or submitted to Him. It is critical in the sense that there are crucial junctures in our Christian lives where we tell God from our hearts, "I will do anything or go anywhere You want; my life is Yours." According to Romans 12:2, we will enjoy His full empowerment, direction, and influence only once we come to this point of submission.

When we see people who have been Christians for twenty years exhibiting little life change, it is often because they've allowed the Spirit only "sips" of their lives. In contrast, we may meet others who are relatively new as Christians but whose lives have been radically transformed. They have allowed the Holy Spirit to consume every area of their lives, withholding nothing, and so have changed lives to show for it.

2. Confession. Sin is choosing to go our own way, rather than God's way, in an attempt to satisfy our needs, wants, and desires. When we sin, we take control of our lives away from the Holy Spirit and turn it over to our sinful desires. When we've sinned, we need to confess it to God. *Confession* literally means to "agree with God." We agree that we have sinned (not rationalizing or justifying our actions). We agree that Christ's death has paid the price for our sin, enabling us to be forgiven. We repent—we turn back to God and agree to do things His way.

How do we maintain the Spirit's maximum influence in our lives? We keep short accounts of sin. As soon as the Spirit brings awareness of sin to our minds, we confess it immediately.

3. Reliance. Have you ever watched cigarette smokers? Every time they sense a need in their lives, they light up. If they feel lonely, they light up. If they feel scared or nervous, they light up. If they need confidence, they light up. I find myself doing the same thing with food, music, and coffee. Did you ever eat when you weren't hungry? You realize later that you were relying on food to fill your loneliness. Throughout each day, we sense the need for empowerment. Whether we're eaters, coffee drinkers, or smokers, all of us have this reflex. When these needs—or "thirsts"—arise,

God wants us to reflexively turn to Him and ask for comfort, empowerment, wisdom, and direction: "Oh, God, please give me wisdom," "Oh, God, please strengthen me," and so on.

Perhaps you're one of the many who carry a water bottle with you wherever you go, fearful that at any moment dehydration will set in and your parched and cracking lips will need a swig of the life-saving elixir of glacier water, green tea, and honey. (Why not just be escorted by one of those Saint Bernards with the barrel under its collar rather than court disaster?) Anyway, the water-bottle phenomenon is a good picture of a life reliant upon the Spirit, all day long taking sips of "living water" (John 7:38) to meet our many thirsts that arise throughout the day.

4. Cultivating our hearts toward God. In Ephesians 5:19-20, Paul talks about singing spiritual songs and hymns and having a thankful heart. The important lesson here, as it relates to maximizing the Holy Spirit's influence over us, is that we can foster an environment in our hearts that facilitates the control of the Holy Spirit. Just as going to the mall might foster materialism's control, so activities such as thanksgiving, praise, singing, and prayer enhance the Spirit's influence in our hearts and mind. As we sing spiritual songs and fill our hearts with thanksgiving throughout the day, we find ourselves more in tune with the Holy Spirit's presence and direction.

5. Community. In community with other Christians we experience a dynamic of the Spirit-filled life that we can never experience alone, because there we encounter the Spirit who indwells others. We are empowered to live the Christian life as we receive encouragement, acceptance, and teaching from others. We find fresh life when we share our sins and struggles. We are blessed as we pray together and minister to one another. The Christian life was never meant to be lived independent of the Spirit-empowered ministry of the body of Christ.

A PARADIGM OF INFLUENCE

We have looked at alcohol as a biblical teaching aid for understanding the idea of a foreign influence at work in our lives. Alcohol differs in some significant ways from the Spirit, but it is nonetheless helpful to us in understanding the concept of influence. Therefore, we shouldn't think of the Holy Spirit as being like a light switch (either on or off) but instead as being an influence that we can cultivate, maximizing the Spirit's control in our lives.

All Worship
By Rick James

Worship is one of those words, like the word *holy*, that we kind of understand but would be hard-pressed to define. And the problem with words we can't define is that their meaning can shift without our even noticing. Such is the case with *worship*. It has come to be synonymous with singing and praise music, even though those aspects of worship really only hint at the word's full meaning.

Worship means "saturation." Being saturated with the presence of God, we overflow back to God (in praise, service, thanksgiving, singing, and so on), and in turn, He refills us. Us pouring ourselves into God and Him pouring Himself back into us—this cycle is worship. Our souls have been designed by God to carry on this function.

Because it's a part of our design, everyone worships. Everyone lives to be saturated.

Picture a sponge with all of those empty pockets and caverns. This is the anatomy of our soul, created for wringing and absorbing (worship). But apart from God, like a fish flapping for oxygen on dry land, we are desperate for saturation. Therefore, everyone finds something to worship. The drunk saturates himself with alcohol. The greedy person looks to money. The workaholic buries herself in activity. The worrywart becomes saturated with worry, and the lustful, with lust.

Why do people fill themselves with these toxins? Because the only thing worse than being a sponge saturated with fear, worry, greed, activity, lust, or alcohol is being an empty sponge. No one can long endure the pain of feeling empty, so we all saturate ourselves with something. Then that which saturates us oozes back out of us, making room for more of the same. Unfortunately, even though whatever we choose to saturate ourselves with momentarily feels good, if it's not God, it becomes the very thing that kills our souls. It's like drinking saltwater: a momentary quenching of the thirst is followed by dehydration and even greater thirst.

When we become Christians, it's not that we *begin* to worship; it's that we restore worship to its original design. We reboot our lives with the process of being saturated with God.

Worship is critical to the topics of lust and relationships because both are primary forms of false saturation (read: worship). True worship is their corrective. And when the Bible speaks of worship, the following three elements are in view.

REPENTANCE AND HUMBLING

I'm non-hygienic. My toenails are long. I shave once a week and seldom clean my hands after going to the bathroom unless there are sufficient people in the restroom to create shame. So it will come as no surprise that I will not hesitate to use a dirty sponge for cleaning.

My wife, on the other hand, was horrified one time to see me using the same sponge to clean the dishes that I had used to wipe the mayonnaise off the kitchen floor. To make her point, she asked me to wring out the sponge in the sink. As I did, out came the most vile, putrid flow of bubonic-plague fluid I've ever seen. Point made.

The first component of worship is this wringing out of our souls toward God. We drain the bile and create a vacuum to be filled with God's Spirit. We pour out our sin in humility and repentance; God fills us with His grace, mercy, and love.

I think that most people understand how the first part of this cycle works. We have all at times confessed, repented, and humbled ourselves before God. What is often missed is the way we are resaturated. Look at this passage:

> Why does the wicked man revile God?
> Why does he say to himself,
> "He won't call me to account"?
> But you, O God, do see trouble and grief;
> you consider it to take it in hand.
> The victim commits himself to you;
> you are the helper of the fatherless. (Psalm 10:13-14, NIV)

Do you see that glorious "But ..."? That is the refill mechanism. But You, O God, are good, are kind, act completely out of love ...

"But" is the great refrain of the Psalms. We vomit out our sin, the lies we have believed, and our self-centeredness, and we pivot on the word "but" before flooding our minds and souls with the truth about God—who He is and what He has done. Watch the dynamic as David humbles himself:

> What is man that you are mindful of him,
> the son of man that you care for him?
> You made him a little lower than the heavenly beings
> and crowned him with glory and honor.
> You made him ruler over the works of your hands;
> you put everything under his feet. ...
> O LORD, our Lord,
> how majestic is your name in all the earth!
> (Psalm 8:4-6, 9)

Do you see the emptying (squeezing out), followed by the drinking in with the phrase "O Lord, our Lord, how majestic is your name in all the earth"? This is the complete rinse cycle. This is worship—pouring yourself out to God and filling yourself with truth (God).

THANKSGIVING AND PRAISE

Ephesians 5:19-20 says, "Sing and make music in your heart to the Lord, always giving thanks to God the Father for everything, in the name of our Lord Jesus Christ." The next aspect of worship, then, is praise and thanksgiving.

It works something like this: You're feeling like a dry sponge, but in faith, you squeeze out a few drops of thanksgiving toward God. You thank Him for the things He's doing in your life. It's a little sandy at first, a little parched and dry: "Thanks, God. Thanks ... thanks that I have a head and my feet are shod with shoes. Thanks that You, in Your benevolence, gave me hair and digits on my hand."

But you stay with it. All of sudden, you begin to notice your sponge starting to fill. There's more meaning in your words. The sphere of your thanksgiving begins to widen. The more you give thanks, through His empowerment and presence, the more thankful you become. You find yourself worshiping!

At first it's like priming a pump. But as you stay with it, the flow begins, first in spurts and then as a continuous stream. In fact, once the saturation cycle gets flowing, you could actually thank God for your head and mean it.

The same dynamic is true of praise. You begin in a rather boring way: "God, You are so sovereignly, benevolently omnipotent." But then you say something a little different, like "God, You're really smart." That's when your mind and soul begin to engage. "Yeah, You *are* smart—a genius, in fact!" The pump starts flowing and you find yourself praising Him for anything and everything. You are overflowing to Him and, concurrently, He's flowing into you. You are having a thankfest. You are worshipping.

When you begin your day like this, then with little effort and at any time, you can dive right back into that flow of worship. Often the pump needs only one priming, leaving you with flowing water for the entire day.

Here's something else you'll find: when your heart is engaged in true worship, it's more immune than before to the gods of false worship. Lust loses its gravitational pull, or as Elrond says of Frodo in *The Lord of the Rings*: "The hobbit shows unusual resilience to its [the ring's] evil." As you worship, there isn't the same craving for relationships and attention; you don't feel as needy. While empty sponges are drawn to any puddle, saturated sponges are not.

SERVICE

Last, we pour ourselves out in service. Here, as we are saturated with God, we overflow into the porous lives of others. Look at the following verses:

Even if I am being poured out like a drink offering on the sacrifice and service coming from your faith, I am glad and rejoice with all of you. (Philippians 2:17)

Brothers, we want you to know about the grace that God has given the Macedonian churches. Out of the most severe trial, their overflowing joy and their extreme poverty welled up in rich generosity. (2 Corinthians 8:1-2)

Do you see the language of saturation? I want you to note that there are two different dynamics of saturation as it relates to service: siphon and overflow.

Have you ever run out of gas and needed to siphon some out of another gas tank? No? Me neither, though I suspect that the illustration would have been powerful if we had. Well, let's proceed with it anyway.

In your spiritual life, the siphon effect occurs when you step out into service completely empty, in faith, believing that God will empower you. Let's take an unlovable person, for example. You initiate in love toward him without a flicker of compassion. But in so doing, you create a spiritual vacuum—a siphon—and that sucking sound is replaced by a sense of God's presence flowing in to fill the void. Now, miraculously, you find yourself overflowing toward the other person with a care and empathy that could only come from God.

The other dynamic of saturation occurs when we minister out of a heart overflowing with God's presence and joy. Your delight in Him is so powerful that you cannot but help overflow in service to others.

Have you ever sat enjoying an amazing meal with a group of friends and not said, *"Mmm, this amazing!"* or *"You've got to try this!"* It's virtually impossible. This is the physics of joy; it seeks to be made complete, and it does so by sharing with others.

It is this type of saturation that John speaks of in 1 John 1:3-4: "We proclaim to you what we have seen and heard, so that you also may have fellowship with us. And our fellowship is with the Father and with his Son, Jesus Christ. We write this to make our joy complete."

John is writing this epistle because he is so saturated with God that he experiences joy, and joy being what it is, it is made complete by overflowing to others. This is the direction the cycle of worship goes in the realm of service. As we are filled with God, we overflow toward others, or we overflow toward others and God fills us.

HOLD OUT OR HOPE

Our greatest hope for a life of purity is learning to worship: to overflow to God and He into us. None of us can remain an empty sponge, no matter how much discipline we have. Sooner or later, we will be drawn back to dirty waters if our souls are not being saturated with God.

The great tragedy within our ministries is seeing well-meaning believers who have never learned to worship (or who don't practice it) valiantly trying to stave off old habits of sin—the places they used to go for saturation. They are fighting against the law of gravity by flapping their arms, mustering all their will in a futile struggle with the inevitable: the need to worship something. That object of worship, if it is not God, will be something else.

If you find yourself inexorably drawn back to old watering holes, it is a warning that your soul is dry and in need of worship. Don't simply say no to those desires; satisfy them in God.

A Love Story, Part 1 For Better or For Worse

By Will Walker

My wife has been fighting a battle with anxiety and sometimes depression. It feels like more like a war, actually, a never-ending war. At times we feel that this is just how life is going to be and that we will always be frustrated by our helplessness. It really pisses us off, if you want to know the truth. Why won't God answer our prayer for healing? Why can't Debbie just have one day without worry or fear? One day!

The most troublesome times for me are the days when Debbie says she doesn't feel like God loves her and isn't even sure that He exists. I can hear the despair in her voice as she articulates the thought that her life might be meaningless. I don't know what to say on those days. If hope for change is linked to our experience of God's love for us, which I think is true, then you can imagine my concern for Debbie.

Everybody has their battles, and relationships are perhaps the largest battleground there is. Our emotions toward the opposite sex are so inexplicably strong, and many have been hurt so badly. And as if relationships were not hard enough by themselves, we also carry around the baggage of personal struggles—neglect, abuse, shame, addiction, loneliness. On one hand, we may wonder how God could love us as we are. On the other hand, we may doubt God's love precisely because He has allowed us to be as we are. These are real issues, troublesome questions. I don't know what to say, exactly, except that these feelings are actually quite normal when it comes to our relationship with God, as normal as they would be in any love relationship. I mean, how do you know anyone loves you?

DATING GAMES

You could say that you know someone loves you because he tells you he loves you or because he acts in such a way that would indicate that he loves you. But I'm not sure these are always reliable sources of knowledge. Having watched college students date for a decade now, I can say with confidence that everything is backward in the world of dating. At first it feels as if it is all about this person you like and how you want to do things for him because you like him. But really, you are doing those things to get that person to like you. It's hard to tell if people love other people or just the idea of being loved.

As an observer, I can only conclude that nobody really knows what they're doing in this area. For the most part, it's like taking a multiple-choice test that you didn't study for. One of the things you want to say or do at any given moment is probably the right thing, but then there's the always confusing "none of the above." The reason some people seem to be better at dating than others is the same reason that some people are better test takers. It has nothing to do with real knowledge, I'm pretty sure. This is why books on dating are so popular. Could it be that someone came into possession of the test—discovered the four hidden secrets to unlocking the seven mysteries of relationships? It's unlikely, but we'll give it a try anyway.

When I was in college, the formula for dating success was group dates. This is where a group of people go out and try to pretend that specific people in the group are not attracted to other specific people. No pressure. Everyone is just friends. One time, some guys asked a group of girls out on a geriatric group date. Seriously, they all dressed up as old people and ate dinner at 4:30 in the K-Mart deli. Then they played canasta or something before "retiring to their quarters" at the late hour of 8:30.

Group dates were doomed to fail because guys are always trying to figure out which girl—in any given group of girls—they are most interested in. So we all started listening to this tape series about courtship and decided it was time to get serious about dating. We said things like "I would like to pursue you" and "May I court you with the intention of marriage?" It was pretty intense, but the girls loved it.

A few years later everyone was kissing dating goodbye. I wonder if that is anything like what my friend Jeremy recommends—dating, but without any of the related terminology. It seems to work for people, but I always feel awkward asking a guy how things are going with his girlfriend … that … he's … not dating.

Personally, I was never very good at dating. I was pretty moody in college. A real jerk sometimes, if you want to know the truth. I remember waking up one Thursday morning in February of my freshman year, feeling like I needed to get away for a few days. So I took a road trip. I didn't tell anyone where I was going or when I'd be back. I just left. The following Tuesday night, I finally made it back to campus. The thing about that particular Tuesday was that it was Valentine's Day.

So I was dating this girl, Jennifer. The first thing I did when I got back was go up to her dorm room. Besides being pretty upset that I had been gone for five days and did not call her even once, she was glad to see me. In fact, she started giving me all these cards and gifts. I was quite surprised to see that she had missed me so much. About the time she gave me the third or fourth gift, I realized that I had forgotten Valentine's Day. Oh man, there is no recovering from that. To make matters worse, all the single girls in the hall had drifted down

to Jennifer's room to live vicariously through her Valentine's Day. Witnesses. There was no escape. What was I going to say?

After she finished crying, I went back to my dorm room and tried to sleep it off. Jennifer, on the other had, did not merely sleep it off. That's one thing about girls. They can't let bygones be bygones. Seeing as how Jennifer would never forget that I forgot, and how I would not be able to go to her room anymore on account of the fact that all those girls sat up all night talking about how I was the devil, I didn't know what to do. So I broke up with her. I told her that I needed to be alone for a while, that I really shouldn't be around people. That was probably true.

I met Debbie three weeks later. Apparently three weeks was all the alone time I needed. Isn't that the worst—to be the last person that someone else dated before he got married? The only thing that could be worse is if that person decided to write about it in a book. Some people.

That's probably more than you wanted to know about my dating woes. All I want to say is that dating involves a lot of games—always putting your best foot forward, worrying about what you just said, discerning what everyone else thinks about the relationship. And worst of all is the ever-present reality that it could all end. I'm not against dating. There are many wonderful things about the dating world. I am just saying that it's difficult to know if anyone really loves you—the real you—because of all the games. That is why we must not think of our relationship with God in the same way we think of dating.

Maybe nobody would say they think of God that way, but we certainly act like it at times. We perform so God will notice us, which somehow makes us feel like we are more loved by God. When we mess up, we act as though God will react by giving us the silent treatment or by breaking up with us. We plead our case with other Christians in an attempt to gain the momentum of peer approval, as if God could be swayed to forgive if enough of His friends were on our side. And when things go bad—when my wife seems like she will never get better—I am tempted to think that God is just not that interested in me anymore. Maybe the romance is over and this is all coming to an end. We may not say it, but we definitely play the dating

games with God. But God does not think of us that way. He thinks of us as His bride.

DEATHBLOWS

Marriage is nothing like dating, because you live with each other. You can't hide the real you. Debbie and I had no idea how opposite we were or how hard marriage would be. We had told each other going in that divorce would not be an option for us. That is how we made it through the first year. We had to. The second year was better, having learned to communicate and work through things. Now we have been married nine years, and we are perfect. Well, we are prefect in every way, except…we have lots of problems.

Since Debbie is more relationally in tune that I am, she usually notices the problems before I do. And since she is always thinking about the future of our relationship, she is able to forecast the problems that are coming, sort of like a tornado warning. She loves me and has nothing but our best interests in mind, but because I never see the warnings coming, I refer to them as deathblows. The first deathblow occurred six months into our marriage when she said she missed her dad (serious threat to my manhood). Then there was the time when she said something along the lines of "I love you, but I don't have any feelings for you." (Translation: I love you because I vowed to love you, but I don't

feel like I love you.) I never see it coming, I tell you, never.

We work through the deathblows, and though the process can be painful, it is deeply meaningful and satisfying. We never think about giving up on each other. We're married. You don't just break up in marriage.

Relationships are frustrating if you want them to get better. Debbie would never be frustrated with me if she didn't want to experience greater intimacy. Deathblows lead to honesty and hard conversations, which produce character and hope. Marriage is like any commitment in that you don't suddenly get to a point where you are ready. Rather, it is the binding commitment of marriage that forces you to persevere and grow. I cannot prove that Debbie loves me, but I believe her. The same goes for God.

ANYONE WANT TO MARRY A PROSTITUTE?

God knew we would have a difficult time believing that He loves us, which I think is why He used the metaphor of marriage throughout Scripture as a way to describe His love for us.

One thing I notice in Scripture is that we are not portrayed as a stunningly pure bride. In fact, we are usually depicted as whores and adulterers, dirty outcasts. It's as though God wants to make it clear that His love for us is pure and unconditional. This is illustrated powerfully in the Old Testament book of Hosea. Basically, God told Hosea to marry a prostitute, knowing that she would be unfaithful to him. This does not sound like good advice. Why would God do that?

> 1 The LORD said to me, "Go, show your love to your wife again, though she is loved by another and is an adulteress. Love her as the LORD loves the Israelites, though they turn to other gods and love the sacred raisin cakes." 2 So I bought her for fifteen shekels of silver and about a homer and a lethek of barley. (Hosea 3:1-2)

God wanted to illustrate the radical nature of His love for His people, unfaithful as they may be. Notice the emotion and power of His love:

> When my people were young, I loved them like a son, and I called them out of slavery in Egypt. But the more I called them, the farther they departed from me. They ignored my voice and worshipped other gods. But I did not leave. I held them by the hand and taught them to walk. I rescued them, but they never acknowledged my help. My people are obsessed with turning away from me.
>
> But how can I give up on them? How can I let them be destroyed? I can't bear the thought of such things. My compassion is aroused for them. I will not forsake them, because I am God and not a man (Hosea 11:1-9, paraphrased).

God is God and not a man. He does not play our games or waver in His affection like we do. Maybe one reason we do not always feel like God loves us is that we are not listening to Him. Maybe we are obsessed with other lovers. Maybe we are all too aware of how unlovable we are. These are deathblows. But God would say such things only because He cares about the relationship. He would never think about leaving us. We're married.

HOW DO YOU KEEP BELIEVING?

I ran into an old friend from college recently at a coffee shop. I hadn't seen Jeff in seven years. I remember him as this commando Christian guy who listened to the Bible on tape while he ate dinner. The first thing he told me was that he had "chucked the faith." I inquired, " 'Chucked it' as in you left and came back to the faith, or 'chucked it' as in you still don't believe?" It was the latter. We talked for a while after that.

The conversation was refreshing because I didn't feel like I needed to explain or prove anything. Jeff already knew everything. At one point we started talking about the Bible. He said, "Man, Paul was either freaking brilliant or tripping on something. His arguments are airtight." I agreed, then told him that I had mostly been reading the Gospels for the past couple of years.

I started talking about the way Jesus interacted with people and how simple and revolutionary His ideas were. As I recounted my discovery of the person of Christ, I began to talk about how Jesus never really asked anyone what they knew or what they could do. He was always asking people things like "Do you love Me? Will you follow Me? Who do you say that I am?" All of His invitations were so overtly relational. It's like Jesus wants us to marry Him. I was thinking these things out loud, and at this point Jeff interrupted me, "It's weird that you say that. I never read the Gospels much. I was always reading the Epistles. Maybe I married a set of ideas and arguments instead of a person."

He asked me how I could keep believing.

The only thing I could think to say, the only thing that I felt was true, was "Dude, I married Jesus. I'm in."

He asked me if I ever had questions or doubts.

"Of course I do," I said. "There are all kinds of things I don't know, and the life that Jesus has led me into is frustrating sometimes, but I'm not breaking up with Him because of it. We're married. I couldn't imagine life without Jesus."

Jeff countered, "But you would be okay if you stopped believing. You really would. At first it felt really weird to me, but after a while, I was okay. I learned different ways to cope and found other things to give my energy to. You don't think you would be okay, but you would be after a while."

I sat there for a minute and tried to imagine what it would be like to break up with Jesus and whether I could actually be okay someday. I sat there quietly, looking away in thought. Thinking about it made my heart hurt. After a minute or two, I looked at Jeff and said, "I wouldn't be okay. It would feel like divorce to me. In marriage you become one with the other person. Divorce would literally feel like death. If Debbie or Ethan died, I would never get over that. Sure, I would cope and get on with life, but I would always feel a sense of loss, like part of me died. That is how it would be if somehow I walked away from Jesus. It would never be okay. We are married."

A BETTER QUESTION

I do not always feel loved by Debbie, and she does not always feel loved by me. That's just the nature of being human—finite and insecure and self-centered. If we were dating, I might react by trying harder to be lovable or else by giving up and moving on to someone else. But we are married. We vowed to love one another through thick and thin, good and bad. And that is exactly the kind of commitment God has made to us. He loves us no matter how many times we turn away from His voice. It makes me think that there is a better question than "Does God love me?" Perhaps the better question is "Are we married?"

If God and I are married, then I can be confident of His love toward me. That doesn't automatically make me feel better about my struggles, but it is a necessary starting point. Once I take Him at His word—that He loves me—then I can move on to trust that His love is good. Even in hard times I am compelled by God's love to believe that He has not forgotten me and is in fact working things out for my best interest. Granted, my best interest may not be the kinds of material and temporal pleasures that I often want. But protecting me from such things is part of the way God builds my character and helps me become the radiant bride I was meant to be. So when I feel like God doesn't love me, one possibility is that my idea of love is simply not as good as God's idea of love.

While we are taking God at His word, we can also reflect on His undying—even irrational—commitment to His people throughout history. He always wants what is best for His people. He provides what they need and protects them in times of trouble. He even disciplines them when they start thinking that someone else could love them better than God. I'm sure they did not feel loved in times of discipline, but that again shows our tendency to see things only from our perspective.

When your relationship with God is hard, even painful, don't settle for wondering if God loves you. Go back to the marriage vows. God said He will never leave nor forsake you, that He loves you as a daughter, and that He will present you as a spotless bride. You can probably even think of times in your life when you have experienced God's love. Those times help us remember God's commitment to us and give us hope for the future. This is why we can't merely date God, because we need the anchor of His unfailing commitment.

WHEN THE HONEYMOON IS OVER

The difficulty of marriage is day-to-day life. It's not always exciting. You argue about the position of the toilet seat and worry about finances. Life tends to occupy so much of your energy that it's hard to focus on things like intimacy and a growing appreciation for each other. Sometimes that's the way it is with God. Our day-to-day lives drown out God's presence and work in our lives. So, how do you gain deeper intimacy with God?

There is a lot of advice out there about how to grow in your relationship with God. Much of it is good, but we often go wrong by turning advice into formulas—trusting a set of activities to produce intimacy. The reality is that you are a person in a relationship, and relationships do not have formulas. You mature and change and find new ways to relate to God. You may go through season of deep intimacy with God, as if He is right next to you all the time. And then there may be seasons of life when God seems silent. The same advice will not be adequate for all seasons and dynamics of a relationship. That said, marriage is not a passive endeavor. Intimacy with God will require intentional effort on our part—not to impress God, as in dating, but to love and serve God, as in marriage.

The problem with hard work, of course, is that we usually don't feel like working all that hard. We have good intentions, but we get sidetracked or tired or simply weighed down by the worries of life. We are prone to want something easier and less permanent, like dating. And that gets us back to where we started, playing games and feeling at times like God does not love us. So, how do you make the marriage work? What do you do?

A Love Story, Part 2 Because He Loves Me

By Will Walker

This is only a book. It cannot make you do anything. In fact, nobody can *make* you do anything. Even God, though I'm sure He is able to, will not force His will upon you. You have the freedom to think and believe and do whatever you desire. And that is a good way to characterize the fall of humankind—we are all bent on doing what we want to do. But in the case of wanting to do good, we often do not do what we want to do, and in the case of not wanting to do bad, we in fact do exactly what we did not want to do. We are complex that way.

Don Miller says that, many times in life, the things we want most are not the things we need.[1] C. S Lewis described the dilemma in terms of first and second wants.[2] He said that when first wants come first, we get the second wants thrown in. But when the second wants take priority, we end up with nothing. For example, feeling valuable is a legitimate first want. And let's say that feeling the approval of your friends is a second want. It's not wrong to want it, but it is not the most important thing in terms of your identity and sense of worth. If you derive your value more from what people say about you than you do from what God says about you, then you end up insecure, because people's opinions are subjective and fickle. You also come off looking pretty needy and will probably not sense that people like that about you. So in the end you don't feel valuable or liked. But if you derive your value from what God thinks about you—that He knows everything about you and still loves you more than you could ever imagine—then you are likely to feel incredibly secure about your identity as a child of God. That kind of quiet confidence is attractive and will quickly gain the favor of people around you, not that you need it.

So, in our lives, and in the realm of relationships specifically, there are all kinds of thoughts and feelings and wants swirling around. Some of them are more important than others. These desires are strong currents in our lives, pushing us in directions that we may or may not want to go. This is part of what it means to go with the flow, to act without thinking. Whatever the reasons, we don't evaluate our wants much. We do what we want, not always in a rebellious sort of way, but usually in an autopilot sort of way. This causes a lot of frustration and disorder in our lives because, frankly, our autopilot is not that good. Sometimes we want and do what is good, but usually our natural course is one of unrealized intentions and regret.

But what if all your wants were written on a piece of paper and I could simply tell you which ones should be of primary and secondary priority? That would make things a lot easier for you. Of course, it may turn out that the primary things are not the things you currently want the most. What would you do then? It's not easy to change what you want. It's difficult to even explain why we want what we want. We just do. We have preferences and tastes and habits. We are sometimes blinded by temporary pleasures. So, how do you make yourself want something—want to wait for lasting pleasure, want to date the right guy, want to be pure, want to do what God has been telling you to do lately?

PUNCH-DRUNK LOVE

I was talking with some fraternity guys about this recently—you know, trying to help them get in touch with their feelings. Actually, we have been talking all semester about how we can become the kind of people who want what God wants. This conversation often makes us feel helpless before our natural desires and the cultural tide against what God wants. It took us nearly a semester to articulate that it is difficult to make yourself want something you don't want. (Don't laugh. You'll stifle our progress and we'll end up stuffing our emotions forever.) We also concluded that this is why we sin, because at least in that moment, we want to.

One day we were talking about how people who are in love do stuff they never would have imagined doing. For example, a guy we all know went to the mall recently to get something for his girlfriend. On top of that, he went to a store where, apparently, you build your own teddy bear. Somehow he talked a friend into going with him. So there they were, two guys trying to maintain coolness while assembling a teddy bear together.

I rode an undersized mountain bike from Fort Worth to Dallas (thirty-five miles) on a Texas summer day because my car was in the shop and I wanted to see my girlfriend. It took me four and half hours, and I almost collapsed from dehydration. Nobody in their right mind would do such a thing. But I was not in my right mind. I was in love with a girl named Debbie.

So the frat boys and I decided that if those two guys could build a teddy bear, and if I could brave the entrance and exit ramps of Dallas freeways on a mountain bike, then people's wants could be changed if they were in love.

As we talked about the relationship between love and want, we discovered that it is difficult to intentionally fall in love, even with God. I mean, I did not decide to love my wife. We just fell in love. It wasn't even glamorous. We met in a roller skating rink, in college. But there was something about the way she turned the corner during reverse skate that caught my attention. Something inexplicable that made me ask my friends who she was. Something that made me want to be with her. A few weeks later, I was on my spring break vacation and I couldn't stop thinking about her, the way she had smiled at me when we said goodbye on campus. I had to see her. I didn't know her phone number or how to get to her house, only

that she lived in Dallas. I left in the middle of the night and tracked down Debbie's number through my roommate, who knew her roommate. I finally found her and asked her out on a date.

I thought a concert would be a pretty cool date. The problem was that I didn't have any money. Being broke is what turned this romance into a comedy … or maybe a tragedy. I figured, if my parents wanted to come, they would pay for everything. So that is how our first date went down, me and my parents picking up Debbie in my dad's company car to go to a concert. On top of that, I invited Debbie's roommate to come with us for some reason. You would have thought we were thirteen and going to the mall. The good part, I guess, is that I could only go up from there. So, having failed miserably at being cool, I opted for being weird. I'm convinced that Debbie kept seeing me simply because she was intrigued.

Love has a strange effect on people, which is why people who follow Jesus are hard to account for. They die to their desires and adopt an entirely different way of seeing things, like "It's better to give than receive,"[3] "Do not store up treasures on earth,"[4] "Do not worry about your life,"[5] and "Consider others as more important than yourself."[6]

HOW TO FALL IN LOVE

I know I just said that you can't decide to fall in love, but I do think you can become the kind of person who is more likely to fall in love. Thinking about Jesus, it seems like people loved Him because they had an encounter with Him in which they experienced His love for them. So it seems that we could pursue Jesus with the intent of experiencing His love for us, and then His love would in fact transform our desires in ways that rules and willpower never could.

In my opinion, that's where many of us have gone wrong. We have reduced a relationship with God to a set of rules to keep and activities to do. I can tell you this from experience: the checklist of Christian activity does not love you, no matter how much you may love it. We don't experience God's love because we are lovable. Just the opposite: we experience His love because, knowing exactly how unlovable we are, He loves us more than we can imagine. This is the heart of the gospel.

That may sound too religious or simplistic, but that's because our understanding of "gospel" has become cliché. We tend to think of the gospel only in terms of the four or five points that we need to agree to in order to go to heaven when we die. But it's more than that—bigger, longer, broader, in the way a marriage far transcends the list of vows. So, how can we begin to think about the gospel more relationally, in a way that would help us experience God's love? Remember, experiencing God's love is how we come to want, and actually live, a life of purity and devotion to God.

For the sake of space and clarity, I am going to list some ideas I have found helpful. Please do not take the list to be a formula. Relationships do not have formulas, only discernible patterns or rhythms in how we relate—a dance, not operating instructions.

We were created for relationship. When God said, "Let us make man in our image, in our likeness," [7] I think he was primarily talking about community. Think about the Trinity for a moment. The Father and the Son and the Holy Spirit are always deflecting glory to one another and serving each other. It is a community of mutual submission and love. Wouldn't you like to have a group of friends like that, always trying to give each other credit and always serving the desires of one another in love? This is what God wanted for us: that we could experience community like the members of the Trinity have community. This kind of trinitarian community would, of course, be possible only for people who were satisfied and secure in their relationship with God.

We are isolated because of sin. Sin is our reality. We love it and hate it, and we hate that we love it. We readily admit that we are sinners, but we try to hide specific sins. Sin, personified, has been with us longer than anyone else in our life. We literally don't know how to live without it, can't even imagine that. And even though we are all in this together, we try to hide it as if we are doing just fine. But we aren't fine. We are frustrated and often lonely. Trinitarian community feels like a far-off land. But we still have our dignity.

Jesus exposes our sin. The encounters I mentioned—the ones where people fall in love with Jesus—usually involve a moment in which the persons find out that Jesus knows their deepest darkest secrets. He knows they are afraid, adulterous, prideful, materialistic, ashamed. He does not harp on people's immorality in these situations, but He does want them to know that He knows everything about them. That's what meaningful relationships are all about. Intimate knowledge.

Jesus forgives our sin. In the case of people who do not think they need to be forgiven of very much—that they are plenty lovable—those people do not really experience God's love for them. They are generally too preoccupied with loving themselves. But in the case of those who understand the magnitude of the forgiveness they need, these are the people who fall in love with Jesus. They never imagined that He would love them as they are, no strings attached. But when He did, they were overcome with love. It plays out like John said: "We love God because he first loved us."[8]

Jesus restores our relationships. Once God's love is poured out in our hearts, we are free to love others as they are, no strings attached. We find ourselves closer and closer to the kind of relationships for which we were created.

We are here on purpose. Jesus prayed that we would "be brought to complete unity to let the world know that God sent him and has loved us even as He have loved Jesus."[9] Our mission to tell the world about Jesus is not programmatic but rather is simply an expression of what a God-centered, human-shaped-void-filling community would do.

Community. Intimacy. Forgiveness. Mission. This is only a glimpse of the good news about Jesus. But it's enough to see how overtly relational the gospel is. The Christian life is not a performance or an isolated effort.

Living a solitary life reflects a distorted reality. What's more, it rarely produces the kind of love-driven desire that we have been talking about. In a "just me and God" relationship, the effects of a depraved character are often difficult to grasp. By contrast, in honest and below-the-surface relationships with other people, the effects of sin are evident. Grace stops feeling so cheap as we witness the real consequences brought about by our selfish ambitions. To think other people unnecessary in our relationship with God is shortsighted at best and a different gospel at worst.

COMMUNAL LIFE

So much of what this book has to say comes down to your relationship with God. Do you want what He wants? Do you trust Him? Do you want His love more than anything else? These are the primary questions. And I am saying that you will not be able to discover the true answers to these questions apart from community—a group of people who are committed to following Christ together, putting on display the kind of love God has poured out into our hearts. We need each other to experience God. There is much to say about community, but again for the sake of space and clarity, I'd like to offer a few things that I believe will help you experience God's love and want to do the hard work of marriage.

Honesty is the most essential aspect of a relationship. Not common interests or love. We can only know each other to the degree that we are honest with each other. Dishonesty is usually our attempt to manipulate others and spin perception. At the very point where what I think and what I say I think differ, you can only relate to a fake version of me—even if the fake me is just the real me, slightly twisted. True relationship is suddenly off the table. I'm not saying that honesty is the cure-all, but I am saying that this is one thing that will go a long way toward meaningful relationships.

Confession is personal but not private. Want to know why it's so hard to overcome sin? It's because we don't tell people about it. Look what John says:

> This is the message we have heard from Him and announce to you, that God is Light, and in Him there is no darkness at all. If we say that we have fellowship with Him and yet walk in the darkness, we lie and do not practice the truth; but if we walk in the Light as He Himself is in the Light, we have fellowship with one another, and the blood of Jesus His Son cleanses us from all sin. If we say that we have no sin, we are deceiving ourselves and the truth is not in us.[10]

The thing that sticks out to me is the fact that Jesus cleanses us from sin while we are in the light, which implies that we have sin while we are in the light. How does that work? How can I be in the light and yet have sin? I have always assumed that walking in the light means having some sort of sinless purity about me. I mean, John says that God is light. But then he says that if I say I have attained this sinless purity, I am a liar. It's a tough spot. It seems that "light" is better interpreted as "truth" or "honesty."

God is up-front, totally honest. He doesn't shade things or neglect our relationship. Fellowship with God and with each other means we reciprocate this kind of honesty. Confession is not a spiritual additive, something you can get by without. It is the kind of honesty and truth that makes relationship possible. Jesus is willing and able to cleanse us and restore our relationships if we will just get our sin—the real us—in the light. If we do not talk about our sin, then we are liars in our actual lives, regardless of what we know or say.

We always need to hear the gospel.

Community does not fix our brokenness. Actually, it magnifies our brokenness. Close relationships bring out the worst in people. Ask anyone who is married. Our tendency is to withdraw from one another when those things are exposed. But that is not the gospel. The gospel is God moving toward us while we are running in the opposite direction. God demonstrates His love for us in that while were still sinners Christ died for us. Ultimately we all need acceptance and forgiveness from God, but it's sobering to realize how often He chooses to express those things through each of us. It makes a privatized faith highly unlikely. I need the people in my community, broken as they are, and at the same time they need me, broken as I am. Helpless as we are, we tell each other the good news about Jesus, and in Him we find life.

I realize that this is not the typical advice that people offer for growing in your relationship with God—things like Bible reading and prayer and worship. I wholeheartedly believe that you need to do those things. But I also think that you already knew that. Doing stuff for God is easy. Wanting to do stuff for God is love.

WILL WALKER has been on staff with Campus Crusade for Christ at The University of Texas for seven years. He is the author of a forthcoming book about the necessity of community to fully experience the gospel. He and his wife, Debbie, and son, Ethan live in Austin.

[1] Don Miller, Blue Like Jazz: Nonreligious Thoughts On Christian Spirituality (Nashville, TN: Nelson, 2003), p. 63.

[2] C. S. Lewis, ``First and Second Things'' in *God in the Dock* (Grand Rapids, Mich.: Eerdmans, 1970), pp. 278-81.

[3] Acts 20:35

[4] Matthew 6:19

[5] Luke 12:22

[6] Philippians 2:3

[7] Genesis 1:26

[8] 1 John 4:19

[9] John 17:23

[10] 1 John 1:5-10

Blurbs

This is the part of the book where I offer some random thoughts about stuff—some perhaps more relevant than others. But this is, after all, my book, and after this I may never be allowed to write another one, so I feel obligated to say everything I know and think at this point in time.

These thoughts are here because (1) they are not important enough to merit their own chapter, (2) I didn't have enough consecutive thoughts on the same topic to constitute a chapter, (3) I just ran out of time to write a whole chapter, or (4) they're some actual random thoughts. But nonetheless they are all thoughts you should consider. You never know what nugget of wisdom, what kernel of truth, what gem of wit the Lord will use to radically change your life.

FLIRTING: GOOD OR BAD?

So I'm at this party and I see out of the corner of my eye my friend Shileilei (obvious fake name) guffawing in a most dramatic fashion—mouth open, silent laugh, bent over, knee slapping. She is in conversation with the only two available and mildly attractive guys at this party. She manages to engage one of them for a good portion of the evening and leave with his e-mail address.

On the drive home I ask what was so dang funny.

Shileilei retells the story. It is not that funny, not worth repeating here.

"But why, pray tell, did you laugh so hard?" I beg.

"I was flirting. You know, you've got to show some interest."

"That's flirting?! No wonder I haven't had a date in years."

I have another friend who likes to tell how she went to therapy to learn how to flirt, and lo and behold, she was married within the year.

Now, I don't know about you, but I was always under the impression that flirting was not what nice girls do. In fact, the official definition of *flirt* is

something like "to tease with intent to cause sexual arousal." By that definition, we have certainly clarified by now that is not something we want to participate in. That's what I'll call "bad flirting." However, I think I'm becoming more convinced that there might be such a thing as "good flirting." That is to say flirting that is not so self-serving, that is not about seeking out attention and affirmation from the opposite sex for the sake of your own ego, it's about being open and getting to know people.

Here's the thing. Traditional flirting—the inappropriate touching of the arm or leg as she giggles and says something about how strong he must be—is all about manipulation. It's about acting like someone she isn't, in order to please someone so that he might like her in return. But of course, he doesn't know her, really, since she was pretending to be the person he would like instead of who she really is. It's about flattery and charm. Blick!

Good flirting is not about getting a boyfriend or finding a husband. It's about being open, getting to know people, all kinds of people, and increasing your circle of friends. As you get to know people, you learn more about what type of people you enjoy and connect with, and the more people you know, the more opportunities you might have to date. I'm going out on a limb here to suggest that dating is not about finding a boyfriend or a husband. Flirting and dating both are more enjoyable when the objective is about having fun, trying new experiences, and learning about yourself, about people, about men, about God, about love, and about life.

Within the realm of Christendom, we have some closely held tenets of dating and mating. One of them is that girls do not initiate. In principle, I still hold to this principle. (Was that redundant?) But I do think such thinking has led to the expectation that if we just sit tight and wait long enough, God is going to drop a husband in our lap. I confess I was highly skeptical at first, but I've come to agree with Dr. Henry Cloud on this topic in his recent book, *How to Get a Date Worth Keeping* (destined to become the next dating trend as the pendulum swings away from kissing dating goodbye).

> For some reason people are taught that in every area of life, except dating that they are to be diligent and responsible. ... If you want to be involved in a church, you don't hope one will find you. You visit a number of churches, check them out. ... If you want to build a community of friends, you don't just sit at home. You seek them out.[1]

There's a valid point. If I want to have relationships with men, even just friendships, I should probably have some conversations with at least one or two. Since they're not knocking on my door, I should probably go where they're hanging out. And I think I should possibly flirt—in the good sense, of course.

Flirting is just practicing good social skills. And I do mean practicing. It takes time and effort. It's not easy to meet new people and get to know them. College is probably the greatest opportunity to master the skill. Learn to focus on other people. Ask good questions. Discover how to make people feel at ease.

Of course, there will be some awkward and embarrassing moments along the way. And one day you'll write a book or give a talk and be so glad you have a story to tell, like that time you had a whole conversation with a cute boy, only to discover later that your shirt was missing two strategic buttons. Oh, wait—that's me, not you.

So here are some thoughts:

GOOD FLIRT ...
- Makes friendly eye contact
- Asks questions that show genuine interest in a person
- Focuses on encouraging and affirming others
- Finds common ground
- Is comfortable being herself
- Includes others in the conversation
- Possibly uses some sort of appropriate physical touch—shaking hands, putting a hand on his shoulder while saying, "Nice to meet you" upon departure
- Waits until he asks for contact info, but offer him clues of how he can reach her if he wants to (such as who they know in common, where she works)
- Has a few good questions in mind as well as some interesting facts she likes others to know about her
- Has the objective of finding a new friend and a potential date
- Dresses appropriately

BAD FLIRT ...
- Makes suggestive eye contact
- Touches inappropriately
- Communicates with innuendo
- Becomes whoever her target wants her to be
- Laughs too much (apologies to Shileilei)
- Focuses on gaining attention and self-affirmation

- Uses provocative words or actions or poses (the classic is sitting in a backward chair, with legs spread on either side)
- Competes with other women
- Offers personal contact info (writing it on his arm with lipstick is a nice touch)
- Has a few pick-up lines in the arsenal that work every time
- Has the objective of sex
- Dresses accordingly

LIVING TOGETHER

Don't.

Here's what you're thinking:
1. It will save money.
2. We need to live together to decide if we are compatible for marriage.
3. We're going to get married anyway.
4. We can live together and not sleep together.
5. It's a viable option.

Here's reality:
1. It may save you a few dollars right now, but your divorce attorney down the road is going to suck up any savings you might enjoy now.
2. When you live together, you have an escape clause built in. And trust me, one of you is going to take the escape clause at some juncture. Statistics say that only 55 percent of couples who live together actually end up getting married within five years. (You may think those are good odds, until you note the next point.)
3. Statistics say that couples who live together before marriage have an 80 percent higher chance of divorce than do those who don't live together (and that rate is already at 50 percent).[2]
4. Riiiight.
5. It's not an option.

One last thought: A recent survey published in *USA Today* showed that most women viewed living together as the "the next step toward marriage", while most men viewed it as, "the step prior to commitment."

"GUARDING YOUR HEART"

When a woman in the Christian world begins a dating relationship, it is not uncommon for an older female sage to advise her to "guard her heart." I know that because I am usually the older sage. I learned it from someone older and wiser who said it to me once. It sounds so … Bible-y and wise counsel-ish, doesn't it? When spoken among a group of women, they often nod their heads and "*Hmm*" simultaneously in agreement with such profound wisdom.

But what does it mean, exactly?

Oddly, it's often spoken in connection with a verse in Proverbs that says, "Guard your heart, for from it flows the wellsprings of life."[3] That is a profound truth, to be sure, but it does not really fit the context here. It's preceded by some verses about hiding wisdom and truth in your heart so that you can guard it from sin, because that affects every area of your life. That's a good principle to live by, and it certainly applies in the context of a dating relationship, but it's not what we mean when we tell it to the newly dating.

Really, "guard your heart" is a sort of code for a whole host of things. Your "heart," in this case, represents your mind, emotions, and will. So you can think about protecting those areas. Being older and wiser, we sages know the nature of women and have seen and experienced the consequences. We usually mean the following: Don't do the things we've done. Don't let your emotions run ahead of the relationship. Don't spend too much time thinking and fantasizing about a future with this guy. Don't allow wrong thinking or emotions to sway your judgment. Don't allow him to consume or control your thoughts, your time, or your energy. Don't allow a guy to shape you or change you just because you want him to like you. Don't share all of your innermost thoughts, hurts, struggles, experiences, and insights until he's pursued those things and has proven trustworthy to care for them. Be careful about how much verbal and physical connection you have. Make him pursue your heart; don't force it on him or let him have it for nothing—he may not want it.

Practical ways to guard your heart include hiding God's Word in your heart. This means, not just memorizing passages, but also meditating on them and thinking about how they apply to your life. When you are focusing on what is right and true about you, about God, and about His nature and character, it helps to keep your priorities in check.

This is where the discipline of "taking every thought captive"[4] can come in handy. Granted, this is not necessarily battling for God's truth, as the context of that verse implies, but it's a good discipline to learn to control your thought life. Be intentional. Don't just go with the white noise in your head. Choose what you think about.

Since I'm all about taking verses out of context, I've got one more for you. Jeremiah talks about the heart as well. He says, "The heart is deceitful above all else and desperately sick——who can understand it?"[5] When it comes to relationships, I could not agree more. I generally consider myself wise and discerning. However, I don't trust my own judgment when it comes to matters of the heart—— my own heart, I mean. My emotions hold far too much sway over my perspective. I need objectivity. I need someone who knows me well, someone who can observe our relationship firsthand, and someone who cares enough about me to ask hard questions and speak truth.

Communicate well in the relationship. If something is unclear, don't make assumptions or read between the lines. Ask for clarification. Pretty much, if a guy doesn't say it straight up, don't assume he's thinking anything more than what he's said.

Continue to fill your life with other people and activities. Just because you're dating does not mean you should abandon the rest of your schedule and friends. Include him in your life; don't replace your life with him. And whatever you do, don't hold on to him for dear life. You'll drown him and yourself.

All of this guarding is important, because relationships are high risk. A broken heart is never pleasant, though I think everyone needs one or two in life. It's a rite of passage, and it can be a part of our spiritual and emotional growth. All the don'ts are lessons we sages have learned as we've gone before you, even though someone offered the same wisdom to us. Chances are, you're going to learn it for yourself firsthand as well, but perhaps you'll be quicker to recognize your mistakes. And you'll find yourself saying it to someone else soon thereafter. "Hmm. … You're so right."

"PURSUING"

I know there are some guys reading this book and trying to solve the mystery that is womanhood. So I'm throwing you guys a bone. If we're all about guarding our heart, we're expecting to be pursued. Here's what we mean when we say that: Take the initiative. Step up to the plate. Get in the game. (That's the end of my sports analogies—I was trying to communicate in your heart language.)

In other words, ask a girl out—ahead of time, preferably a couple of days ahead of time. Be proactive. Plan your time together. Have questions in mind that will help you get to know her. Guide the conversation. Communicate when there is something to communicate about. Treat her with respect, honor, and dignity, not because you like her, but just because she's a woman. Be a gentleman. Prove yourself trustworthy.

Do the right thing. Even if it means you've got to take one for the team.

ONE WOMAN FOR ONE MAN VS. OPTIONS

There's a debate about whether God has created one particular man to be the husband of specifically one woman. And if that's the case, what if we screw that up? What if we marry the wrong person? Or what if he's got commitment issues and never marries? And if one person marries the wrong person, then who he was supposed to marry marries the wrong person. … Doesn't that have a domino effect on all humankind and mess up who everyone else is supposed to marry? But then again, maybe God in His foreknowledge knew ahead of time who you were going to marry, whether that was the original plan or not, and so even though he's the wrong person, he's really the right person in God's plan for you now. There are lots of what-if's in this scenario, but that's where we can trust God's foreknowledge to orchestrate the details. In this camp, I have the freedom to sit at home and wait or to go to a remote village somewhere in Tyjaigasdjkstan and trust that God will bring me His good and perfect provision regardless of where I am. Because it's not about the odds; its about being where and who God wants me to be. If there's just one guy, then God will work out the details. There's some comfort in that.

On the other side of the debate are those who say you can marry whomever you want, or even if you want. You have free will to choose, and God will work in your life regardless of the context. He can and will be involved, and while there are wise choices and poor choices, there is not one specific person He intended for you. There are options. This gives you a lot of freedom, along with a lot of responsibility. Suddenly, it really is up to you to go out and find someone and to try to win his heart with all your feminine powers. In this scenario there is a lot left up to the likelihoods of the world. A person who is less attractive or who maybe has some issues is probably less likely to find a mate. Odds do play a factor. But God can certainly trump any odds.

All of this is tied up in the whole free will/predestination/foreknowledge debate. We don't really get it. There is probably some truth in both scenarios. (Though, given some of the couples I know, I may be more convinced of the first scenario, because they are so obviously perfect for each other. I can't imagine that there'd be another person quite like them.)

This debate may or may not have some effect on how you approach dating and marriage. It probably does influence your contentment level. Trust me, you were going to think of all these questions on your own someday; I just threw it out there to say that it's an age-old debate. It will really mess with your head if you let it. So just know this: either way, God is sovereign and in control and has your best interests at heart.

DIFFERENCES BETWEEN MEN AND WOMEN

There have been way too many books written on this topic for me to take up valuable space and ink repeating their content. But I do think a book like this should at least include some basics that will give you a grid for understanding the opposite sex until you have a chance to read the others. So a short list will do for now.

If women are like a casserole, men are like a TV dinner (global vs. compartmental). (Do you even know what a TV dinner is? Frozen meal, foil tray, unidentifiable red dessert? Maybe think of it as a lunchable—divided compartments.) Men and women think differently. For us, everything is thrown in one big pot. The flavor of one area of our life affects the flavor of every other area. Men, not so much. They can compartmentalize. Where this will cause you grief is when you have your first big fight and he goes to play basketball with the guys and you are paralyzed with heartache. He really does care; he can just choose to not think about it.

Women—25,000; men—12,000. Average words per day, that is (communication vs. activity). It is no surprise that women are much more communicative. We value conversation, while men value doing things together, having shared experiences. This will bite you when you feel like your relationship has moved so much further along when you have had some deep conversation and he doesn't see it that way. For him, the more stuff you do together, the deeper the relationship.

The princess and the king (wanted vs. respected). The nature of men and women really is fairy tale–like, and that's why we like fairy tales. It's been said throughout this book over and over: women need to be wanted, pursued, and known, like a princess. But you might be surprised that guys are more motivated by respect. They want to be the good king or at least the noble prince (though they'd never admit it in those terms).

I can't believe I'm confessing this in print, but it's too classic an example to not use. After a serious breakup when I was much younger, I actually wrote the guy a forty-five-page letter—over the period of a month. I know that's so wrong, but I really needed to be understood and known. His response was twelve points of rebuttal. Basically, he needed me to know where he was right and he wanted to know that I still respected him. (for the record, I am a much healthier person now.) Anyway, it might be helpful for you to think through what communicates respect and disrespect to a guy.

So … that may help explain some things for you.

(Disclaimer: these are broad and sweeping stereotypes. Statements may not apply to all men and all women.)

ARE WOMEN BECOMING MORE LIKE MEN?

In their sexuality, I mean. Or is that just the wishful thinking of men? I don't know the answer to that question. But as I have been paying more attention to such things, I've noticed several advertisements that show women responding like men—referring to waiters as "lunch," for example. Basically, it appears that women are becoming more visually stimulated. *Sex and the City* would certainly make it seem as though women are just looking for sex. Samantha, for sure. The others maybe want the relationship *and* the sex. (Not that I watch *Sex and the City* or anything.)

It's not uncommon these days to go into a girls' dorm room and find posters of attractive, scantily clad men adorning the walls. That used to be such a guy thing. Is it just the male marketing and media execs who are making women think they should be that way, or are women actually changing? There's an interesting project for your next sociology or human sexuality or marketing or some other kind of class. Send me your paper when you're done.

WORDS

words I like: *succulent, pumpkin, paprika, persnickety, edamame, smidgen, svelte ,-esque added to the end of any word (e.g., she was very Oprah-esque in her communication style)*

words I hate: *sliver, slit, pus, booths, moist, slather, slab, vulva (hey, it's a women's book!)*
words I find funny: *wienie (commonly misspelled "weenie", but in fact, it is the shortened version of wiener)*
words or phrases I tried to work into the content of this book but was unable to do so: *hoi polloi; vexed; nota bene; Jimmy Choos, Manolo Blahniks & $1,000 bags; Jingleheimerschmidt, John Jacob*

BROTHER/SISTER RULE

I know I'm not the first to have this theory, but I like to claim it as my own. It seems to me that most happily married couples I know look as though they could be brother and sister. That is to say they have similar body styles, hair color and skin tones Which I would say is evidence of our own vanity—we are attracted to ourselves. Case in point: the Schwarzeneggers. (*nota bene:* That is not to say that there are not some exceptions. See Kate Hudson and Chris Robinson, that is if they're still married. Really, it's more of an observation than a rule.)

A corollary is the Ken and Barbie Principle. Unusually attractive people are drawn to each other, often in opposites—tall, dark, and handsome to the blond, blue-eyed movie star. (see most of Hollywood)

The rule can also be applied to people and their pets as well as, on occasion, to people and their cars.

The point is to be on the lookout for someone who looks as though he could be your brother. (Or my brother, as far as that goes—tall, big, pale, brown hair. Anyway ...)

THE TALKING POINT

The point of this whole book, just in case you missed it, is to fall in love with Jesus, and the other stuff will work itself out.

Okay, I can't think of anything I else I have to say right now.

[1] *How to Get a Date Worth Keeping* by Dr. Henry Cloud (Grand Rapids, MI : Zondervan, 2005) p. 27
[2] http://www.marriagebuilders.com/graphic/mbi5025b_qa.html
[3] Proverbs 4:23
[4] 2 Corinthians 10:5
[5] Jeremiah 17:9

How to Get a Date Worth Keeping

By Dr. Henry Cloud

Another Friday night alone. It stinks, doesn't it. But what can you do to fix it? More than you've ever imagined. You can put an end to the datelessness. Starting today—right now—you can begin a journey that will bring fun, interesting people into your life, broaden your experience of others and yourself, and lead you toward that date of all dates—a date worth keeping.

Zondervan Publishing House

Be Dating in Six Months or Your Money Back

How to Get a Date Worth Keeping

Dr. Henry Cloud

DEVOTIONALS

THIS IS NOT YOUR MOTHER'S DEVOTIONAL GUIDE...

To Know Him Is to Love Him:
Falling in Love with Christ
Daily Reflections from the
Gospel of Luke
By Rick James

The point of *Fantasy* is that rules will not lead to a life of purity. Rather, a passionate relationship with Christ causes us to end affairs that fail to satisfy us in the way that only He can. Here are a month of reflections that walks you through the Gospel of Luke with the purpose of rekindling—or even beginning for the first time—your love affair with Jesus. These reflections help you to see Jesus in a fresh light, so that your attraction to Him would make other attractions loosen their grip on your heart.

This is probably a little different than any sort of "devotional" thing you've done before. The answer is not always "Jesus," "the cross," or "John 3:16" (although those are fine answers). Think of it as sort of a blog—slightly random, but hopefully helpful insights into the nature and character of the Father, the Savior, the Spirit, yourself, and how we all interact.

Use this guide as you will, but here's a suggested plan. Each day read the passage and insights. You may need to read the chapter to understand the whole context. Then answer the following questions in your own journal or blog to share with your group of friends to discuss insights and applications.

1. What questions or thoughts does this raise in my mind?
2. What can I learn about the nature of Jesus, the Spirit, or the Father? (Don't restrict your thinking and observations just to our insights—read the passage a few times and come up with your own.)

3. What can I learn about my own nature? How do I feel about that? How does my experience relate to this insight?
4. What do I need to act on, pray about, or apply in some way to my life?

In the end, I hope that you do sense an intimate knowledge and connection with Jesus that would cause you to live a life that gives glory and honor to the Father, as well as create a hunger for more of Him. Now that you're in the habit, feel free to move on to another one of the Gospels on your own.

By the way, this month of devotionals has only twenty-eight days, so you got a couple of freebies in there to sleep late. Unless, of course, it's February. And not a leap year.

DAY 1

In those days Caesar Augustus issued a decree that a census should be taken of the entire Roman world. (This was the first census that took place while Quirinius was governor of Syria.) And everyone went to his own town to register.

So Joseph also went up from the town of Nazareth in Galilee to Judea, to Bethlehem the town of David, because he belonged to the house and line of David. He went there to register with Mary, who was pledged to be married to him and was expecting a child. While they were there, the time came for the baby to be born, and she gave birth to her firstborn, a son. She wrapped him in cloths and placed him in a manger, because there was no room for them in the inn. (Luke 2:1-7)

Mary has never slept with a man. Imagine Mary having to tell Joseph that she is spontaneously pregnant. After an angel speaks to Joseph in a dream, he believes Mary. It must have been some dream, for in the history of unwanted pregnancies, this is probably not the first time someone has told this story, but I'm sure it was the first time anyone believed it. From other historical sources, we know that those who didn't believe the story referred to Jesus as a bastard, and Mary had to live with the whispers and rumors of adultery. It's interesting that God allows Mary to be thought of as an adulteress and Jesus to be raised in a home that was the subject of rumors of sexual infidelity. This spurs many thoughts in my mind: that God values humility over our reputation, that Jesus didn't have an idyllic childhood, that Jesus was teased, that sexual stigma has no bearing on how God feels about us.

DAY 2

The child's father and mother marveled at what was said about him. Then Simeon blessed them and said to Mary, his mother: "This child is destined to cause the falling and rising of many in Israel, and to be a sign that will be spoken against, so that the thoughts of many hearts will be revealed. And a sword will pierce your own soul too." (Luke 2:33-35)

You would think that being the mother of Jesus would give Mary card-member privileges, that she might be exempt from the common worries associated with parenting—He's not going to dress goth or smoke in the bathroom. But Mary's child, Jesus, would in fact pierce her soul, the prophet tells her. Children: wanting them, not having them; having them, not being able to have them—it's a mixed bag of hope and hurt. Even Jesus would one day pierce the soul of His mother when He willingly chose death upon the cross, leaving her to grieve and listen to people who rejected Jesus. Men and children, since the Fall, seem to be our crucibles of spiritual growth. Neither will ever be easy.

DAY 3

When he was twelve years old, they went up to the Feast, according to the custom. After the Feast was over, while his parents were returning home, the boy Jesus stayed behind in Jerusalem, but they were unaware of it. Thinking he was in their company, they traveled on for a day. Then they began looking for him among their relatives and friends. When they did not find him, they went back to Jerusalem to look for him. After three days they found him in the temple courts, sitting among the teachers, listening to them and asking them questions. Everyone who heard him was amazed at his understanding and his answers. (Luke 2:42-47)

Everyone assumes Mary and Joseph were perfect parents. Funny, in the only story of Jesus's childhood, they lose Him for three days. They didn't even realize He was missing for at least a day. These days the state can take away your children for such an oversight. No parents are perfect, and we all bear the imprint of our parents' imperfections. Yet God in His wisdom choose Mary and Joseph, whatever their shortcomings (apparently missing short-term memory), and God did in fact choose your parents. What He had in mind was sort of like a salad bar: embrace what's good and leave behind what's not, always grateful that you had a free meal. What have you embraced of your parents, and in what ways is your life a reaction to their failings? God intended both in shaping you.

DAY 4

When all the people were being baptized, Jesus was baptized too. And as he was praying, heaven was opened and the Holy Spirit descended on him in bodily form like a dove. And a voice came from heaven: "You are my Son, whom I love; with you I am well pleased." (Luke 3:21-22)

The Gospels bring out many aspects of the relationship between Jesus and His Father. This one is either taken for granted or overlooked. The Father is well pleased by the Son, and the Son lives to please His Father—not simply to obey, but to please. Obeying and pleasing are different, and the nuance leads to reflection: Am I pleasing God? Is He happy with me, does He like me? *Obedience* and *love* are words with different feels to them. We know God loves us—He kind of has to—but does He like us? My parents love all my brothers and sister the same; I do not know if they like us the same! The feeling of being pleasing, not simply loved or obedient, comes through intimacy. Only in day-to-day closeness does our nagging sense that God is not "for us" disappear. No amount of obedience apart from that intimacy can produce the same sense.

DAY 5

Jesus, full of the Holy Spirit, returned from the Jordan and was led by the Spirit in the desert, where for forty days he was tempted by the devil. He ate nothing during those days, and at the end of them he was hungry.

The devil said to him, "If you are the Son of God, tell this stone to become bread."

Jesus answered, "It is written: 'Man does not live on bread alone.'"

The devil led him up to a high place and showed him in an instant all the kingdoms of the world. And he said to him, "I will give you all their authority and splendor, for it has been given to me, and I can give it to anyone I want. So if you worship me, it will all be yours."

Jesus answered, "It is written: 'Worship the Lord your God and serve him only.'"

The devil led him to Jerusalem and had him stand on the highest point of the temple. "If you are the Son of God," he said, "throw yourself down from here. For it is written: 'He will command his angels concerning you to guard you carefully; they will lift you up in their hands, so that you will not strike your foot against a stone.'"

Jesus answered, "It says: 'Do not put the Lord your God to the test.'"

When the devil had finished all this tempting, he left him until an opportune time. (Luke 4:1-13)

I love shortcuts. I'll find them even if it takes twice as long and twice as much energy to find them (the same mindset, incidentally, that leads me to pay more than retail for items on eBay). At the heart of Jesus's temptation is a shortcut, a chance to declare His identity and establish His kingdom while bypassing the cross. Same goal, different means and timing. The heart of many of our temptations is taking matters into our own hands and not following God's plan or timing: If He isn't meeting my needs the way I want, when I want, I'll meet them myself—a shortcut to the promised land. Jesus wants us to see and follow His example of submitting to God's plan and timing, choosing to limit ourselves to God's provisions, whatever they may be. The remarkable thing is that Jesus had the power to do otherwise, while we often do not. If you could blink Joe Perfect into your life, would you still refrain and wait for God's timing? Or even let Joe go if he wasn't a part of God's plan?

DAY 6

He went to Nazareth, where he had been brought up, and on the Sabbath day he went into the synagogue, as was his custom. And he stood up to read. The scroll of the prophet Isaiah was handed to him. Unrolling it, he found the place where it is written: "The Spirit of the Lord is on me, because he has anointed me to preach good news to the poor. He has sent me to proclaim freedom for the prisoners and recovery of sight for the blind, to release the oppressed, to proclaim the year of the Lord's favor." (Luke 4:16-19)

In the book of Luke, this marks the beginning of Jesus's public ministry. Jesus announces Himself by quoting the prophet Isaiah—specifically, Isaiah 61. Look at the interesting spot where He stops the quote. Jesus said He had come to proclaim "the year of the Lord's favor." The passage in Isaiah goes on to say "and the day of his vengeance." We can never know what thoughts went through Jesus's mind, but from a thorough study of the Gospels, it's safe to say that "Dude, I can't say that; it's going to make people angry" isn't one of them. Rather, the reason for the editing was to signify the nature of His ministry. When Jesus returns, the second part of that verse will be fulfilled: the Day of Judgment. But the essence of Jesus's ministry then, as now, is to proclaim grace, forgiveness, and the year of the Lord's favor—come in now and all debts will be canceled. Buy six sandwiches and get the seventh free. This general description, more than any specific statement, allows us to see the heart of Jesus's ministry as Jesus defined it.

DAY 7

In the synagogue there was a man possessed by a demon, an evil spirit. He cried out at the top of his voice, "Ha! What do you want with us, Jesus of Nazareth? Have you come to destroy us? I know who you are—the Holy One of God!"

"Be quiet!" Jesus said sternly. "Come out of him!" Then the demon threw the man down before them all and came out without injuring him.

All the people were amazed and said to each other, "What is this teaching? With authority and power he gives orders to evil spirits and they come out!" (Luke 4:33-36)

I have all kinds of questions about exorcisms, like why a Ouija board? Would any piece of plywood cut to the same dimensions summon the satanic host? Is the evil in the lettering, the font? I have had relatively few verbal encounters with Beelzebub, which, I believe, is why I tend to think of sin in my life as simply rebellion or poor choices, oblivious to the third party who is active in both temptation and sin. In the "Our Father" prayer, Jesus instructs us specifically to pray that we might be kept from temptation and delivered from evil. Yet how often do we pray and see the battle for our holiness on the spiritual level? I assure you that if Jesus tells us only a few things for which to pray and two of them are deliverance from temptation and evil, it is not simply a suggestion but a necessity. I believe our spiritual and sexual lives would be quite different if we prayed daily for protection from the evil one.

DAY 8

When he had finished speaking, he said to Simon, "Put out into deep water, and let down the nets for a catch."

Simon answered, "Master, we've worked hard all night and haven't caught anything. But because you say so, I will let down the nets."

When they had done so, they caught such a large number of fish that their nets began to break. So they signaled their partners in the other boat to come and help them, and they came and filled both boats so full that they began to sink.

When Simon Peter saw this, he fell at Jesus' knees and said, "Go away from me, Lord; I am a sinful man!" For he and all his companions were astonished at the catch of fish they had taken, and so were James and John, the sons of Zebedee, Simon's partners.

Then Jesus said to Simon, "Don't be afraid; from now on you will catch men."
(Luke 5:4-10)

When you bring anything into sharp light, it becomes well defined. All grays become black or white. As Peter is now parked only a few feet from the sun, he is aware immediately that his life is a shadow. Knowing the fear and conviction his presence brings, Jesus hands Peter these sunglasses: "Don't be afraid." This phrase is repeated enough in the Gospels that we know for sure that Jesus does not want us to be afraid of Him. The reason, as exemplified in Peter's story, is that He has not come into our life for the purpose of judgment or punishment but to know us—to come into our world and have us come into His. Like Peter in this story, I spend much time groveling on the ground due to my failure, when Jesus would like me to put it behind and move on—*we have things to do.*

DAY 9

While Jesus was in one of the towns, a man came along who was covered with leprosy. When he saw Jesus, he fell with his face to the ground and begged him, "Lord, if you are willing, you can make me clean."

Jesus reached out his hand and touched the man. "I am willing," he said. "Be clean!" And immediately the leprosy left him. (Luke 5:12-13)

Few of us struggle with the doctrine of omnipotence, the fact that God is all powerful—I wonder if God could lift that school bus? We easily believe that God can do anything, and we truly believe He can heal and make us whole. The question is not usually about His power but His intent, not "Can He?" but "Does He want to?" I think the words of this man are preserved for us so we can see it in ink: "Are you willing to?" "I am willing to." Jesus wants us to know that, not only can He do something about our situation, but also He wants to—He is favorably disposed to the idea. It's helpful sometimes to picture Jesus saying these words and put in our own request. Then we get to hear Jesus say to us, "I am willing." For most assuredly, He does want to help us.

DAY 10

One day as he was teaching, Pharisees and teachers of the law, who had come from every village of Galilee and from Judea and Jerusalem, were sitting there. And the power of the Lord was present for him to heal the sick. Some men came carrying a paralytic on a mat and tried to take him into the house to lay him before Jesus. When they could not find a way to do this because of the crowd, they went up on the roof and lowered him on his mat through the tiles into the middle of the crowd, right in front of Jesus.

When Jesus saw their faith, he said, "Friend, your sins are forgiven." (Luke 5:17-20)

You could easily miss an important little phrase in here. "On the roof"? No, not that phrase; that's pretty unimportant. I was thinking of "And the power of the Lord was present for him to heal the sick." Luke is careful to show us that Jesus, though He was God, relied on the Holy Spirit to perform mighty works and to accomplish the will of the Father. Jesus models a life of reliance upon the Spirit of God. We do not simply go out and do things for God, but as we abide in His Spirit, He leads us in His will and empowers us to carry it

out. Abiding is keeping connected to God all day long and in constant reliance: "Lord, give me the strength to say no." "Help me to make a good choice." "What would You have me do with the rest of my afternoon?" "What should I say to her?" Constant abiding and dependence is how we access the supernatural power God has given us to live a life pleasing to Him.

DAY 11

Do not judge, and you will not be judged. Do not condemn, and you will not be condemned. Forgive, and you will be forgiven. Give, and it will be given to you. A good measure, pressed down, shaken together and running over, will be poured into your lap. For with the measure you use, it will be measured to you. (Luke 6:37-38)

My cell phone bills are usually twice what they should be due to small, illegible contingencies—overage fees for anyone who dials with her right hand or laughs like a schoolgirl. Who knows what's in there? The reception of forgiveness seems to have an up-front contingency clause that we in turn forgive others—the friends and family plan. If you think about everything God has forgiven us for, it's an understandable request. The backbone of the clause is that we are not God; judging others and dealing out payback are His prerogative, not ours. We are forgiven and reconciled through Christ's death alone. For the believer, this relates to our day-to-day experience of God's forgiveness as well as being turned over to the consequences of our sin. If we are not forgiving others, we will have a hard time experiencing God's forgiveness, for we reflexively attribute to God and His judgments the standards we impose on others. If we force others to pay for the consequences of their sin, we should expect no "get out of jail free" cards when our sin brings painful consequences. In the area of dating and relationships, in particular, hurt brings plenty of opportunities to forgive. Are you holding anyone ransom with unforgiveness because he wronged you?

DAY 12

No good tree bears bad fruit, nor does a bad tree bear good fruit. Each tree is recognized by its own fruit. People do not pick figs from thornbushes, or grapes from briers. The good man brings good things out of the good stored up in his heart, and the evil man brings evil things out of the evil stored up in his heart. For out of the overflow of his heart his mouth speaks. (Luke 6:43-45)

Question: What do Jesus and Pavlov's dog have in common?
Answer: Nothing. Jesus focuses on the heart more than behavior. He says our actions invariably flow from the inside out. What we think, what we dwell on and dream about—these are the seeds that will sprout in actions. Here is where we fight the battle. Minds filled with lust, worry, and envy are our downfall. We often minimize the importance of guarding our hearts and eyes, thinking only a prude would not read this or watch that. We look at the action, not its effect. How could watching *that* be a sin! The issue is not so much watching or reading *that*, but what *that* becomes when it's incubated in our fallen minds and hearts. So, well, maybe it's time to use discretion when it comes to *that*.

DAY 13

So Jesus went with them. He was not far from the house when the centurion sent friends to say to him: "Lord, don't trouble yourself, for I do not deserve to have you come under my roof. That is why I did not even consider myself worthy to come to you. But say the word, and my servant will be healed. For I myself am a man under authority, with soldiers under me. I tell this one, 'Go,' and he goes; and that one, 'Come,' and he comes. I say to my servant, 'Do this,' and he does it."

When Jesus heard this, he was amazed at him, and turning to the crowd following him, he said, "I tell you, I have not found such great faith even in Israel." (Luke 7:6-9)

This is one of only two times the Gospel says that Jesus was amazed. The other time was due to the people's unbelief in His hometown (Mark 6:6). Faith amazes Jesus, which is just cool to think about. I wonder what it would be like to trust Jesus enough to amaze Him. If you were able to take to Him the dearest things on your heart, like the centurion did, and say, "Listen, I really trust You with this, so I'm not going to sweat it," I bet

He would be absolutely delighted. And like the centurion, you can believe that He will.

DAY 14

Soon afterward, Jesus went to a town called Nain, and his disciples and a large crowd went along with him. As he approached the town gate, a dead person was being carried out—the only son of his mother, and she was a widow. And a large crowd from the town was with her. When the Lord saw her, his heart went out to her and he said, "Don't cry."

Then he went up and touched the coffin, and those carrying it stood still. He said, "Young man, I say to you, get up!" The dead man sat up and began to talk, and Jesus gave him back to his mother. (Luke 7:11-15)

Jesus's heart has left the building. It went out from Him, pulled by the pain and sorrow of this woman. As you study the Gospels, you'll note that Jesus has an agenda. He always has a reason for what He does. He walks on the water, and, of course, an Old Testament passage says, "Only God treads the seas" (Job 9:8). Oh, so it's an object lesson. Here we have a story captured to show that Jesus was diverted by need. That God's plan is not just a big brain but a big heart. Jesus is moved by your hurt and disappointment. His heart is moved when He sees us in pain.

DAY 15

Now one of the Pharisees invited Jesus to have dinner with him, so he went to the Pharisee's house and reclined at the table. When a woman who had lived a sinful life in that town learned that Jesus was eating at the Pharisee's house, she brought an alabaster jar of perfume, and as she stood behind him at his feet weeping, she began to wet his feet with her tears. Then she wiped them with her hair, kissed them and poured perfume on them.

When the Pharisee who had invited him saw this, he said to himself, "If this man were a prophet, he would know who is touching him and what kind of woman she is—that she is a sinner."

Jesus answered him, "Simon, I have something to tell you."

"Tell me, teacher," he said.

"Two men owed money to a certain moneylender. One owed him five hundred denarii, and the other fifty. Neither of them had the money to pay him back, so he canceled the debts of both. Now which of them will love him more?"

Simon replied, "I suppose the one who had the bigger debt canceled."

"You have judged correctly," Jesus said.

Then he turned toward the woman and said to Simon, "Do you see this woman? I came into your house. You did not give me any water for my feet, but she wet my feet with her tears and wiped them with her hair. You did not give me a kiss, but this woman, from the time I entered, has not stopped kissing my feet. You did not put oil on my head, but she has poured perfume on my feet. Therefore, I tell you, her many sins have been forgiven—for she loved much. But he who has been forgiven little loves little."

Then Jesus said to her, "Your sins are forgiven." (Luke 7:36-48)

I'm thankful to God for a lot of things, but over the years, I have especially become thankful for the sin that God rescued me out of. It was a considerable stink pit, and I'm thankful that God allowed me to wander far enough into it to realize just how bad it stank, how bad I stank. I see many Christians who lack a zeal or passion in their lives, and I wonder if they will ever realize just how sick they are. Some of the greatest heroes of the faith were often the worst of sinners, profoundly grateful for being pulled from their own paths of destruction. Jesus is obviously talking about perception. The Pharisees were equally sinful, sick; they simply couldn't see, wouldn't see it. We can rejoice in whatever God allowed in our past to produce our current gratitude. It is better to have been a worse sinner and be grateful than a lesser sinner and complacent.

DAY 16

This is the meaning of the parable: The seed is the word of God. Those along the path are the ones who hear, and then the devil comes and takes away the word from their hearts, so that they may not believe and be saved. Those on the rock are the ones who receive the word with joy when they hear it, but they have no root. They believe for a while, but in the time of testing they fall away. The seed that fell among thorns stands for those who hear, but as they go on their way they are choked by life's worries, riches and pleasures, and they do not mature. But the seed on good soil stands for those with a noble and good heart, who hear the word, retain it, and by persevering produce a crop. (Luke 8:11-15)

Sometimes we believe that when we become Christians we will be spared all difficulty. Wrong. Not that this is an illogical assumption—after all, we're now following God's plan for our lives. It just isn't totally accurate. Jesus implies that we will have worries and lack certain things, and this will cause some to fall away. Perhaps for these people Jesus was a means to an end. They thought He could get them what they wanted, and when they didn't get it, they moved on to the next big thing. They wanted a genie and not a Savior. They subscribed to the oxymoron "selfish marriage." More tragic are those who seem to have a good heart and yet are wooed to the world or ensnared by it. I do not know if the list was meant to be comprehensive, but worry, riches, and pleasure seem to cover most things that steal our hearts. As I think of seed, I ponder what seeds of desire I still cherish for things that, when grown, will choke out my love for Christ.

DAY 17

Now Jesus' mother and brothers came to see him, but they were not able to get near him because of the crowd. Someone told him, "Your mother and brothers are standing outside, wanting to see you."

He replied, "My mother and brothers are those who hear God's word and put it into practice." (Luke 8:19-21)

This is kind of funny when you picture it. Jesus's family is waiting for a VIP pass, and the bouncer won't let them in. It's not that Jesus is being heartless to dear Mum and the boys, but He must make clear that, unlike the religious priesthood, membership in the kingdom is a matter of faith, not lineage. Whenever possible, we are to love, serve, and respect our parents. This is not possible when Jesus calls us to do something other than what our parents want. In such cases, Jesus trumps parents (and of course, uncles trump cousins, and brothers trump uncles—such is the family food chain). Jesus wants us to have good friends and a great family, but He insists on being chief in our affections. This gets at the point Scripture often makes that God is jealous. Many perversions of jealousy are sinful, but in its righteous sense, jealousy is rightful desire for exclusivity in a relationship, accompanied by anger when it is violated. Jesus loves us jealously. Be aware of rivals to His affection; He is.

DAY 18

As Jesus was on his way, the crowds almost crushed him. And a woman was there who had been subject to bleeding for twelve years, but no one could heal her. She came up behind him and touched the edge of his cloak, and immediately her bleeding stopped.

"Who touched me?" Jesus asked.

When they all denied it, Peter said, "Master, the people are crowding and pressing against you."

But Jesus said, "Someone touched me; I know that power has gone out from me."

Then the woman, seeing that she could not go unnoticed, came trembling and fell at his feet. In the presence of all the people, she told why she had touched him and how she had been instantly healed. Then he said to her, "Daughter, your faith has healed you. Go in peace." (Luke 8:42-48)

Just as you begin to identify with Jesus, He does something suprahuman, letting us know He is not absolutely of our species. Like someone with a strange organ or a spare thyroid, Jesus apparently could sense faith, knowing when He was approached with or without it. The woman apparently was fearful to ask for help: fearful of Jesus, fearful of embarrassment, but perhaps most fearful that He would say no. All of us would like to be healed secretly from many things without going public. But getting well involves both humility and a community that makes private healing a rare occurrence. We cannot remain in the shadows with our brokenness. It might be helpful to think through what ailment or sin you have kept concealed. Ask yourself if you want to be well enough to go public to a few friends.

DAY 19

Late in the afternoon the Twelve came to him and said, "Send the crowd away so they can go to the surrounding villages and countryside and find food and lodging, because we are in a remote place here."

He replied, "You give them something to eat."

They answered, "We have only five loaves of bread and two fish—unless we go and buy food for all this crowd." (About five thousand men were there.)

But he said to his disciples, "Have them sit down in groups of about fifty each."

The disciples did so, and everybody sat down. Taking the five loaves and the two fish and looking up to heaven, he gave thanks and broke them. Then he gave them to the disciples to set before the people. They all ate and were satisfied, and the disciples picked up twelve basketfuls of broken pieces that were left over. (Luke 9:12-17)

Hmm. Twelve baskets, twelve disciples. I wonder if there's a lesson here, or if Luke just thinks that's a neat coincidence. I'm going to bet it's a lesson. Jesus was showing the disciples that while they were inadequate to meet the needs of others, He could make them adequate. He wanted to provide food for others through His disciples. Our walks with Jesus can be rather self-absorbed—"Let's talk about me"—looking always at our own sin, needs, and wants. But the focus of a true disciple is feeding others. The danger of a completely personal walk is that it can spiral into therapy, having a quiet time on the couch while Jesus takes notes and nods. But we will never feel whole until we focus on the needs of those around us, losing our lives in order to find them.

DAY 20

As they were walking along the road, a man said to him, "I will follow you wherever you go."

Jesus replied, "Foxes have holes and birds of the air have nests, but the Son of Man has no place to lay his head."

He said to another man, "Follow me."

But the man replied, "Lord, first let me go and bury my father."

Jesus said to him, "Let the dead bury their own dead, but you go and proclaim the kingdom of God."

Still another said, "I will follow you, Lord; but first let me go back and say good-by to my family."

Jesus replied, "No one who puts his hand to the plow and looks back is fit for service in the kingdom of God." (Luke 9:57-62)

Without close examination, Jesus seems a little harsh in these vignettes—or more to the point, demanding. Maybe more is going on here than meets the eye. Jesus seems to be clarifying what it means to love and follow Him. The three things are these:
- a willingness to sacrifice
- a willingness to make Jesus a priority above all else
- a willingness to persevere in our commitment

These really are the measurements of love. Love is measured by the degree to which we will sacrifice; it is measured by priority; and it is measure by endurance. These are the height, depth, and width of love. That's why most wedding vows contain these phrases: "in sickness and in health," "forsaking all others," "till death parts us."

In essence the call to follow Jesus is a marriage proposal. Jesus is saying, "Will you marry Me?" Well, will you?

DAY 21

As Jesus and his disciples were on their way, he came to a village where a woman named Martha opened her home to him. She had a sister called Mary, who sat at the Lord's feet listening to what he said. But Martha was distracted by all the preparations that had to be made. She came to him and asked, "Lord, don't you care that my sister has left me to do the work by myself? Tell her to help me!"

"Martha, Martha," the Lord answered, "you are worried and upset about many things, but only one thing is needed. Mary has chosen what is better, and it will not be taken away from her." (Luke 10:38-42)

Mary and Martha are types. You know them both. Mary appears reserved and soft-spoken, while Martha has a strong personality. "Get that car out of my parking space, skillet head." In the story of Jesus and Lazarus, Martha is bold and brash. Notice whose house it is—Martha's. Martha gets things done. But she has focused on doing for Jesus rather than being with Jesus. In the final verse, Jesus says that Mary has chosen the better portion. The word "portion" is rich in Old Testament meaning, usually referring to food.

"The Lord is our portion" means the Lord is our food: our sustenance, our strength, our motivation. Martha chose the food source of busyness and activity—a sugar high. Now she's out of energy, frustrated, and looking for someone to blame. The passage points to our need to begin our days with Jesus, being nourished by Him, making a choice to have Him, not activity, as our food source.

DAY 22

Then Jesus said to his disciples: "Therefore I tell you, do not worry about your life, what you will eat; or about your body, what you will wear. Life is more than food, and the body more than clothes. Consider the ravens: They do not sow or reap, they have no storeroom or barn; yet God feeds them. And how much more valuable you are than birds! Who of you by worrying can add a single hour to his life? Since you cannot do this very little thing, why do you worry about the rest?

"Consider how the lilies grow. They do not labor or spin. Yet I tell you, not even Solomon in all his splendor was dressed like one of these. If that is how God clothes the grass of the field, which is here today, and tomorrow is thrown into the fire, how much more will he clothe you, O you of little faith! And do not set your heart on what you will eat or drink; do not worry about it. For the pagan world runs after all such things, and your Father knows that you need them. But seek his kingdom, and these things will be given to you as well. "Do not be afraid, little flock, for your Father has been pleased to give you the kingdom. Sell your possessions and give to the poor. Provide purses for yourselves that will not wear out, a treasure in heaven that will not be exhausted, where no thief comes near and no moth destroys. For where your treasure is, there your heart will be also. (Luke 12:22-34)

Has anyone ever told you not to worry? How dumb is that? You can't just stop worrying anymore than you can cease being a carbon-based life form. The genius of Jesus's words is that He doesn't simply tell us not to worry. Instead, Jesus tells us to set our hearts on the kingdom. But this also is abstract and nebulous. I want to set my heart on the kingdom, but how? Practically speaking, Jesus says to give: give time to the kingdom, give money, give everything. For our hearts follow where we place our treasure. If you want to stop worrying, seek the kingdom. Seek the kingdom by giving your treasure to it, for we cannot love in the abstract.

DAY 23

Be dressed ready for service and keep your lamps burning, like men waiting for their master to return from a wedding banquet, so that when he comes and knocks they can immediately open the door for him. It will be good for those servants whose master finds them watching when he comes. I tell you the truth, he will dress himself to serve, will have them recline at the table and will come and wait on them. It will be good for those servants whose master finds them ready, even if he comes in the second or third watch of the night. But understand this: If the owner of the house had known at what hour the thief was coming, he would not have let his house be broken into. You also must be ready, because the Son of Man will come at an hour when you do not expect him. (Luke 12:35-40)

If I said to you, "Just stay sexually pure until your ninetieth birthday," that would be hard. The finish line is a long way off. But this is not the biblical finish line. The encouragement of Jesus is that the end, or His return, could come at any moment. So stay ready. The finish line is right around the corner. When we think of living for a finish line seventy years away, we get sluggish and we want to make the trip as comfortable as possible—carry a refrigerator in our knapsack. Jesus said be holy and alert, because He might return at any moment. This theme is repeated throughout the New Testament. In the period until His return, He wants His followers to stay loyal, pure, and alert.

DAY 24

Or suppose a woman has ten silver coins and loses one. Does she not light a lamp, sweep the house and search carefully until she finds it? And when she finds it, she calls her friends and neighbors together and says, 'Rejoice with me; I have found my lost coin.' In the same way, I tell you, there is rejoicing in the presence of the angels of God over one sinner who repents. (Luke 15:8-10)

Luke 15 contains three different stories. A lost coin, a lost sheep, and a lost son. At the moment, I could identify more with a lost set of car keys. The common thread in these stories is loss of something valuable, emotional duress at having lost it, a diligent and panicked search, and great joy at finding what was lost. Jesus tells these stories to show the emotion of God, the joy He feels when His children return to Him and the sorrow when they wander, and His faithfulness to

diligently pursue what is lost. Try reading through these stories and making note of the emotional language. Meditate on what they communicate about the heart of God.

DAY 25

Now on his way to Jerusalem, Jesus traveled along the border between Samaria and Galilee. As he was going into a village, ten men who had leprosy met him. They stood at a distance and called out in a loud voice, "Jesus, Master, have pity on us!"

When he saw them, he said, "Go, show yourselves to the priests." And as they went, they were cleansed.

One of them, when he saw he was healed, came back, praising God in a loud voice. He threw himself at Jesus' feet and thanked him—and he was a Samaritan.

Jesus asked, "Were not all ten cleansed? Where are the other nine? Was no one found to return and give praise to God except this foreigner?" (Luke 17:11-18)

The cure for an infection is penicillin; the cure for laryngitis, well, who the heck knows—honey? The cure for a bitter heart is a thick coating of thankfulness. Throughout the day, giving thanks in all things keeps away thoughts that lead to sin and a sick heart. When our souls are happy in God, they are somewhat immune to the temptation of other gods. At least that's the way we see it from our side of the fence. From Jesus's side, it's just plain ingratitude on our part. I'm not sure if rudeness and bad manners are sin, but when they involve ingratitude for all Christ has done for us, they certainly seem to cross the line. It makes me want to be close to Jesus when I think about the fact that it matters to Him that I say thank you.

DAY 26

Jesus told this parable: "Two men went up to the temple to pray, one a Pharisee and the other a tax collector. The Pharisee stood up and prayed about himself: 'God, I thank you that I am not like other men—robbers, evildoers, adulterers—or even like this tax collector. I fast twice a week and give a tenth of all I get.'

"But the tax collector stood at a distance. He would not even look up to heaven, but beat his breast and said, 'God, have mercy on me, a sinner.'

"I tell you that this man, rather than the other, went home justified before God. For everyone who exalts himself will be humbled, and he who humbles himself will be exalted." (Luke 18:9-14)

Comparison is ugly. We feel ugly for doing it, and others become ugly in our eyes. The Pharisee assesses himself by comparing himself to others: "I don't do what these people do." Humility resides not in self-loathing but in an accurate appraisal of ourselves. We can never be humble as long as we compare ourselves to others. We approach God with confidence because we have been forgiven, we are in Christ, and we are His children. Our confidence is never based on performance. Jesus wants us to come to Him humbly and confidently.

DAY 27

As he looked up, Jesus saw the rich putting their gifts into the temple treasury. He also saw a poor widow put in two very small copper coins. "I tell you the truth," he said, "this poor widow has put in more than all the others. All these people gave their gifts out of their wealth; but she out of her poverty put in all she had to live on." (Luke 21:1-4)

Jesus misses nothing. I guess that's part of being omniscient. Some of the things that seem great to the world may be insignificant to Him, and insignificant things may be great in the kingdom. Jesus always sees the heart. Always. That's powerful. Nothing we do with a pure motivation to love Him will be forgotten or go without reward. In fact, He values most the things you do in secret, just between you and Him.

DAY 28

A large number of people followed him, including women who mourned and wailed for him. Jesus turned and said to them, "Daughters of Jerusalem, do not weep for me; weep for yourselves and for your children." (Luke 23:27-28)

Jesus said, "Father, forgive them, for they do not know what they are doing." And they divided up his clothes by casting lots. (Luke 23:34)

Then he said, "Jesus, remember me when you come into your kingdom."

Jesus answered him, "I tell you the truth, today you will be with me in paradise." (Luke 23:42-43)

We can entrust ourselves completely to this Jesus. In the midst of being tortured, He was still thinking of the best interest of others, even the best interests of His executioners. When we see a love that surpasses all that we can humanly imagine, it's staggering to think that we are reluctant to entrust to Him our deepest desires and reluctant to love Him with every fiber of our being.

RESOURCES

Books can be ordered from www.christianbooks.com

Every Woman's Battle and/or Every Young Woman's Battle by Shannon Ethridge
Sex and the Soul of a Woman by Paula Rhineheart
Lies Women Believe By Nancy Leigh DeMoss
Breaking Free: Making Liberty in Christ a Reality in Life by Beth Moore
Inside of Me: A Story of Love, Lust and Redemtption by Shellie R Warren
A Return to Modesty by Wendy Shallit
Real Sex by Lauren Winner

DATING

Boundaries in Dating by Henry Cloud
How to Get a Date Worth Keeping by Dr. Henry Cloud
Marriable: Taking the Desperate Out of Dating by Hayley DiMarco & Michael DiMarco
Before you Live Together By David Gudgel
When God Writes Your Love story By Eric and Leslie Ludy

MARRIAGE

Preparing for Marriage by Dennis Rainey

To Become One by Chris Seay and Chad Karger
For Women Only: What You Need To Know About The Inner Lives Of Men by Shaunti Feldman
Sacred Marriage: What If God Designed Marriage To Make Us Holy More Than To Make Us Happy by Gary Thomas

SEXUAL ISSUES

No Stones by Marnie Feree, M.A.
Don't Call it Love by Patrick Carnes, Ph.D.
In The Shadows Of The Net-breaking Free Of Compulsive Online Sexual Behavior by Patrick Carnes, Ph.D., David L. Delmonico, Ph.D., Elizabeth Griffin, M.A.
Cybersex Exposed by Jennifer Schneider, M.D., PhD and Robert Weiss, M.S.W.
She Has a Secret by Douglas Weiss, Ph.D.
Secret Step Workbook by Douglas Weiss, Ph.D.
The Final Freedom by Douglas Weiss, Ph.D.

HOMOSEXUALITY

www.exodus-international.org
www.desertstream.org
www.regenbooks.org
www.narth.com
www.pfox.org

My Genes Made Me Do It! A Scientific Look at Sexual Orientation by Neil and Briar Whitehead
Restoring Sexual Identity: Hope for Women Who Struggle with Same-Sex Attraction by Anne Paulk
The Friendships of Women by Dee Brestin
Out of Egypt by Jeanette Howard
Desires in Conflict by Joe Dallas

SEXUAL ABUSE

The Wounded Heart: Hope for Adult Victims of Childhood Sexual Abuse by Dan Allender
The Wounded Heart Workbook by Dan Allender
Beauty for Ashes: Biblical help for Sexually Abused by John Coblentz
No More Hurting: Life Beyond Sexual Abuse by Gwen Purdie
Into Abba's Arms by Sandra Wilson
Learning to Trust Again a Young Woman's Journey of Healing from Sexual Abuse by Christa Sands
A Safe Place: Beyond Sexual Abuse by Jan Morrison
The Courage to Heal Workbook: For Women and Men Survivors of Child Sexual Abuse by Laura Davis
On The Threshold Of Hope: Opening The Door To Healing For Survivors Of Sexual Abuse by Diane Langberg / Tyndale House
Shattered Innocence: A Revealing Story of Sexual Abuse, Its Aftermath, and Recovery by Kelly Vates / Evergreen Press
Listen to the Cry of the Child: The Deafening Silence of Sexual Abuse by Barbara J. Hansen / Winepress Publishing

Mercy Ministries of America
P.O. Box 111060
Nashville, TN 37222
615-831-6987
615-315-9479 – fax
info@mercyministries.com
http://www.mercyministries.org
*Ministry that provides residential programs for young women ages 16-28 with life controlling problems such as unplanned pregnancy, drug and alcohol abuse, victims of physical and sexual abuse, eating disorders, and emotional difficulties resulting from past abortions. They produce a quarterly newsletter.

 BODY IMAGE
Wanting To Be Her: Body Image Secrets Victoria Won't Tell You by Michelle Graham
Thin Enough: My Spiritual Journey Through the Living Death of an Eating Disorder by Sheryle Cruise
Hope- Help and Healing for Eating Disorders by Gregory Jantz
Starving: A Personal Journey through Anorexia by Christie Pettit
Breaking Free from Anorexia and Bulimia by Linda Mintle

www.lfed.org (Lifelines Foundation for Eating Disorders)

http://familylife.com/articles/article_detail.asp?id=279 – article By Dennis and Barbara Rainey

Mercy Ministries of America
P.O. Box 111060
Nashville, TN 37222
615-831-6987
615-315-9479 – fax
info@mercyministries.com
http://www.mercyministries.org
*Ministry that provides residential programs for young women ages 16-28 with life controlling problems such as unplanned pregnancy, drug and alcohol abuse, victims of physical and sexual abuse, eating disorders, and emotional difficulties resulting from past abortions. They produce a quarterly newsletter.

National Association of Anorexia Nervosa and Associated Disorders
Box 7
Highland Park, IL 60035
847-831-3438
847-433-4632 – fax
info@anad.org
http://www.anad.org

*This national non-profit and educational self-help organization seeks to meet the needs of anorexics and their families. It provides counseling, information and referrals, self-help groups for victims and their parents, educational programs, and a listing of therapists, hospitals and clinics that treat these illnesses.

Remuda Ranch Programs for Anorexia and Bulimia
1 East Apache St.
Wickenburg, AZ 85390
928-684-3913
928-684-5222 – fax
800-445-1900
Drema.stroud@goodnet.com
http://www.remudaranch.com
*Offering a specialized treatment system for women, this organization is dedicated exclusively to the treatment of anorexia, bulimia, and related problems. Services are available for Spanish Speakers.

LEADER'S GUIDE
SMALL GROUP ANSWERS

Study 1: Quenched Satisfaction

Opening questions: Share some of your own examples to get the group going. Our dreams share common threads because we have similar core needs and desires.

1. It seems to be an attempt to engage her in a spiritual discussion. The vulnerability of asking her for something opens a dialogue in which the conversation would have, under normal conditions, been one sided.

2. Religious leaders of the day did not address women, as they were seen as second-class citizens. Jews certainly would not have talked with a Samaritan.

3. The time to get water would have been at a cooler point in the day. Her going at this time probably hints at the fact that she is a social outcast. The Jews deemed all Samaritans to be social outcasts, so she is an outcast among outcasts.

4. He is offering a spiritual solution to her real problem, her true thirsts.

5. She is obviously thirsty to be loved and known. She has sought to meet that thirst through a succession of empty and unsuccessful relationships with men.

6. Share as a group. Be as vulnerable as you can and set the pace for the group.

7. Share as a group.

8. The cycle can vary, but unlike "living water," it's more like saltwater. The more you drink, the thirstier you get. You come to a relationship for love, security, and acceptance, and when the relationship doesn't work out, you feel even more unloved, less secure, even rejected. You leave thirstier or needier than when you began, creating not simply a desire for another relationship but a need for one.

9. Because of the stigma attached. Nothing summarizes failure like a string of broken relationships, and nothing says "immorality" like living together.

10. You are not looking for any specific answer.

11. Share as a group.

12. Jesus is extremely honest and genuinely interested in this woman's life and well-being. He is not put off by her sin. He engages in her attempts at sidetracking the discussion.

13. Have the group share. Don't be afraid to ask "Why?" as people share their thoughts. This is really the heart of the study, as it is meant to diagnose where people are getting their "water" and what their "water" is.

14. We all come to Jesus with our thirst. But do we treat Him as the object of our thirst or simply as the vehicle to get what we really thirst for: relationships? If it is the latter, we are no better off than the woman.

Study 2: Sex Offenders
Purity

Opening questions: These are just to get the group going; they are not looking for any specific answers. But the discussion should lead to a greater realization that women's standards are often far from biblical.

1. Our motives and thoughts are important. Sin occurs in the heart first.

2. You're not looking for any specific answer, and you might get several different responses ranging from "Just like men" to more relational fantasies. Be willing to share first to get the ball rolling.

3. Yes, sexual immorality is biblically defined as sexual relations outside the confines of a monogamous heterosexual marriage. The adultery principle, then, is about having sex with someone who does not belong to you. (If a man is not your spouse now, he probably will be someone else's spouse eventually.)

4. Jesus's intent is to show that sexual sin and its ramifications don't just begin at intercourse, but rather they begin with our thought life and heart attitude. By this expanded definition, Jesus makes it clear that we're all sinners.

5. "More and more" is found in verse 1 ("live to please God") and verse 10 ("Love each other"). He encourages his readers by saying that they are doing well, but he says they could excel still more. He desires to see them makes steps of continued growth.

6. *Sanctified* means "to be made holy." *Sexual immorality* is a general term referring to anything that deviates from God's design for sex. *Passionate lust* is a lust that has been cultivated and has become a large sexual appetite. It also speaks of unbridled desire. *Heathen* are the nonreligious, the godless.

7. Specific challenges might include the Internet, pornographic movies and lyrics, as well as the late age at which we tend to marry in our culture. There is no right answer for the next two questions.

8. Have the group look up the verses and summarize.

9. A key thought is that our bodies are the temples of the Holy Spirit. Therefore, we have a responsibility to keep our bodies pure from sexual immorality. Our bodies belong to God.

10. Someday a man with whom you've been intimate may get married and belong to another. Sexual immorality, from this perspective, is like robbery—taking something that doesn't belong to you.

11. Discuss. (It might be nothing more than a kiss.)

12. This is just for discussion. There are pros and cons to engaging an ex-boyfriend on this issue. It might be best left alone.

13. The phrase contains a warning and an exhortation to be holy. This imperative to be holy, coupled with Paul's reminder that God gives us His Holy Spirit, seems to be a reminder that we are to remember that the Spirit indwells our bodies,

making sexual impurity unthinkable (hopefully). Also, it is the Spirit who gives us the power to remain pure.

14. It is how God designed sex, and therefore, how it works best. Sex is a degree of intimacy best protected by the commitments of marriage. It also reflects our relationship with God, which is purity and intimacy reserved for God alone.

15. Give people the freedom to discuss this. Basically, anything that begins to cause sexual arousal is stepping over the line of lust.

16. This is for discussion, but look to see whether people have used the Scriptures to inform their standard.

17. You are hoping there might be some consensus on this, and perhaps as a group, you could make this your standard.

18. You might share something you've done or written as an example.

Study 3: Getting Back Together
Forgiveness and Restoration

Opening question: Part of the answer may be cultural: sexual sins bring the most condemnation. It might be physical, something about the raw and fleshly nature of the act. And last, sex involves a deep part of us. Failure in this area seems to go right to our core.

1. There is no right answer. Let the group discuss.

2. There is no biblical passage that states this—both are accountable. But there is the principle of stewardship: of her to whom has been given, much is required. If women's sexual drive were less then men's (a far from proven fact), then they might have greater responsiblity. Without hard facts, it is simply an interesting issue to discuss.

3. Discuss as a group and pray for sensitivity.

4. The Law of Moses stated that a woman caught in adultery was to be stoned. If Jesus had said, "Let her go," He would be breaking the Mosaic

law. Israel was under Roman occupation, and as such the Jewish leaders were not allowed to carry out capital punishment. So, on the other hand, if Jesus said, "Stone her," He could be breaking the Roman law and making Himself subject to execution.

5. There is often a natural desire to be free, coupled with self-loathing.

6. Perhaps this is an opportunity to self-reflect and an open door for repentance.

7. The Old Testament states that the law was written by the "finger of God" (Ex. 31:18). And here we find Jesus writing in the ground with His finger. Here is the author of the law that they have come to trap by the law.

8. Have the group share. Sometimes there are creative ideas that help us to digest God's forgiveness.

9. Jesus tells her to leave her life of sin because He knows how destructive it is both for her and for others involved. He doesn't hate sin for the sake of hating it; He hates sin because it's so damaging to those He loves.

10. There is clearly a time when we come to Christ and leave our old life behind. This does not mean we never fall back into such sins. But the trajectory of our new life as a whole moves in a different direction.

11. Jesus repeats the question three times because Peter denied him three times. This is an opportunity for confession, to repeat "I love you" for every time he had denied it. It is important to see that Jesus is helping Peter to feel forgiven and restored, not rubbing salt in a wound.

12. Just prior to his betrayal, Peter claimed that even if all the disciples would fall away, he would not (Matt 26:33). Peter was claiming a greater level of commitment. Here, Jesus is reminding him that his true failure was not the denial but the pride that precipitated it.

13. The essential components include acknowledging that we have sinned, acknowledging that Jesus's death has paid for our sin and that all is forgiven, and then turning from sin to God in repentance. While sin does not hinder our relationship with God, just as in a family, it hinders fellowship.

14. We can confess our sin, but if we don't trust in God's Word and His incredible mercy, we will still feel that He is angry with us. We must believe that what the Bible says is true.

15. All are human ways to aid us in feeling forgiven: trusting in our ability to obey in the future; minimizing the sin so it will be easier for God to forgive; or berating ourselves to help pay for the sin.

16. These are alternatives to faith, which chooses to believe that we are forgiven because of Christ no matter what we've done.

17. A major reason we do not grow in holiness is because we don't have the courage to hear painful truth about ourselves from God, our conscience, or others. When we filter out hurtful truth, we spare ourselves pain. But that pain is the needed fuel of repentance. Repentance, in turn, leads to growth. True repentance also helps us to feel forgiven.

18. Have the group follow the exercise. Say that this is one way to help yourself metabolize the forgiveness that's yours. Some additional passages about forgiveness and restoration include Psalm 32, Psalm 103:12, Isaiah 38:17, and Romans 8:1.

Study 4: Bride by Design
Self Worth

Opening question: The first question is to identify with Christ in His abilities—to be able to create a person who would connect with you and accomplish your purposes.

1. As far as being created by Him and through Him, there is evidence through this and other passages that Jesus's primary role in Creation was to carry out the plans and direction of the Father (John 1:3; 1 Corinthians 8:6; Hebrews 1:12). As far as being for Him, the sole reason for our existence is to glorify Christ (in other words, it's not about you; it's all about Him).

2. We all have things that we like about ourselves and things we wish we could change. Go around and share one of each. Be careful to distinguish between things that are physical characteristics, personality, gifts, and so on, and things that really are sin issues. For example, someone may wish she wasn't so critical all the time. Really, that's not so much a personality thing as a sin habit. It may actually be that she has the gift of prophecy or discernment but she has not learned to use that gift in the power of the Spirit.

3. Discuss. There are no right answers.

4. Maybe a person tends to be loud and gregarious. She could use that to gather people to help build community. Maybe a person has bad acne scars or some other imperfection. Those are the types of things that God allows so that He can meet you in your personal pain to connect with Him more intimately and He can be more manifest in your character.

5. A bridegroom delights in every aspect of his bride—in her appearance, her quirkiness, her gifts and personality, her imperfections, her character. He longs to be with her, to look at her. He carries a picture with him always. He delights in showing her off. He wants to talk with her, share his life with her, and be a part of her life. He wants to know everything about her and be known by her.

6. The answers should be the same as above. Discuss whether it is easy or difficult to believe that's true.

7. "Fearfully" means "with awe and reverence." God made you with intent and purpose, and you are a wonderful creation.

8. The problem with imperfections and deformities and disease is the problem of evil in the world. Why does God allow it? He can redeem even what is the result of sin in the world and bring glory to Himself through it, perhaps by drawing people to Himself, by bringing healing at some point, or by using it to help other people.

9. It's the difference between head knowledge and heart knowledge. When you know something in your soul, you know it experientially. You know it emotionally. You are more fully convinced.

10. Discuss. This could be a good opportunity to bring up issues with food. In any group of college women, chances are strong that someone in the group struggles with an eating disorder.

11. Discuss. There's no specific answer. But it should come out that it gives you a sense of purpose in life. You and your life have been intentionally planned (Ephesians 2:10).

12. Do on your own. But if the group is comfortable, they could share some of their praises and ways God has used those things to glorify Himself.

Study 5 : Gripes, Complaints and Compliments
Worry and Distractions

Opening question: Let the group discuss. If people are having a hard time describing their relationship, suggest using only three or four adjectives to describe it.

1. She's upset that Mary is not helping her, that Mary gets to be spending time with Jesus, and perhaps that she is not getting done all she had hoped to.

2. Mary is reserved, more passive, and perhaps quiet. Martha seems more extroverted, has a take-charge personality, and is bold—a leader.

3. Discuss.

4. As in the story of Lazarus, Martha does not settle for the status quo. She initiates and gets things done. Marthas accomplish a lot. The negatives can be having a lack of sensitivity and being prone to become too busy and driven.

5. There are no right answers. You're simply looking for people to identify when and how they experience stress and worry.

6. Discuss.

7. The emphasis upon many things is in contrast to the one thing she has failed to do: spend time with Jesus. Jesus plainly tells her she has focused on the wrong thing.

8. "Portion" can refer to a tithe, which in context speaks of giving to the Lord the first part of our time. "Portion" can also refer to food: Jesus is our sustenance, our power source, our energy and motivation.

9. Busyness, cell phones, activities, coffee, to-do lists, e-mail, music—all these provide energy, a buzz of life. But we run ahead, over commit, run out of energy, and then, like Martha, we start looking for someone to blame—why aren't other people doing their jobs or working hard enough?

10. Discuss.

11. If Martha were to show the same persistence in prayer as in other effort, much more might happen. Reliance upon God to provide our needs. Expectancy that God will intervene and act on our behalf. As we pray in these ways, we go about the work of the kingdom in the right way, not running ahead and trying to do stuff for God, but walking with Him, reliantly, expectantly, persevering in prayer as much as in daily effort.

12. Have the group share what they've written down.

Study 6: Lies that Bind
Believing Lies

Opening questions: Discuss as a group.

1. Jesus is hungry and physically needy and therefore vulnerable. Satan makes use of our physical, emotional, and mental vulnerability.

2. Discuss as a group.

3. You are not looking for a right answer, but in asking the question, you are clarifying that a component of temptation is meeting our needs in a way that is outside God's plan.

4. Have people share with the group.

5. Discuss. You might ask follow-up questions: In what ways do these lies affect you? On a scale from 1 to 10, how powerfully do you feel them?

6. Have the group share. (You might spend some time before the study writing down some passages to common lies.)

7. You aren't looking for a "correct" answer. It might be a new idea for some that may be of

benefit. There also may be some biblical support in that "faith comes through hearing the word of God" and that many times the Scriptures encourage the public reading of Scripture. (Romans 10:17)

8. An application of truth is bringing falsehood out of the darkness and into the light. In essence, that's what took place. Lies lose power when they are exposed.

9. Speak truthfully. Don't manipulate. Be honest about our lives and feelings. Confess our sins to others. Avoid falsehood of any kind.

10. Have everyone share.

11. It is an attempt to manipulate God, using love as the leverage to get what is wanted. It dictates to God the means by which He is to show His love. Testing God involves satisfying a doubt about His love, not affirming our faith in His love.

12. Discuss.

13. You might read a page from your journal as an example to the group.

Study 7: Group Date Community and Accountability

Opening questions: as the leader be prepared to share first and create a comfortable environment for vulnerability. They can share funny things or more serious things. Think of some questions to prompt their thinking.

1. Benefits of friends: We are more productive when working with a friend (verse 9). Friends pick us up when we fall, physically, emotionally, or spiritually (verse 10). Friends keep us "warm" (verse 11). Friends can help defend us from attack (verse 12). Negative consequences of isolation: There's no one there to pick us up when we fall (verse 10). We won't be able to keep "warm" (verse 11). We might be overpowered when we are attacked (verse 12).

2. Discuss.

3. Among other things, people have hurt us in the past, relationships take effort, and people can become annoying. To get the group talking, share your own reasons for why you isolate yourself.

4. The media make us momentarily less conscious of our isolation and boredom, but ultimately, they increase both.

5. This is just for discussion.

6. Among other things, other Christians can point us to the truth of God and are able to pray for us. Christian community is a place where we are encouraged to walk with God and where we are known by others. It is also a place where we get and give encouragement and learn about God.

7. This is just an exercise. People might end up saying all kinds of ridiculous things, which is quite all right. It still serves the point that there is enjoyment and life in being known.

8. Among other things, it involves biblical teaching, encouragement, honesty, and prayer.

9. The focus of 1 John 1:9 is confessing to *God* and *being cleansed*. The focus of James 5:16 is confessing to *others* and *getting better*.

10. All of us will have to give an account someday before God. Relationships of accountability are ones where we've chosen to "give account to," to agree to disclose our lives in total honesty. These relationships provide strength, prayer, help, and encouragement and ultimately enable us to give a good account before God.

11. E-mail or IM one another at night to keep each other accountable while on the computer. Meet regularly to discuss sexual struggles. Decide together on certain practices and standards to guard purity.

12. Grace is expressing unconditional forgiveness. Truth means we ask difficult question, such as "What will you do differently so that this doesn't happen again?" Truth is upholding standards, while grace grants forgiveness if standards are violated.

13. People will tend more to one side or the other.

14. Have the group share what they've listed.

15. Discuss.

Study 8: Love Connection Commitment

Opening question: Start your discussion with defining love, both as the world defines it and as God defines it. You could add to the discussion by asking, how do you know someone loves you?

1. Wedding vows are a commitment to persevere through all circumstances, to prioritize that relationship above all others, and to commit for life. Jesus tested this person's commitment level similarly. To follow Him may mean having no home—no place to lay one's head. It means prioritizing the gospel over everything else, and it means committing to follow Him for the long haul, without looking back. It's not just a seasonal commitment.

2. Discuss and share.

3. The obvious answer is the cross. Jesus gave His own life in exchange for ours. As marriage is for the long haul, so His commitment to us is an eternal commitment. Once we become a Christ follower, we are sealed with the Holy Spirit and cannot be lost (John 10:28-29). He chose us. He can only act in our best interests. He gives good gifts. Read Ephesians 1 and make a list of all that He's done on our behalf. Have people share how they've experienced these things personally in their lives.

4. Keeping His word, His commandments—basically, obedience.

5. He and the Father will make their home with you and He will disclose Himself to you and the Father will love you. I don't think that's implying a conditional love on the Father's part; I think it's more about our experience of the Father's love. In an experiential sense, the more we take steps of obedience out of love for the Father and Jesus, the more we understand their character and heart and the more we recognize their involvement in our lives. God does make Himself known to us more and more.

6. Often people want to find a religion or something that meets their need and makes them feel good about themselves more than they want to find truth. As in dating, they want to keep their options open in case something better comes along. There is little or no commitment involved. Marriage, on the other hand, is a commitment based on love for the spouse. It is not about having needs met as much as it is about giving your life to another person.

7. Dating is much more tentative and uncertain. There is a fear that the other person will leave you or fail you or hurt you. It feels more performance driven. You have to earn the other's love and admiration. It's an emotional roller coaster based on circumstances. Dating tends to be self-focused—is this right for me? Marriage is about sacrifice, giving yourself to another. A healthy marriage is secure. There's freedom to completely be yourself. There will be hurts and disappointment, but not with fear of abandonment. You know that you will work things out. Marriage is more stable and consistent in spite of circumstances.

8. Discuss and share.

9. Discuss and share, but trust is probably a foundational answer.

10. Discuss and share. Suggestions: Take a day with the Lord—just go somewhere with your Bible, pen, and journal and spend an extended period of time praying, worshiping, reading the Word, studying, journaling, and so on. Add variety to your daily time with the Lord: one day, write your own psalm; another, spend time meditating on a passage and journaling about how it applies to your life; another, go on a prayer walk. Have someone that you consistently talk to about your relationship with the Lord. If you are not doing so already, start praying for some specific things and keep track of how God answers. Share your ideas.

11. This is a culmination of this study. I hope that through these articles and study times you have fallen more in love with Jesus and want to love Him by honoring Him with every area of your life, especially the areas of sexual purity and dating relationships. Hopefully, you've built enough community in your group that you each feel the freedom to share your vows with each other. You may want to come up with vows as a group and sign them together.